# TERRORISM AND
# THE CONSTITUTION

Also by David Cole

*Enemy Aliens:*
*Double Standards and Constitutional Freedoms*
*in the War on Terror*

*No Equal Justice:*
*Race and Class in the American Criminal Justice System*

# TERRORISM AND
# THE CONSTITUTION

## Sacrificing Civil Liberties
## in the Name of National Security

David Cole

James X. Dempsey

FOREWORD BY

NANCY TALANIAN AND KIT GAGE

THE NEW PRESS

NEW YORK
LONDON

Requests for permission to reproduce selections from this book should be mailed to:
Permissions Department, The New Press, 38 Greene Street, New York, NY 10013

Original edition published by the First Amendment Foundation, 1999, 2002
This edition published in the United States by The New Press, New York, 2006
Distributed by W. W. Norton & Company, Inc., New York

The authors gratefully thank Lynne M. Baum, Erin Corcoran, John J. Donoghue,
Ben Karpf, Greg Smith, and Daniel Williams for invaluable research assistance.
Research and writing for this third edition were supported in part by grants to the
Center for Democracy and Technology from the Open Society Institute and the
John D. and Catherine T. MacArthur Foundation.

ISBN-13: 978-1-56584-939-6 (pbk.)
ISBN-10: 1-56584-939-6 (pbk.)
CIP data available.

The New Press was established in 1990 as a not-for-profit alternative to the large,
commercial publishing houses currently dominating the book publishing industry.
The New Press operates in the public interest rather than for private gain, and is
committed to publishing, in innovative ways, works of educational, cultural, and
community value that are often deemed insufficiently profitable.

www.thenewpress.com

Printed in Canada

2  4  6  8  10  9  7  5  3  1

342.73
C

To Don Edwards,

for his lifetime commitment to the First Amendment,
from his leading role in the successful campaign to abolish the
House Un-American Activities Committee to his still-unfulfilled effort
to enact a law prohibiting the FBI from undertaking investigations
infringing on the First Amendment. As longtime chairman
of the Civil and Constitutional Rights Subcommittee of the
House Judiciary Committee, Don Edwards cheerfully and
tirelessly pursued a principled and consistent oversight of the FBI.
His vision was simple and enduring: that domestic tranquillity
can be secured without sacrificing the blessings of liberty.

# Contents

## Part I: Investigating First Amendment Activities: The FBI Before September 2001

## Part II: Control vs. Discretion: The Limits of Legal Restrictions on the FBI's Authority

# Preface
## to the Third Edition

The terrorist attacks of September 11, 2001, marked a quantum leap in the deadliness and audacity of terror. They revealed a vulnerability that many in the United States had never before appreciated. And they sparked a fundamental debate about the tension between liberty and security in the United States, and in particular about the capability of our government to keep us secure within the confines of due process, respect for freedoms of speech and association, and a system of government powers subject to checks and balances. This third edition of *Terrorism and the Constitution,* like the first, addresses these questions, and provides important historical perspective on the dangers of affording the government unchecked power in an effort to attain greater security.

The first edition of this book, written in 1999, did not foresee the devastating scope of the attacks of September 11. However, in that first edition, we predicted that there would be terrorist attacks against the United States and against U.S. interests abroad. We also warned that the federal antiterrorism effort then in place was flawed and ill suited to meet the terrorist threat. Unfortunately, despite some important improvements in the counterterrorism programs of the U.S. government, we must repeat those warnings today. Major

elements of the government's reaction to terrorism have been misguided not merely because they sacrifice civil liberties but also
because, as is becoming clear, unchecked government power ultimately undermines security.

By their very scale, the events of September 11 have required all
of us to reassess what is thinkable and unthinkable. The failure of
U.S. authorities to detect the September 11 attack in advance, despite its scope and scale, mandated comprehensive reconsideration
of our intelligence capabilities and powers. Yet this reexamination
did not even begin until after the USA PATRIOT Act was adopted
and after many other constitutionally suspect initiatives were
launched. These steps were taken without asking what went wrong
before September 11 and what measures would be more effective in
preventing such failure in the future. The joint inquiry of the Congressional Intelligence Committees in 2003 and the 2004 report of
the 9/11 Commission shed important light on the failures, chief
among them turf battles, lack of skilled professionals, misplaced priorities, and an inability to analyze information. Notably, neither of
the inquiries found fault with the constitutional principles of due
process, accountability, or checks and balances.

To the contrary, one of the lessons of the four years since September 11, 2001, is that, even as we face new and more difficult challenges, the fundamental principles that ought to govern the
response of a democratic society to terrorism remain unchanged: we
should focus on perpetrators of crime and those planning violent
activities, avoid indulging in guilt by association and ethnic profiling, maintain procedures designed to identify the guilty and exon-
erate the innocent, insist on legal limits on surveillance authority,
bar political spying, apply checks and balances to government powers, and respect basic human rights. Departing from these principles, as the military and intelligence agencies have done, for
example, in abusing detainees at Abu Ghraib prison in Iraq, is not

only wrong but actually harms national security by fueling anti-American sentiment. The first edition of this book foresaw and discussed all of these issues, illustrating them with specific historical examples. These issues are all the more pressing in the wake of September 11, and the history all the more important to keep in mind. If we are to learn from our mistakes, we must not lose sight of how we have gone astray in the past.

Much has changed since September 11, however, and therefore this third edition includes a thoroughly revised text, with particularly substantial changes to Chapter 6 (addressing, among other issues, the changes in attorney general guidelines on terrorism investigations) and a new Part IV, detailing and assessing the antiterrorism measures adopted in the wake of the September 11 attacks.

The need for a revised third edition illustrates the ever-developing nature of the struggle to preserve liberty while providing security. We hope that our book offers some contribution to the ongoing debate, as this issue is likely to define the character of our nation for generations to come.

David Cole
James X. Dempsey
October 2005

# Foreword
# to the Third Edition

The indiscriminate arrests from 1919 to 1921 of thousands of immigrants and suspected radicals, known as the "Palmer Raids"; the internment of Japanese-Americans in World War II; the House Un-American Activities Committee hearings in the 1940s and 1950s; and the FBI's Counter-Intelligence Program (COINTEL-PRO) in the 1960s and 1970s were all U.S. government programs that dealt harshly with individuals considered to be "subversive." In all these cases, the government reacted to real and perceived security threats by sacrificing the rights and liberties of immigrants, citizens who opposed government policies, or both. Limited public opposition and overly broad government secrecy helped sustain some of those policies for decades, until enough people found the courage and clarity of purpose to mobilize sufficient opposition to bring them to an end.

*Terrorism and the Constitution* takes a critical look at the history of government abuses and people's mobilization to stop them—in the courts, in Congress, and in the court of public opinion—offering a compelling case for the claim that sacrificing civil liberties does not necessarily make us safer, but more often than not results in gratuitous abuse of the rights of the most vulnerable without appreciably advancing security. It is our hope that this book can serve as a tool for organizing the kind of political support for civil liberties that is critical to restoring the principles of liberty and justice that characterize this nation at its best. That work has already begun, in part with the help of this book's earlier editions.

After September 11, 2001, it was impossible for those familiar with the U.S. government's history of overreaching in times of crisis not to recognize the patterns, as Arab, Muslim, and South Asian immigrants were rounded up indiscriminately, the Justice Department's surveillance powers were expanded through executive fiat, and Congress steamrolled passage of the USA PATRIOT Act in late October 2001.

Two weeks later, a small group of Northampton, Massachusetts, residents convened to consider the significance of the Patriot Act and other ominous government actions. They knew it would be futile at that point to appeal to Congress, where only sixty-six House members and one senator had the courage to oppose the Patriot Act at final passage. They recognized that the general public was still traumatized by September 11 and the subsequent anthrax attacks and appeared willing to support whatever government action might appear to help to prevent further attacks, even if it meant sacrificing basic rights.

When change inside the Washington Beltway seemed impossible, the Northampton Bill of Rights Defense Committee formed to organize locally. In Northampton the group tested a strategy that has since been repeated in several hundred locales, involving local education and debate about federal policies, followed by passage of a city council resolution enabling the municipal government to take a stand—objecting to the civil liberties abuses of the "war on terror," and telling local law enforcement not to infringe on locals' constitutional rights even if the Patriot Act and other federal laws and policies might encourage them to do so. As the work of the committee caught on nationally, the group shortened its name to the Bill of Rights Defense Committee (BORDC).

The Northampton resolution passed unanimously, and the BORDC pursued similar efforts in two nearby towns. At a town meeting in Amherst, Massachusetts, Anne Awad explained her support for a town resolution, stating, "As members of the select board, we want to know that all residents and visitors to our town feel safe. We do not want to support profiling of particular types of people. If one group is viewed suspiciously today, another group will be added to the list tomorrow." Amherst and Leverett town meetings overwhelmingly passed resolutions.

Meanwhile, Ann Arbor, Michigan's city council passed a resolution inspired by the immigration authorities' December 2001 arrest of Ann Arbor resident Rabih Haddad for a minor immigration violation, and Denver's city council passed a resolution following the discovery that the Denver Police Department had been keeping extensive files on peaceful protesters.

To support local education and action to restore civil liberties nationwide, BORDC created a website providing information about the local resolutions, invited people to start local groups, and offered to help them organize. The website, www.bordc.org, includes a time line for local organizing, petitions, resolutions, press releases, suggestions for local education, contact information for local groups, and links to helpful websites of other civil liberties organizations.

As news of the grassroots movement spread, people who had privately been concerned about the government's actions welcomed the opportunity to organize locally as part of a national movement. The acronym "USA PATRIOT Act," chosen to immunize the bill from scrutiny or opposition in Congress or elsewhere, gradually became a liability as people used it as shorthand for the broad array of laws and executive initiatives that the government was using to bypass constitutional rights and liberties in the name of protecting our national security.

The local groups' organizing and education quickly showed results, as each resolution that passed inspired more communities to form local Bill of Rights Defense Committees. The American Civil Liberties Union added national support and alerted its affiliates and members. By the end of 2002, twenty-two resolutions had been passed. Four months later, there were a hundred, including the first statewide resolution, approved by the Hawaii legislature. As Justice Department spokesperson Mark Corallo dismissed the resolutions as confined to "left-leaning" communities, the true nature of the defense of civil liberties became evident as the state of Alaska and the cities of Detroit, Los Angeles, Dallas, and Kansas City joined the growing list of "civil liberties safe zones." The American Library Association, American Association of Law Libraries, United Electrical, Radio and Machine Workers of America, National League of Cities, Unitarian Universalist Association, Veterans for Peace, and several state chapters of the League of Women Voters were among the many organizations that also passed resolutions.

Congress began to listen: In March 2003, Rep. Bernard Sanders (I-VT) proposed the Freedom to Read Protection Act, to exempt libraries and bookstores from Patriot Act Section 215, which gave the government sweeping powers to demand records from libraries, bookstores, and all other businesses. Other bills soon followed. In July, Rep. C.L. "Butch" Otter (R-ID) offered an amendment to the Commerce, Justice, State, and Judiciary Appropriations Act of 2004 to defund Patriot Act Section 213, popularly known as "sneak and peek," which authorized secret searches of citizens' homes in ordinary criminal cases. In a blow to the Justice Department, Otter's amendment prevailed in the House with a bipartisan vote of 309 to 118.

After the vote, Attorney General John Ashcroft tried to revive support for the now-tarnished Patriot Act with a speaking tour in August and September 2003, in which he refused to speak in public but instead praised the Act before closed-door, invitation-only gatherings of uniformed law enforcement officers. His defensive tour only fanned the flames of opposition as press reports of Ashcroft's appearances and of the demonstrations at each stop made still more people aware of the controversial Act. During his thirty-city tour, dozens more communities started local Bill of Rights Defense Committees, and twenty-nine cities passed resolutions.

In October 2003, more than 200 members of local committees from twenty-seven states and representatives of national civil liberties and civil rights organizations gathered in Silver Spring, Maryland, for the Grassroots America Defends the Bill of Rights National Conference. Coordinated by the First Amendment Foundation and the BORDC, among others, the meeting brought together people from the grassroots movement and nationally known voices from across the political spectrum to strategize about how to advance the work they had begun.

Since September 11, 2001, nearly 400 state and local governments in forty-three states have enacted resolutions upholding the constitutional rights of their 62 million residents, and hundreds more resolution efforts are under way. In the meantime, federal judges have found parts of the USA PATRIOT Act and the laws it expanded to be unconstitutional, and the U.S. Supreme Court has rejected the executive branch's claim of extraordinary powers to hold U.S. citizens and foreign nationals as enemy combatants indefinitely without judicial review.

The grassroots movement has helped make millions of people aware of the dangers of unchecked power within the executive branch. A truly remarkable diversity of people now speak out fearlessly about their concerns. They speak with many voices, led by no one group but connected to an expanding array of local and national networks. This movement's impact, combined with lawsuits, human rights reports, Freedom of Information Act requests, and press accounts of wrongful arrests and ruined lives, increases the onus on members of Congress and the courts to restore the U.S. system of checks and balances.

With this message of hope and activism, we welcome this revised and updated edition of *Terrorism and the Constitution,* confident that it will continue to provide a solid foundation of information for those fighting with us for our freedoms.

Nancy Talanian
Bill of Rights Defense Committee
www.bordc.org

Kit Gage
First Amendment Foundation
www.firstamend.org

# 1

# Introduction

Terrorism presents a special challenge to a democratic society: how to prevent and punish ideologically motivated violence without infringing on political freedoms and civil liberties.

Nothing presented that challenge more urgently and sharply than the terrorist attacks of September 11, 2001. The horrific attacks of that day indelibly underscored the reality that the United States and its citizens are the targets of dangerous groups and individuals at home and abroad. Government agencies must have the legal authorities and resources sufficient to prevent terrorism when possible and to prosecute it when it occurs. In responding to terrorism, however, we must adhere to the principles of political freedom, due process, and protection of privacy that constitute the core of a free and democratic society.

The record of our nation's response to the threat of political violence is unfortunately one of repeated infringements of these principles. As the Supreme Court itself has acknowledged, "History abundantly documents the tendency of Government—however benevolent and benign its motives—to view with suspicion those who most fervently dispute its policies."[1] This is by no means a problem unique to the United States, but unfortunately our consti-

tutional commitment to civil liberties has not protected us from recurring official abuses. With confounding regularity, our government has, in the name of protecting national security, subverted the
very rights and liberties "which make the defense of the Nation
worthwhile."[2]

The Federal Bureau of Investigation, our nation's premier law enforcement agency, has the central role in fighting terrorism at
home.[3] It brings to this task impressive resources, significant legal
powers, and a jurisdiction that even extends overseas. In recent decades, the Bureau has penetrated and prosecuted a wide array of organized criminal groups. It has pursued public corruption at all
levels of local, state, and federal government, while demonstrating a
resistance to the kinds of corruption that have sometimes plagued
police forces at the municipal level or in other countries. It has successfully investigated terrorist acts at home and abroad.

Yet this same FBI throughout its history has all too often violated
First Amendment rights of freedom of speech and association. In
the name of national security, it undertook the disruption and "neutralization" of peaceful protest. It devoted resources to monitoring
political activity rather than focusing on the investigation of criminal conduct. It relied on sweeping theories of guilt by association
rather than undertaking the harder but more productive work of
identifying those individuals who were planning violent activity. It
resisted public accountability and limits on its discretion.

In the wake of the first bombing of the World Trade Center in
1993, and the bombing of the federal building in Oklahoma in
1995, Congress enacted the Antiterrorism Act of 1996,[4] at the time
one of the worst assaults on the Constitution in decades. That law, a
precursor to the more infamous USA PATRIOT Act, resurrected
guilt by association as a principle of criminal and immigration law.
It created a special court to use secret evidence to deport foreigners labeled as "terrorists." It made support for the peaceful humanitarian

and political activities of selected foreign groups a crime. And it repealed a short-lived law forbidding the FBI from investigating First Amendment activities, opening the door once again to politically focused FBI investigations.

The 1996 Act has yet to yield any measurable protection against terrorism, although it has led to substantial incursions on constitutional rights. The Immigration and Naturalization Service, for example, took the Act as a green light to violate a fundamental principle of due process: that everyone has the right to confront his or her accusers. In dozens of cases after the 1996 Act passed, the government detained and sought to deport noncitizens (almost all of them Muslims) on the basis of secret evidence regarding their political affiliations with "terrorist organizations." In virtually every instance, it became apparent that those the government sought to deport were not dangerous terrorists. In case after case, the INS was forced to release aliens when its charges against them were revealed to be nothing more than guilt by association. None of the nineteen men who participated in the attacks of September 11 were among those, or had any connection with those, targeted by the government for deportation based on secret evidence. Indeed, not one of the government's "secret evidence" targets had *any* connection to al Qaeda. In addition, under the 1996 Act, the State Department published a politically selective list of "foreign terrorist organizations" to which it became a crime to give even humanitarian assistance of food and educational supplies, chilling political support but again yielding no impact on violent activity. Measures aimed at terrorism struck only the Constitution.

Civil liberties suffered a second blow in February 1999 when the Supreme Court ruled that immigrants selectively singled out for deportation in retaliation for their mere association with a faction of the Palestinian Liberation Organization had no right to challenge their deportations on First Amendment grounds.[5] The Court ruled both that Congress had cut off all access to the courts for such claims in a 1996 immigration law, and that in any event foreign nationals have no constitutional right to object to being targeted for deportation based on activities that would clearly be protected by the First Amendment if engaged in by United States citizens. In effect, the Court put immigrants on notice that if they engage in political activity of which the government disapproves, they are vulnerable to selective retaliatory enforcement of the immigration laws.

And now, in the aftermath of the September 11, 2001, atrocities, the nation is in deeper crisis than it has been in many decades. Once again, we are faced with undocumented claims that surrendering liberty will purchase security. We have seen numerous measures adopted or proposed that run counter to fundamental constitutional principles: military tribunals, torture, detention—even of citizens—without due process, secret deportation proceedings, and extralegal renditions. In the Patriot Act adopted in October 2001, Congress expanded government surveillance powers, changed the relationship between law enforcement and intelligence agencies, and broadened the discretion of the executive branch to detain foreign nationals indefinitely based on their associations and beliefs, rather than their acts.

Outside of the Patriot Act or any other legislative authority, based only on assertions of executive power, the government has engaged in literally worldwide abuses, including torture of detainees at Guantánamo Bay, Cuba, in Afghanistan and Iraq, and at other, secret locations;[6] roundups of foreign nationals in the United States; and the imprisonment of even U.S. citizens in military jails without charge.[7] A previously little known "material witness" law has been used to jail people without criminal charges.[8] Attorney General John Ashcroft rewrote guidelines governing intelligence gathering inside the United States, cutting surveillance loose from any grounding in suspicion of involvement in crime, much less terrorism.[9] Government agencies embarked on a range of "data mining" programs without privacy guidelines.[10] And Congress created powerful new intelligence agencies (the Department of Homeland Security, the office of the Director of National Intelligence, and the National Counter-Terrorism Center) without clearly defining rules for domestic spying.

The purpose of this book is to examine the civil liberties issues raised by government responses to terrorism, and to identify what is necessary to ensure that counterterrorism activities (especially those conducted inside the United States) are reliably consistent with the Constitution. The book seeks to place the terrorism problem in historical context by reviewing the government's persistent infringements on the First Amendment and its avoidance of meaningful controls. Part I recounts several recent instances where "counterterrorism" investigations consisted largely of monitoring First Amendment activity. These cases all arose after the reforms of the Watergate era, which were supposed to have reined in the FBI in response to earlier abuses. Part II outlines the legal framework that permitted such intrusive investigations even before the Patriot Act and other changes. Informed by this background, Parts III and IV examine the Antiterrorism Act of 1996, the Patriot Act of 2001, and other recent antiterrorism intitiatives. The conclusion proposes an alternative approach to fighting terrorism that is likely to be both more effective and more consistent with the Constitution than the path the government has taken.


## FIVE STORIES

To understand the recurring nature of the government's misguided response to ideological threats, we start with five stories:

## The Fifties: McCarthyism

In August 1952, Frank Wilkinson was testifying on behalf of the Los Angeles Housing Authority as an expert witness in an eminent domain hearing against slum property in the Chavez Ravine area.[11] The Housing Authority wanted to clear the slum to build public housing. Wilkinson had been on the Housing Authority staff for ten years, campaigning for the racial integration of public housing. His support for social justice had long since brought him to the attention of the FBI, which had secretly begun an investigation in an attempt to link him to the Communist Party. As Wilkinson finished his testimony at the condemnation hearing, he was asked on cross examination, "Mr. Wilkinson, will you now tell us of all the organizations, political or otherwise, with which you have associated?" In those times, the mere posing of the question carried an implied accusation that one was a Communist.

Wilkinson refused to answer the question, launching a public odyssey that included a trip to federal prison and a lifetime of defending the First Amendment. His insistence upon his constitutional rights made headlines the next day in the *Los Angeles Times.* The eminent domain court disqualified him as an expert and struck his testimony from the record. The Los Angeles City Council called upon the House Un-American Activities Committee to investigate the Housing Authority. The California Senate subpoenaed both Wilkinson and his wife, a high school teacher. When they refused to answer questions regarding their political affiliations, they were both fired from their jobs.

Wilkinson went on to organize community and legal efforts to defend the Constitution, helping to found what is today the National Committee Against Repressive Legislation (NCARL). The FBI continued to investigate, harass, and disrupt his First Amendment activities. In July 1958, Congress subpoenaed Wilkinson and again asked about his political associations. He again refused to answer, invoking his First Amendment rights. With Carl Braden, the civil rights activist, he was cited for contempt and convicted in federal court. He appealed all the way to the Supreme Court, where he lost by a vote of five to four.[12] In 1961, he served nine months in prison. When he came out, the FBI stepped up its neutralization campaign, as field offices were invited to interfere with his speaking engagements through "disruptive tactics." In all, Wilkinson was under surveillance for thirty-eight years. The FBI generated 130,000 pages of detailed reports on him and his friends at a cost of several million dollars. At the end of it all, the FBI concluded that Wilkinson and the group he founded to fight for the First Amendment had engaged in no illegal activities.

## The Sixties and Seventies: COINTELPRO

On April 22, 1970, thousands of people gathered on Washington, D.C.'s mall to celebrate the first Earth Day. Rallies in cities across the nation brought the total to twenty million Americans participating in what has been described as the "birth of the modern environmental movement."[13] The FBI was there. Headquarters had ordered agents in at least forty cities to spy on Earth Day events. Their reports identified groups and individuals associated with planning the event. They attempted "to link the environmental activists with organizations the bureau [had] already targeted for surveillance, infiltration, and disruption."[14] In Denver, the FBI's surveillance team recorded the remarks of Senator Gaylord Nelson. In Washington, D.C., agents carefully wrote down the slogans on signs carried by marchers and summarized each of the speeches, noting, for example, that Phil Ochs "made a few anti-war, anti-administration remarks."[15]

The Earth Day surveillance was part of a massive FBI program known as COINTELPRO, a set of secret investigations and disruptive actions against political activism across a wide range of issues. A special Senate committee chaired by Idaho Democrat Frank Church (the "Church Committee") in 1975 and 1976 found that the FBI had conducted a wide-ranging campaign of monitoring and disrupting political groups that were not engaged in any illegal conduct.[16] At the peak of its efforts, the FBI was investigating all major protest movements, from civil rights activists to Vietnam war protesters to women's liberation advocates. Standard FBI methodology included bugging of homes and offices, wiretapping, break-ins, and informants. In addition, the FBI sought to spread misinformation, foment internal dissension, and even provoke illegal activity. The effort consumed tremendous resources and sowed distrust and fear among many seeking peaceful change in government policies, but it produced little evidence of criminal conduct.[17]

## The Eighties: Central American Activists

"Please call me about Nicaragua. This will be a friendly chat." A New York law student returning home one day in 1985 found that message written on an FBI business card left at her door. The student had never been to Nicaragua, but had recently attended a meeting about the Nicaraguan conflict at City University. As public opposition to U.S. intervention in Central America mounted in the early 1980s, many others also received visits from the FBI. Daisy Cubias, who worked with the Ecumenical Refugee Council in Milwaukee, was visited once at her job and twice at home by FBI agents who asked her about members of a coalition to which she belonged that opposed U.S. policy in Central America. A Santa Cruz man was called by the FBI after returning from a trip to Nicaragua; when the man declined to meet for an interview, the agent commented that he "sounded guilty." One FBI agent seeking to interview a Detroit woman explained, "We try to interview everyone who makes a trip to Nicaragua. We do it for positive intelligence gathering."[18]

FBI agents tried three times to contact Jill Clark, a member of the New Orleans chapter of the Committee in Solidarity with the People of El Salvador (CISPES). Questioned about the visits at a 1985 hearing, FBI Director William Webster defended the visits and testified, "We are not keeping track of the membership of CISPES as such."[19] Three years later, however, the Center for Constitutional Rights, a public interest legal organization in New York City, released thousands of pages of documents obtained under the Freedom of Information Act, showing that the FBI had conducted a nationwide investigation of CISPES and other domestic groups whose only common feature was that they opposed American assistance to the military of El Salvador. The documents showed that, contrary to Webster's assurance, some FBI field offices in fact did undertake to identify CISPES members "as such." In the name of investigating "support for terrorism," agents monitored campus meetings, photographed peaceful rallies, checked license plate numbers in church parking lots, sent an informant into CISPES offices to copy or steal records, and questioned activists at home and at work. While the investigative efforts were nominally focused on CISPES, they ultimately collected information on the political activities of 1,330 groups opposed to U.S. policy in Central America.[20] Throughout, the FBI gave little attention to uncovering criminal conduct, and never found any evidence of terrorism or support of terrorism.

### The Nineties: Palestinians and Muslims

Khader Musa Hamide immigrated to the United States in 1971. He earned a bachelor's degree in psychology and an MBA. He also became active in the Palestinian community. He distributed copies of a newspaper published by the Popular Front for the Liberation of Palestine (PFLP). The PFLP, the second-largest faction within the umbrella Palestine Liberation Organization, had engaged in violent activities in the Middle East, but it was also engaged in a wide range of lawful activities, including the provision of education, day care, health care, and social security, as well as cultural activities, publications, and political organizing. Hamide participated in demonstrations advocating Palestinian self-determination and helped organize large public dinners which featured political speeches, cultural performances, and humanitarian aid fund-raising attended by hundreds of Palestinians and Arab-Americans.

In 1984, Hamide's activities brought him to the attention of the FBI. He and others in the Los Angeles area suspected of being PFLP members became the subject of an intensive FBI investigation. An undercover FBI agent moved into the apartment next door to Hamide for nine months. With the assistance of local police officers, the FBI documented in detail Hamide's participation in political demonstrations, his distribution of literature, and his speeches at public events. It painstakingly (but not very accurately) translated hundreds of pages of Arabic-language newsletters. Yet the FBI made no attempt to follow the trail of the money allegedly collected by Hamide and the others to determine whether it supported lawful or violent activities. Once the FBI had characterized the PFLP as a terrorist organization, it did not matter to its investigation that Hamide and his friends were engaged in entirely lawful and peaceful protest activity.

After three years of investigation, the FBI found no evidence of criminal activity by Hamide or other alleged PFLP members in Los Angeles. But rather than close its investigation and move on, the FBI asked the Immigration and Naturalization Service (INS) to deport Hamide and several others in order to "disrupt" their political activities and hamper the PFLP. In 1987, shortly after Hamide applied for U.S. citizenship, FBI and INS agents arrested him and his Kenyan-born wife and six others and sought to deport them immediately. The government, invoking long-unused provisions of the McCarran-Walter Act, charged them with being deportable for being associated with a group that advocated "world communism." In a chilling preview of what was to come in other cases, the INS sought to detain the "Los Angeles 8" on the basis of secret evidence, but an immigration judge refused to go along, and released them. Federal courts blocked the deportations, characterizing the government's case as based on "guilt by association," but the Justice Department appealed to the Supreme Court, which ruled that aliens can be singled out for deportation based on their legal, political activities.[21] The government is still seeking deportation, more than eighteen years after the case began. It is now proceeding under the Patriot Act, claiming that conduct dating back to the 1980s violates a law passed in 2001.

### *Post-9/11: Material Support and an Idaho Student's Website*

In March 2004, Attorney General John Ashcroft announced the federal indictment of Sami al-Hussayen, a Saudi student at the University of Idaho. Ashcroft described al-Hussayen as part of "a terrorist threat to Americans that is fanatical and . . . fierce." What was al-Hussayen's crime? Creating a website.

The government alleged that running the website violated the Patriot Act, which made it a crime to provide "expert advice or assistance" to terrorist groups. Al-Hussayen had done so, the government charged, by including on his website links to other websites. Those other websites in turn featured the texts of speeches by Muslim clerics, some of which preached violent jihad.

The government never claimed that al-Hussayen himself had advocated violence. Nor did it maintain that al-Hussayen had intended to further terrorism by including these links among many on his website. The government's claim was that, under the Patriot Act, it did not matter why al-Hussayen had included the links. Any support to a terrorist group is a crime, the government argued, without regard to the intention of the individual providing the support, and even if the support consists of placing a link on a website. On this theory, the *New York Times* could be prosecuted for providing material support to al Qaeda if it included a link to one of Osama bin Laden's recorded messages in connection with a news story about the message.

Before it indicted him, the government wiretapped al-Hussayen. All told, it collected 20,000 e-mails and listened in on 9,000 of his phone calls over the course of a year. Yet in a lengthy criminal trial, the prosecution offered no evidence that al-Hussayen intended to support terrorism. In June 2004, an Idaho jury acquitted al-Hussayen on all terrorist charges. He had sat in jail for nearly a year and a half. As one juror said later, "He never spoke a word supporting terrorists. He just did what a university or a television station does—he posted the stuff." [22]

## THE LIMITS OF POST-WATERGATE REFORMS

These stories, spanning five decades, reveal a troubling pattern of surveillance and "disruption" of legitimate political activity. After the Church Committee in 1975 and 1976 documented the intelligence agencies' illegal tactics, public and congressional outrage spawned a series of reforms intended to prevent political spying and harassment. The reforms were significant and many of them remain in place today but, as the CISPES and LA 8 cases illustrate, the changes were by no means as deep or as permanent as many had believed. And the executive branch's recourse to arbitrary arrests and torture after September 11—justified by legal analyses citing the Constitution—shows just how little is resolved. While the Supreme Court held in the enemy combatant decisions in June 2004 that the president does not have a "blank check" in the "war" on terrorism, intrusions on privacy, ethnic and religious targeting, guilt by association, and assertions of unfettered executive power remain central to the government's approach to national security and counterterrorism.

The FBI, the Justice Department to which it reports, and the government as a whole still have not defined a concept of "intelligence" that fully respects civil liberties. Consequently, through the 1980s and 1990s, the FBI continued to undertake investigations that, while lacking the extreme tactics of COINTELPRO, shared the philosophy and approach of the counterintelligence investigations condemned by the Church Committee. Arab-American community leaders, Palestinian students, Amnesty International members, and environmental activists were among the subjects of FBI counterintelligence or antiterrorism investigations whose focus on political activity recalled the abuses of the past.

The adoption of the Antiterrorism Act of 1996 and the Patriot Act of 2001 show how little has been learned from the abuses of the past and how alluring the concept of unrestrained intelligence investigations remains. The 1996 Act's explicit criminalization of support for peaceful activity effectively authorized FBI surveillance and infiltration of political, religious, and ethnic groups engaged in peaceful humanitarian and political work. Its repeal of a prohibition against using First Amendment activities as the sole basis for an investigation further encouraged politically motivated investigations. Its reintroduction of guilt by association into the immigration laws allowed the exclusion and deportation of foreign nationals not for what they have done but for the causes and groups with which they have associated. And the endorsement of secret evidence in immigration proceedings against alleged "terrorists" denied the most fundamental of rights—the right to defend oneself by confronting one's accusers. And this was pre–9/11.

As 9/11 grimly underscored, the 1996 Act's provisions had little direct impact on the fight against terrorism. Before 9/11, the support for terrorism provisions had resulted in only three prosecutions, none involving al Qaeda. (After September 11, the material support provision was used to prosecute men who had received training at al Qaeda camps.) The "Alien Terrorist Removal Court" of the 1996 Act has to this day never been used—in part because the Justice Department claimed authority outside the Act for using secret evidence in deportation proceedings with even fewer due process protections. Prior to 9/11, the government carried out a number of successful prosecutions of terrorists, but did so without relying on the 1996 Act authorities.

The Patriot Act and other post–9/11 initiatives present several new themes. One is the breaking down of the "wall" that had existed between intelligence and law enforcement agencies (and between the intelligence and law enforcement units within the FBI). To some extent, the wall had become perverted to the point where it served neither civil liberties nor national security, but the result of the changes is to allow government agents in criminal cases to take advantage of the less restrictive rules applicable to intelligence investigations, while also allowing intelligence agencies like the CIA to enjoy the fruits of the considerable powers of law enforcement agencies. Second, the Patriot Act gave the government new powers to acquire the vast databases of personal information generated in the course of everyday life in the digital age at the same time that commercial databases and the power of technology to analyze data for patterns increased. And while FBI agents interviewed activists planning protests at the Democratic and Republican conventions in 2004,[23] ethnicity and religion seemed to have replaced politics as the most dangerous basis for investigations and detentions, as noncitizens bore the brunt of many of the most troubling antiterrorism campaigns.

## CHILLING EFFECT ON THE FIRST AMENDMENT

In the past, the FBI intentionally used investigations to intimidate. An FBI memorandum in September 1970 urged questioning members of one group in order to "enhance the paranoia in these circles and . . . further serve to get the point across that there is an FBI agent behind every mailbox." [24] When confronted with charges of harassment today, the government responds that its *intent* is not to intimidate. Viewed objectively, however, government monitoring and questioning of people regarding their political activities, particularly when targeted at Arabs and Muslims, has an inescapable chilling effect. For protest groups already at odds with the government, or for minority ethnic or religious groups, such attention inevitably inhibits and reduces the level of political activities in which the group's members feel free to engage. Word travels fast that the FBI has been to visit somebody and has asked about the group's activities, membership, or funding.

The government's case against the LA 8, for example, had a devastating chilling effect on the activities of Palestinians throughout the United States. And when the FBI began interviewing Arab-Americans during the Gulf War in 1991, many were afraid to speak out, both because of concern that neighbors and co-workers would assume that there was a reason for the FBI visit and for fear of being subjected to racial harassment. [25] These tactics simultaneously silence the community targeted and build suspicion of law enforcement. As Casey Kasem, a Los Angeles radio host and prominent Arab-American, said, "When Arab-Americans become suspect, then

Arab-Americans tend to want to carry a low profile and not speak out on issues they believe strongly in. The interviews are thus impeding our First Amendment rights."[26] And the Gulf War interviews of Arabs were mild compared to the targeting of Arabs and Muslims in the wake of the terrorist attacks of September 11. In just the first few weeks after 9/11, hundreds of noncitizens, almost all of them Arabs or Muslims, were locked up in a process the Department of Justice Inspector General later found to be "indiscriminate and haphazard."[27] The government instituted special registration requirements against Arab and Muslim males, forcing 80,000 of them to report to immigration offices to be fingerprinted, photographed, and interviewed.[28]

Enforcement or investigative efforts that follow lines of politics, ethnicity, or religion have an inevitable chilling effect. Yale Law School professor and First Amendment scholar Thomas Emerson described the impact of government surveillance on what he called "the dynamics of the system of freedom of expression":

> Suspicions that government infiltrators are reporting the discussions at meetings dampen the spontaneity or destroy the harmony of a political gathering. Thus many people will hesitate to attend a meeting where the police are taking down license numbers or engage in a demonstration where they are being photographed.[29]

This chilling effect undermines the political and social integration necessary to the maintenance of security in a democratic society. To promote security, we need to avoid engendering the sense that dissenters or immigrants are excluded from society. This alone is a powerful reason to adopt a model of intelligence that does not define threats in terms of politics, religion, or ethnicity and to develop counterterrorism strategies that do not devolve into the monitoring of entire religious or ethnic communities.

## POLITICAL MONITORING VERSUS
## CRIMINAL LAW ENFORCEMENT

For much of its modern history, our nation has grappled, often unsuccessfully, with the question of how to separate the few who resort to violence from the many who criticize the government, the few who are dangerous from the many who are different. In the 1950s, this challenge was posed by the threat of Communism. Today's challenge is terrorism.

What are the means to prevent attacks like those of September 11, and to promptly identify, arrest, and convict the perpetrators of such acts, without casting a net that sweeps in peaceful dissent or ethnic identity? If a fundamentalist religious group or a militia group is preaching the propriety of violence or advocating support for terrorism, when should the FBI be permitted to investigate, and how long and intensively should it continue investigating? If a person or group is involved in violent activity, should the FBI identify and monitor others who share the same ideology? If a group is raising money and sending it to a politically active foreign group, should the FBI be permitted to investigate? Should the government be able to prohibit all support for a group that engages in both violent and peaceful activities? These questions are central to the fight against terrorism.

One approach, followed throughout much of our history, has been to designate certain ideologies or groups as suspect, to attempt to identify their adherents, members, supporters, or associates, and then to monitor the activities of all those identified. This "guilt by association" intelligence model presumes that all those

who share a particular ideology or political position must be monitored on the chance that they will slip into criminal activity in
order to achieve their political objectives. It blurs the distinction
between "support" for a cause and participation in violence. Thus,
even if an investigation begins with an allegation of violent conduct, it often expands to include many who share the same ideology, without any evidence linking them to the crime. At its worst,
this approach has led to investigations aimed mainly at disrupting,
discrediting, and neutralizing "targets," whether or not there was
any evidence that they were planning criminal activity.

A better approach recognizes the critical distinction between
criminal conduct and ethnic, religious, or political identity. This approach accepts angry criticism of government as healthy to a democratic society and constitutionally protected. It requires the
government to have suspicion of personal involvement in past, ongoing, or planned criminal conduct before it investigates a group or
an individual; if there is no reason to suspect criminal conduct, persons and groups should be left alone, regardless of their beliefs or the
actions of those with whom they associate. The goal of this model is
not to draw the widest possible picture of an enterprise, but to narrow the scope of inquiry to the true threats. Rather than viewing advocacy and violence as part of a continuum, the approach tries to
draw a distinction between the two.

Professor Emerson described the choice as follows:

> The problem is not the government's power to investigate a crime
> that has been or is about to be committed, . . . since, in such
> cases, any impact upon the right of an individual to freedom of
> expression has never been considered to be of constitutional di-
> mensions. . . . Rather, the issue arises where the collection of
> data is not related, or only remotely related, to law enforcement
> and is principally designed to inform the government about the

political beliefs, attitudes or activities of individuals or organizations in the community. It must be conceded that the distinction involved is often difficult to draw; it is, however, fundamental to the constitutional issue.[30]

Especially after September 11, some have argued that the law enforcement approach is limited to prosecuting terrorist attacks after they occur and is therefore inadequate to prevent terrorism. According to this view, a more expansive intelligence approach is more effective. This argument ignores the fact that the 9/11 attacks were plotted mainly overseas, where our intelligence agencies already operated with very few constraints, and yet the intelligence agencies failed to predict and prevent the attacks. It also ignores the fact that one of the principal goals of the criminal justice system is the prevention of crime.

Adherence to a criminal standard does not mean that the FBI must remain deaf to statements calling for violent activity, nor, as some have irresponsibly said, does it require the FBI to wait until a bomb goes off before it can act.[31] While a person cannot be prosecuted under the Constitution merely for saying that federal buildings should be blown up, law enforcement agencies may constitutionally investigate to determine if a person making such statements plans to act on them, for conspiracy to blow up federal buildings is a crime. What the First Amendment demands—and what proponents of an "intelligence" approach to terrorism too often forget—is that an investigation must be narrowly limited to determining whether violent activity is in fact being planned. The government should not extend its attention to an individual without reason to suspect—apart from ideology, ethnicity, or religious belief—that he shares in the criminal plans or activity. And if evidence is not developed that a suspected group is in fact engaging in or planning violent activity, the government should withdraw its attention, until and unless new evidence provides reason to suspect that the group or individual is planning acts of violence.

## THE CONSTITUTION AND AN EFFECTIVE COUNTERTERRORISM STRATEGY

A focus on criminal conduct, critics claim, is too narrow. In order to maintain security, government officials and terrorism experts tell us, we must surrender some of our liberty.[32] But in the past, we have all too often sacrificed liberty without benefit to security. There is no necessary contradiction between a robust application of constitutional rights and an effective counterterrorism strategy. To the contrary, an antiterrorism policy that cuts corners constitutionally is likely to be ineffective.

Terrorist acts are criminal regardless of ideology and are best handled by strategies that are as divorced from ideology as possible. Much of the 1996 Antiterrorism Act and the immigration provisions of the 2001 Patriot Act focus not on acts of violence but on the political or religious ideology that motivates them. This approach is inevitably imprecise and inefficient. First, for practical reasons alone, the government cannot monitor all adherents of certain religions or ideologies or all members of certain ethnic groups on the chance that they may engage in terrorism sometime in the future. Our nation harbors too many diverse religions, ideologies, and nationalities for the government to monitor effectively. Second, the ideological approach encourages stereotyping that not only stigmatizes the innocent but may lull security services into ignoring genuine threats that do not fit an ideological or ethnic pattern. The ideological approach is bound to be static, while the "face of terrorism" can change rapidly: Muslim fundamentalist one day, white separatist the next, anti-technology loner the next. The Oklahoma

City bombing demonstrated the frightful destructiveness of a person of little ideology and no apparent affiliation.

Third, politically focused investigations are likely to be counterproductive and may actually contribute to violence. Political freedom is a society's safety valve, allowing the passionately critical a nonviolent way to express their dissatisfaction with the status quo. Dissent is the mechanism for initiating social change. Shutting off this safety valve only encourages those who have no desire to see the process of peaceful change work. Further, if entire groups are identified as enemies, the cohesiveness of the group may harden against society, substantially diminishing the likelihood that law enforcement agencies will find cooperative witnesses. If the FBI treats an entire nationality or group as suspect, members of that nationality or group will in turn treat the FBI as suspect, making even legitimate investigation much more difficult.

In 1991, Frank Wilkinson and the National Committee Against Repressive Legislation launched a campaign calling for legislation to complete the process of reforming the FBI. At the heart of the campaign was a petition calling for legislation limiting FBI investigations to situations where there are specific and articulable facts giving reason to believe that the person or group has committed or is planning a criminal act, and limiting such investigations to obtaining evidence of criminal activity.

Despite the support of over 500 legal scholars across the country, the proposal was not adopted. As a result, there is no such statutory limitation on the FBI. The principle that the FBI should confine itself to collecting evidence of crimes and potential crimes should be a central premise of our national antiterrorism strategy, yet it is nowhere reflected in our statute books. If it had been, we might have avoided some of the abuses we detail here. In the wake of the events of September 11, the need for reform is more, not less, urgent than ever.

PART I

Investigating First Amendment Activities:
The FBI Before September 2001

# 2

# The FBI's Investigation of Central American Activists, 1981–1985

". . . it is imperative at this time to formulate some plan of attack against CISPES and specifically, against individuals, . . . who defiantly display their contempt for the U.S. government by making speeches and propagandizing their cause while asking for political asylum.

New Orleans is of the opinion that Department of Justice and State should be consulted to explore the possibility of deporting these individuals. . . ."

*—Teletype message to FBI headquarters from*
*New Orleans field office, November 1983*[1]


## OPENING THE INVESTIGATION

In 1981, the Justice Department ordered the FBI to determine whether the Committee in Solidarity with the People of El Salvador (CISPES) was an agent of a foreign power, that is, whether it was controlled or directed from abroad and thus required to register and disclose information about its finances under the Foreign Agents Registration Act (FARA). CISPES was a U.S.-based organization, composed largely of U.S. citizens, many of them college students. It opposed U.S. aid to the military of El Salvador and openly supported the aims of the Frente Democratica Revolucionario (FDR), the political organization for the rebel groups in El Salvador.[2] The organization acknowledged that it had contact with FDR leaders, and that it had provided funding for humanitarian activities in El Salvador. After a brief investigation, the FBI advised the Justice Department that there was no substantiation for the concern that CISPES was a foreign agent. Rather, the FBI told the Justice Department, CISPES appeared to be an independent, domestic group engaged wholly in lawful, nonviolent political activities.[3]

Nonetheless, in March 1983, the FBI opened an international terrorism investigation of CISPES. It did so on the basis of allegations that CISPES was controlled by the Salvadoran rebel organization, the Farabundo Marti National Liberation Front (FMLN), and was channeling funds to it, and that a CISPES chapter was planning terrorist attacks in the United States.

Most of these new allegations came from Frank Varelli, an immigrant with family ties to El Salvador's security apparatus who moved to the United States in 1980 and took upon himself the mission of exposing a Communist underground that he believed was at work here.[4] By the time the FBI opened the counterterrorism investigation in 1983, Varelli had long been providing information to the FBI about CISPES and other Central American groups. Varelli came under the supervision of an FBI agent who gave him free rein to infiltrate the CISPES chapter in Dallas.[5]

Varelli's specific allegation that CISPES was planning terrorist attacks related only to the Dallas chapter of CISPES. Nonetheless, when FBI headquarters approved the Dallas field office's opening of a full investigation against CISPES, it also directed ten other field offices to examine local CISPES activities.[6] From the outset, the investigation had a dual focus: "establishing the extent of CISPES support of terrorism in El Salvador, and the potential of committing terrorist operations in the United States."[7]

The initial phase of the investigation failed to turn up any evidence that CISPES was planning terrorist attacks in the U.S. The FBI's San Diego office recommended on October 7, 1983, that the investigation be closed: "Information to date indicates that the organization is involved with information campaigns, fund raising functions, and promotion of peaceful demonstrations against United States policy in El Salvador."[8]

## EXPANDING THE INVESTIGATION NATIONWIDE

Nonetheless, on October 28, 1983, FBI headquarters officials ordered the investigation to be expanded to all field offices nationwide. In doing so, headquarters instructed its field offices "to determine location, leadership, and activities of CISPES chapters in your respective territories through sources, investigation, and surveillances," and "not to investigate the exercise of First Amendment rights."[9] These were inherently contradictory instructions, for aside from the unsubstantiated allegations by Varelli that the Dallas chapter was planning violence, all the evidence available to the Bureau indicated that CISPES was involved exclusively in activities protected by the First Amendment. Faced with this contradiction, field offices proceeded to collect and report information on a wide range of First Amendment activities.

For more than two years, the FBI conducted surveillance of a nationwide political organization on a scale not seen since the 1960s. Agents took thousands of photographs at peaceful demonstrations, monitored rallies on college campuses, attended a mass at a university, spied on church groups and labor union locals, sent an informant to numerous meetings, rummaged through trash, collected mailing lists, took phone numbers off posters opposing intervention in Central America, recorded license plate numbers of vehicles parked outside public meetings, and obtained long-distance billing records from telephone companies to trace patterns of association of activists. By the time it was over, the FBI had gathered and added to its files information on the political activities of approximately 2,376 individuals and 1,330 groups.[10]

The CISPES case generated 178 "spin-off" investigations of other groups and individuals. Congressional investigators later found that in four of the cases involving other groups, the investigations were apparently "based solely on [the groups'] ideological similarity to or association with CISPES." Three other groups were targeted because the FBI believed them to be CISPES chapters, even though the groups had their own names and no connection with CISPES other than a shared ideological perspective. The FBI opened a case on another group, the Birmingham Committee in Solidarity with Central America ("BCSCA"), without any clear reason at all; when the investigation failed to establish any connection between CISPES and BCSCA, the Birmingham FBI office nonetheless received headquarters' approval to obtain BCSCA's telephone toll records upon the field office's bald assertion that BCSCA was identical to CISPES. Spin-off investigations of individuals were initiated on the basis of attendance at the showing of a CISPES-sponsored film, the appearance of names on lists of participants at CISPES conferences, and similar associations. In one case, the FBI investigated a university professor on the basis of a question he posed on an exam and a speaker he had invited to class.[11]

While the investigation was still in progress, FBI Director Webster denied to Rep. Don Edwards's House Judiciary oversight subcommittee that the FBI was keeping track of CISPES members per se.[12] Years later, the Center for Constitutional Rights obtained FBI reports disclosing that a number of FBI field offices did in fact try to identify all CISPES members in their area. For example, the Phoenix office reported to headquarters in October 1983 (the memo was addressed to Webster, although it is unlikely he ever saw it), "the case will remain open to further identify the local members of CISPES."[13]

Overall, the CISPES investigation and spin-offs generated a broadly comprehensive picture of grassroots opposition to United States policy in El Salvador. Neither the CISPES investigation nor any of its spin-offs, however, produced any reliable information of planned violence or other illegal activity, and no charges were ever brought against any individual or group.

## GUILT BY ASSOCIATION

"In Dallas' opinion, the key word is solidarity. All of these groups M-19 CO, FALN, FMLN, etc, are connected, extent depending on the groups themselves. In regards to CISPES, one must remember that 80[%] of their membership are Anglo middle class individuals, many very well educated, the same profile as WUO [Weather Underground Organization] members in the 1960's."
—*Memorandum from the FBI's Dallas field office to headquarters, January 1984*[14]

The CISPES investigation was driven by the concept of guilt by association. The first application of the concept came in the opening of the case: the FMLN was a terrorist organization; CISPES "supported" the FMLN; therefore, reasoned the FBI, CISPES was to be treated as a terrorist organization. The second application of guilt by association occurred when the Dallas field office's investigation was extended to other CISPES chapters and ultimately nationwide. The Dallas FBI office had allegations that the CISPES chapter *in Dallas* was planning terrorist attacks, yet the FBI opened an investigation on all CISPES chapters nationwide, solely on the basis of their shared ideology and political goals. Guilt by association also led the FBI to open spin-off investigations of groups associated with CISPES. And finally, the FBI turned to guilt by association when it sought to justify the CISPES investigation by reference to CISPES' associations with other, more radical groups.

By April 1994, the FBI had compiled a list of groups "either in support of CISPES or connected with CISPES in some fashion." The list included Oxfam America, the Southern Christian Leadership Coalition, the ACLU, the U.S. Catholic Conference, and Amnesty International.[15] Guilt by association was stretched to the breaking point when the FBI suggested a link between CISPES and two bombings in Washington. Even as it acknowledged that the bombings were "probably not perpetrated or directed by" CISPES, the FBI bootstrapped its case against CISPES by noting that one bombing took place at "about the same time" a CISPES rally was held in Washington and that responsibility for the other was claimed by another group espousing positions "similar to those of CISPES."[16]

As an intelligence concept, guilt by association justifies everexpanding investigations: each association widens the circle of suspects and justifies still further investigations of the new suspects' associations. The purpose of the investigation becomes establishing the broadest possible network. By contrast, domestic criminal investigations may be opened only upon suspicion of specific, individualized criminal conduct. When an investigation is limited by this criminal standard, investigators seek to determine who is engaged in planning or carrying out violent activities, and guilt by association is inapplicable. But under the FBI's foreign counterintelligence and international terrorism investigations, the criminal standard does not apply: the FBI is not limited to investigating criminal conduct. The CISPES investigation, as an international terrorism investigation, was governed by the counterintelligence guidelines and was not subject to the criminal standard, even though it took place in the United States and focused mainly on U.S. citizens.[17]

## MONITORING FIRST AMENDMENT ACTIVITIES

The CISPES investigation involved close monitoring of core political activity. The FBI collected detailed information on a planned march on Washington to demonstrate against U.S. involvement in Central America and passed it on to the Department of Justice Criminal Division, the Defense Intelligence Agency, the Secret Service, and the secretary of state, even as the Bureau noted, "All reports indicate plans for a peaceful march." The reporting included the numbers of buses that were expected from various cities, the times of their departure, and the cost of the trip per individual.[18] One FBI report on CISPES described in detail a campaign by a coalition in San Francisco in support of a local ballot initiative. The FBI report pointed out that the mayor, the local archbishop, and "all local congress people" also supported the initiative.[19] The Louisville office reported that CISPES distributed literature to the public "urging U.S. citizens to write their respective congressmen to express their concerns over increasing U.S. involvement in El Salvador." The Mobile office reported on a two-hour radio program in which a CISPES supporter described the group's political positions. The Pittsburgh office quoted at length from a newspaper article entitled, "Churches and the Peace Movement."[20] An agent in Wichita removed a flyer captioned "Stop U.S. Intervention in Central America and the Caribbean" from a bulletin board in the Liberal Arts Building at Wichita State, and sent a copy to headquarters.[21]

One of the most striking aspects of the CISPES investigation is the amount of confusion that existed within the FBI about what investigation was and was not permissible under the First Amendment. It is not that FBI officials were unaware of the First Amendment implications of the investigation. Indeed, it is clear from internal FBI memos that many agents and supervisory officials involved in the case were anxious to adhere to First Amendment limits. They just did not know what those limits were or how they could be reconciled with the investigation's stated objective of identifying CISPES chapters, leaders, and activities.

One telling example came from the Cincinnati field office. Its investigation of the local CISPES chapter turned up contacts with an order of Catholic nuns. The field office cabled headquarters, asking for "guidelines regarding investigations of captioned matter, vis-à-vis religious organizations—specifically the Roman Catholic Church." [22] The field office sensed that there was something wrong with investigating an order of Catholic nuns, but that is where the guilt by association concept of intelligence monitoring had led it.

In July 1984, FBI headquarters sent a ten-page memorandum to all involved offices "to reiterate . . . guidelines and instructions for these investigations." The headquarters instructions noted that "some offices have reported information recently regarding political statements and political lobbying." Headquarters explicitly directed that "Political activities or political lobbying . . . are not, repeat not, targets of this investigation and should not be monitored." [23]

The directive had no impact. Two weeks after receiving it, the Denver office sent headquarters a memorandum stating that, "in spite of attempts by the Bureau to clarify guidelines and goals for this investigation, the field is still not sure of how much seemingly legitimate political activity can be monitored." [24] The same week, the Chicago field office sent headquarters a progress report describing CISPES as a group that "organizes campaigns to pressure legislators to vote against covert and overt intervention in Central America." [25] The following month, the Cleveland FBI office filed a report on an upcoming public conference on U.S. military involvement in Central America, sponsored by the United Steel Workers Union, the United Auto Workers, the National Education Association, and the United Church of Christ Commission for Racial Justice. The report listed who the speakers would be and what topics they would be addressing, including "The 1984 Elections" and "Winning the Labor Movement to Non-Intervention."[26] The memorandum concluded that "Cleveland plans to follow the progress of the conference."[27]

Monitoring of political activity persisted until the very end of the investigation. On June 4, 1985, weeks before the investigation was closed, the Houston field office submitted to headquarters 104 photographs of "a march conducted in Houston, Texas, on April 20, 1985 by the Texas April Mobilization for Peace, Justice, and Jobs."[28]

What allowed the CISPES investigation to veer out of control was not the lack of headquarters' attention to the First Amendment. It was something more fundamental, something inherent in the nature of intelligence investigations and in the use of guilt by association as an investigative guide. Instead of narrowly focusing its efforts on confirming or denying the specific allegations that CISPES was planning violent acts, this "intelligence" inquiry expanded into an unlimited effort to identify all possible CISPES chapters, activities, and associations. While the FBI headquarters advised field offices not to monitor First Amendment activities, other memoranda directed agents to identify CISPES members and activities. Since CISPES chapters by and large only engaged in the planning and staging of meetings and demonstrations, agents in the field were understandably confused. Some quietly ignored the case—there was remarkably little reporting from the New York field office, for example. Others did as they were told and unreflectively reported every meeting and poster.

## "SUPPORT FOR TERRORISM"—A NEW, UNDEFINED BASIS FOR INVESTIGATION

When the CISPES investigation was opened, there was no specific statutory prohibition against providing support to a terrorist organization. Aiding and abetting others in criminal conduct was, of course, illegal, as was engaging in a criminal conspiracy, but there was no legislation specifically defining "support for terrorism," or authorizing officials to designate certain groups as terrorist. In 1984, after the CISPES investigation had been opened, the Reagan administration proposed legislation to make "support for terrorism" a crime.[29] (The Reagan legislation was strikingly similar to the legislation later proposed by the Clinton administration and adopted in the 1996 Antiterrorism Act.) The Reagan legislation was strongly criticized as inconsistent with the First Amendment, and it was not enacted, but the FBI was undeterred by the lack of statutory authority. It carried on its investigation of CISPES' alleged "support for terrorism," using the broad discretion granted it under an executive order on intelligence activities and guidelines issued by Attorney General William French Smith that ironically were supposed to limit counterintelligence investigations.

The field offices and headquarters never specified what "support for terrorism" meant, but nobody seemed to have thought it was limited to conduct that supported others in planning or carrying out violent attacks. In the absence of a requirement to focus the investigation on illegal or violent activity, the headquarters directives on the First Amendment could not effectively prevent the monitoring of political activity. With only the guidance of broad concepts like "support for terrorism" or "foreign direction or control," agents investigated whatever activities CISPES engaged in: meetings, rallies, and grassroots organizing.

The problem was compounded by the FBI's use of the words

"leftist" and "terrorist" seemingly interchangeably. A March 4, 1985, Dallas memorandum stated, "This investigation was based on reliable asset information that CISPES provides international support to the leftist movement in El Salvador." In another memo, the Dallas office reported, "Source advised the following organizations are active in El Salvadoran leftist activities: Houston Human Rights League, Catholic Charities Refugee Halfway House, Holy Ghost Catholic Church, . . . Nuclear Weapons Freeze campaign. . . ." [30]

The interchangeable use of "leftist" and "terrorist" has deeper significance. The central theme of FBI political investigations from the Bureau's inception through the middle 1980s was the threat of a worldwide Communist takeover. The investigation of Martin Luther King Jr., for example, was nominally begun on the grounds that Communists were among his close advisers. Even the attempted deportation of the LA 8 in 1987, discussed in the next chapter, was based on their alleged membership in a group that supported Communism. As the Soviet Union collapsed, however, Communism ceased to be a guiding principle for FBI counterintelligence investigations. Terrorism emerged as the new threat to which government officials pointed when claiming that a surrender of liberty was necessary to purchase security. The CISPES case was part of this transition from "Communism" to "terrorism" as the continuing justification for the special legislative authority and broad national security powers that the FBI had grown accustomed to during the Cold War.

## WAS CISPES AN ABERRATION?

In 1988, FBI Director William Sessions testified that the CISPES case was an "aberration." Yet between January 1982 and June 1988, the FBI opened 19,500 international terrorism cases, many on subjects *not* suspected of being directly involved in terrorist activity, according to a General Accounting Office (GAO) study.[31] Of 158 cases that the GAO examined in detail, 44 percent contained no allegation that the target was involved in criminal behavior or was even a member of a terrorist group; the only justification for the investigation was a suspicion of the subject's undefined association with or link to a terrorist group.[32] As in the CISPES spin-offs, the link to a terrorist group that provided the basis for opening the investigation was sometimes very tenuous—the subject attended a meeting or had a contact with a group or an individual.[33] In one case, the FBI opened an investigation on a group simply because it was named in a brochure distributed by another group already under surveillance. The FBI monitored meetings, demonstrations, religious services, or other First Amendment activities in 11 percent of the 19,500 international terrorism cases. This means that at least 2,000 separate investigations were undertaken between 1982 and 1988 where the FBI monitored First Amendment activities.[34]

Moreover, in reviewing actual case files in seventy investigations that were based only on the subject's suspected association with or link to a terrorist group, the GAO found the FBI inspecting First Amendment activities 74 percent of the time. Thus, in cases opened without a criminal predicate, the FBI was most likely to monitor First Amendment activities.

In addition to CISPES and its spin-offs, other FBI investigations in the 1980s focused on Central American solidarity groups and foreign policy critics. The Bureau maintained a file captioned "Salvadoran Leftist Activities in the U.S.," which collected information on sanctuary activities and demonstrations. It had files titled "Nicaragua Proposed Demonstrations in the U.S." in eighteen cities. It opened an investigation of the Latin America Support Committee after the CISPES case was closed.[35] It continued to collect information on demonstrations protesting U.S. involvement in

Central America under another case file entitled "Nicaraguan Terrorist Matters." In 1986, a year after the CISPES case was closed, the FBI Chicago field office reported on peaceful demonstrations held by the Pledge of Resistance, a domestic group opposed to U.S. foreign policy, as part of the "Nicaraguan Terrorist Matters" file.[36] And through at least 1987, the FBI conducted a domestic security/terrorism investigation of the Pledge of Resistance.

## OVERSIGHT AND CONTROL

The CISPES case reveals both the potential value and the very real limitations of the system of accountability and control put in place in the 1970s. The Office of Intelligence Policy and Review (OIPR) is the Justice Department's internal watchdog for intelligence and international terrorism matters. Yet it allowed the investigation to go on for twenty-seven months, and ordered the case closed only on June 18, 1985, seven days after Rep. Don Edwards's subcommittee questioned FBI officials about the nature of the Bureau's investigations into CISPES and other Central American–related groups. When Edwards tried then and again in 1986 and 1987 to learn more about the FBI's investigation, FBI officials responded with only fragmentary answers. It was not until January 1988 that the full scope of the investigation was brought to public attention, two and a half years after the investigation was closed, and only as a result of a Freedom of Information Act request filed by a public interest group, the Center for Constitutional Rights (CCR).

At a hearing in 1988, Rep. Edwards described the difficulties his subcommittee experienced in trying to conduct oversight of the CISPES investigation:

> [T]he subcommittee began asking questions about CISPES in 1985, and it has taken us over three years to get the full story. The

Director [of the FBI] states now that CISPES generated 180 spin-off cases. In August 1986, we asked how many spin-offs there were, and the FBI said it didn't understand the question. We first asked to see the CISPES file in 1987. We got access to the file after the case hit the front page of the New York Times in February 1988. In April 1985, Director Webster testified that the FBI was not interested in the members of CISPES per se. Now that proves to be not so. Another FBI official strongly denied in February 1987 that the FBI was passing information to the National Guard in Salvador through Varelli. It now appears pretty clear he did. The FBI assured us it was not investigating the sanctuary movement. It is now clear the FBI surveilled sanctuary churches and investigated some sanctuary activities.[37]

## A FAILURE TO REFORM

In 1988, after the outlines of the story were revealed by CCR, the congressional intelligence committees conducted full investigations, including a review of many documents that had not been released to CCR. Edwards also insisted that the staff of his subcommittee be permitted to review the FBI's classified file. The FBI itself produced a critical internal report, and the FBI director testified publicly that the investigation had been misguided. But the intelligence committees, in their separate investigations, declared that they had found no systemic flaws meriting legislative remedy. The FBI claimed to have improved its internal procedures, and the Department of Justice amended the attorney general guidelines to provide additional guidance for investigations involving domestic groups composed primarily of U.S. citizens. Edwards introduced H.R. 50, the FBI First Amendment Protection Act, to prohibit the FBI from opening investigations on the basis of First Amendment activities. After six years, he finally succeeded in including in the 1994 crime bill a provision prohibiting the FBI from opening or maintaining investigations of "support for terrorism" solely on the basis of First Amendment activities. But two years later, that limitation was repealed in the Antiterrorism Act, meaning that no lasting statutory reform came of the CISPES fiasco.

The FBI admitted that the CISPES investigation had been overbroad, had improperly focused on First Amendment activities, and had been a waste of resources. It appeared to have learned a lesson. But soon, rumblings began again that the FBI's hands had been tied. Officials and former agents complained that criticism of the CISPES investigation had had a chilling effect within the Bureau, that agents recalling the CISPES experience had become overcautious. Following the 1993 World Trade Center bombing, officials grew bolder in these complaints, paving the way for enactment of the 1996 Antiterrorism Act, which repealed the Edwards amendment and adopted a "support for terrorism" provision that essentially legalized the FBI's approach in the CISPES investigation, by making it a federal crime to support the legal activities of designated foreign terrorist groups.

# 3

# The Investigation and Attempted Deportation
# of the Los Angeles 8

"This document hopes to identify key PFLP people in Southern California sufficiently enough so that law enforcement agencies capable of *disrupting the PFLP's activities* through legal action can do so."
—*FBI report, "Popular Front for the Liberation of Palestine (PFLP) Los Angeles Area" (1986) (emphasis added)*[1]

On January 26, 1987, FBI and INS agents in Los Angeles arrested six Palestinians and a Kenyan. Suggesting that it had broken up a terrorist cell, the government held the seven immigrants in maximum security, charged them with being affiliated with the Popular Front for the Liberation of Palestine (PFLP), and sought to deport them under the 1952 McCarran-Walter Act for being associated with a group that advocated the "doctrines of world communism." One week later, the INS arrested another Palestinian on the same charges, making eight "respondents" in all. The government's sensationalized allegations of terrorism and its use of the much-criticized McCarran-Walter Act received national attention, and the detainees were soon dubbed the "LA 8."[2]

In less than a month, however, an immigration judge ordered the eight released from custody because the government was unwilling to present publicly any evidence to support its claim that they should be detained as threats to national security while their deportation cases worked their way through the system. In the eighteen years since the arrests, the case has taken many twists and turns, including an evidentiary hearing lasting six weeks over the course of two and one half years, four trips to the appeals court, and review by the Supreme Court.[3] It produced landmark court rulings upholding the First Amendment rights of noncitizens and rejecting the government's attempts to target political activity, only to see them reversed by the Supreme Court. Other rulings limiting the discretion of the government to use secret evidence in the name of national security still stand. Through it all, the government never showed or even alleged that the LA 8 were engaged in any terrorist activity or supported any unlawful activities of the PFLP. The eight were never charged with a crime, or under any of the deportation provisions addressing actual criminal conduct or conduct threatening national security.

Instead, at the FBI's urging, the government by its own admission targeted the eight for engaging in lawful activity—activity clearly protected under the First Amendment for U.S. citizens—that the government contended supported something else, first "world communism" and later "terrorism." The case highlights the government's tendency to rely on guilt by association as a substitute for investigations focused on establishing individual involvement in violent activity. Like the CISPES investigation, the case provides a window into the FBI's counterterrorism program, revealing another instance in which the FBI's preoccupation with political activity, in particular with statements critical of the U.S. government and its foreign allies, overwhelmed any investigative interest in uncovering evidence of violent crimes.

## TARGETING AND "DISRUPTING" POLITICAL ACTIVITIES

Over the course of eighteen years, as the Justice Department has repeatedly changed its legal theories for deportation of the eight, the one constant has been the government's motive to deport them for their alleged political affiliations and activities. The INS initially charged all eight under provisions of the McCarthy-era McCarran-Walter Act that made it a deportable offense to be affiliated with a group that advocated the "doctrines of world communism." Then-FBI Director William Webster admitted to Congress two months after the arrests of the eight that they "had not been found to have engaged themselves in terrorist activity."[4] Webster admitted, "If these individuals had been United States citizens, there would not have been a basis for their arrest." Nonetheless, Webster asserted, the investigation was properly grounded under the attorney general guidelines governing international terrorism investigations.

When the LA 8 challenged the constitutionality of the initial "world communism" charges under the McCarran-Walter Act, the INS dropped those charges, filed new charges, and announced at a press conference that the change was merely tactical. It explained that it continued to seek deportation because "[i]t is our belief that they are members of [the PFLP]."[5]

The INS charged six of the eight with technical visa violations, such as taking too few credits on a student visa. The other two, Khader Hamide and Michel Shehadeh, were permanent residents, and therefore were not subject to deportation for visa violations. They faced only association-based charges throughout the case. After the INS dropped the charge that they were associated with a group that advocated "world communism," it charged that they were associated with a group that advocated destruction of property, and then with a group that advocated attacks on government officials. (In all instances, it was the same group, the PFLP.) In 1989, a federal district court declared these ideological provisions unconstitutional, but the government appealed. In 1990, Congress repealed these McCarran-Walter Act provisions, but the INS simply added new charges, charging Hamide and Shehadeh with providing material support to a "terrorist organization." Significantly, the INS did *not* allege that Hamide and Shehadeh provided material support to any terrorist *activity*, also a deportable offense, but instead argued that they could be deported solely for providing material support to a "terrorist organization," even though the organization engaged in a wide range of lawful activities and they were alleged to have supported only its lawful ends.

As the case progressed, it became clear that the INS was seeking to deport the LA 8 precisely because the FBI disapproved of their political activities. Internal government documents disclosed in the litigation revealed that, lacking any evidence that they had been involved in criminal conduct, the FBI turned to the INS. The language with which the FBI described its goal was the very language of COINTELPRO, the FBI's discredited domestic political harassment program of the 1960s and 1970s. The FBI said that its purpose was "to identify key PFLP people in Southern California so that law enforcement agencies capable of *disrupting* the PFLP's activities through legal action can do so."[6] The FBI specifically urged the INS to deport Hamide because he is "intelligent, aggressive, dedicated, and shows great leadership ability," and therefore "[b]y removing Hamide through criminal or deportation proceedings the PFLP will be severely hampered in Southern California."

The INS adopted the FBI's COINTELPRO objectives. A senior INS official wrote that the INS's long-term goal was to "seek eventual deportation of [PFLP] members sufficient to disrupt their activities in this District."[7] The INS district director admitted that all eight "were singled out for deportation because of their alleged political affiliations with the [PFLP]." He stated that "there was no ground" for deporting Hamide and Shehadeh "other than their political affiliations and activities," and that "the reason our office devoted such resources and took such steps to deport these individuals is because of their alleged affiliation with the PFLP." He stated that the INS did so "at the behest of the FBI, which concluded after investigating plaintiffs that it had no basis for prosecuting plaintiffs criminally, and urged the INS to seek their deportation."[8]

## ALIEN BORDER CONTROL COMMITTEE

The government's efforts against the LA 8 did not arise in a vacuum. In November 1986, just two months prior to instituting deportation proceedings against the LA 8, the Justice Department was considering internally a document entitled "Alien Terrorists and Undesirables: A Contingency Plan." The document was circulated by the Alien Border Control Committee, a secret interagency task force organized in 1986 to develop, among other things, plans for the "expulsion from the United States of alien activists who are not in conformity with their immigration status." The "contingency plan" proposed building a detention camp in a remote area of Louisiana to hold "alien undesirables" pending deportation. It listed the estimated number of students from Arab countries staying in the U.S. with expired visas, and identified certain countries, all Arab, as being likely origins of terrorist aliens.[9]

Among other tasks, the Alien Border Control Committee sought to develop plans and procedures for deporting aliens critical of U.S. policies. Committee memos indicate that it wanted to "speed up" the removal of "alien activists who are not in conformity with their immigration status." The committee was specifically looking for ways to use secret evidence: "Where criminal prosecution is not practicable for an alien actually engaged in the support of terrorism within the United States, procedures should be developed, utilizing current authorities, if possible, to expeditiously deport such aliens while protecting classified information and the methods by which such information is obtained." [10]

Whether or not the Alien Border Control Committee had any direct connection with the LA 8 case, the documents show that the Justice Department was at the time the case began consciously looking for ways to use the immigration laws to disrupt political activities of "alien activists."


## MONITORING FIRST AMENDMENT ACTIVITIES

The deportation proceedings against the LA 8 were preceded by a three-year FBI investigation that again underscored the dangers of political spying. In 1986, FBI agents wrote a 1,300-page report on PFLP "support activities" in Los Angeles. [11] The report consisted entirely of accounts of lawful, peaceful, and nonviolent political activity. Over 300 pages of the report are devoted to tracking the distribution of PFLP magazines and other literature with an intensity usually reserved for shipments of illegal drugs. Agents intercepted the magazines on arrival at the Los Angeles airport, weighed the boxes, conducted surveillance on the men who picked them up, and reported on meetings of suspected "distributors" of the literature. Agents also wrote detailed accounts of numerous political demonstrations and dinners, and extensive accounts of political speeches, placards, and leaflets.

The FBI was preoccupied with the "anti-U.S." and "anti-Israel" statements of the LA 8. Agents wrote that the eight were "anti-peace, anti-United States peace settlement, anti-Jordanian peace settlement, and anti-Israel." Agents repeatedly noted that individuals made statements or carried placards at demonstrations that were "anti-US, anti-Israel, anti-Jordan." One FBI memo accused Ayman Obeid of carrying an anti-American slogan at a demonstration protesting Israel's invasion of Lebanon, and stated that his "protesting against US foreign policy with the PFLP, which advocates the overthrow of the US government, is assumed to be against his visa status." Another memo charged that Bashar Amer was "devoted to the PFLP and not the US." The report described articles written by Hamide as "anti-REAGAN and anti-MABARAK." It concluded that PFLP members "hate the US."

In later defending its actions in court, the government pointed to three dinner dances held for the Palestinian-American community in Southern California. These events, called "haflis," were a routine part of Palestinian-American political and cultural life across the nation, and were the principal mechanism for raising money for humanitarian aid for Palestinians in the Middle East.[12] According to the FBI itself, each of these events was widely advertised, open to the public, and attended by crowds as large as 1,000.

Judge Stephen V. Wilson, the federal district court judge who reviewed the government's case, found no evidence that any fund-raising at these open public events was intended to support illegal activity.[13] To the contrary, Judge Wilson concluded, FBI agents had ignored evidence available to them showing that the events were legitimate fund-raisers for legitimate charitable organizations. "[T]he government's own evidence shows that at the St. Nicholas event in February 1985, the fund-raising was expressly for the benefit of US OMEN," a U.S.-based, IRS-certified charitable organization. And while the government "ha[d] no evidence of what actually transpired at the San Bernardino VFW dinner in June 1985" (because the agents did not go inside), the FBI had received information that the "fundraising would be represented to the audience as for the benefit of 'the mothers and orphans of Palestinians in the Middle East.' "

Judge Wilson found that the PFLP engaged in a broad range of lawful activities, including the provision of "education, day care, health care, and social security, as well as cultural activities, publications, and political organizing." He concluded that in the government's 10,000-page submission "there is no evidence in the record that could have led a reasonable person to believe that any of the plaintiffs had the specific intent to further the PFLP's unlawful aims."

As the case against the eight progressed, the government's theories became more radical. Ultimately, in the words of Judge Wilson, the government argued that when it is acting in the name of national security, it "can do pretty much what it wants to do." Judge Wilson rejected this contention as "utterly without a basis in law," and "quite disturbing to hear from the government as a justification for its conduct in a case where the plaintiffs have made a preliminary showing that the government in effect treated them as if it could do whatever it wanted."

## ADVANCES—AND A MAJOR SETBACK—
## ON FIRST AMENDMENT GROUNDS

Two months after the arrests, the LA 8, joined by numerous Arab, Irish, and other immigrants' rights and peace organizations, filed suit in federal court against the attorney general and the INS, charging that the McCarran-Walter Act's ideological deportation provisions were unconstitutional under the First Amendment, and that the eight had been selectively targeted for deportation based on constitutionally protected political activity. On January 26, 1989, two years after the initial arrests, Judge Wilson ruled that foreign nationals living here have the same First Amendment rights as citizens, and that the McCarran-Walter Act provisions were unconstitutional.[14] In an attempt to evade the district court's ruling, the INS filed new charges against Hamide and Shehadeh, characterizing the PFLP as a group that advocated the assault of government officials. Wilson, a Reagan appointee, ruled that these new charges were unconstitutional for the same reasons that the earlier charges were—they punished individuals solely for their association with a group that advocates disfavored ideas. After Congress repealed the McCarran-Walter Act in 1990 and enacted a new law making it a deportable offense to "engage in terrorist activity," the INS substituted new charges against Hamide and Shehadeh under the new law. It did not charge them with actually engaging in or supporting any terrorist acts, however. Rather, it charged them only with providing material support to the PFLP, a "terrorist organization," and argued that such support, even for lawful ends, was a deportable offense.

In January 1994, the district court ruled that the LA 8 had been selectively targeted for deportation based on their First Amendment activities while similarly situated members and supporters of the Nicaraguan Contras, Afghanistan Mujahedin, and anti-Castro Cuban groups had not been deported. On that basis, the court blocked the deportation proceedings. In November 1995, the U.S. Court of Appeals for the Ninth Circuit affirmed, squarely rejecting the government's argument that immigrants are not entitled to the same First Amendment protections as U.S. citizens. The court stated:

> [T]he values underlying the First Amendment require the full applicability of First Amendment rights to the deportation setting. . . . Because we are a nation founded by immigrants, this underlying principle is especially relevant to our attitude toward current immigrants who are part of our community. . . . Aliens,

who often have different cultures and languages, have been subjected to intolerant and harassing conduct in our past, particularly in times of crisis. [Citing Alien Enemies Act of 1798 and Palmer Raids of 1919–20.] It is thus especially appropriate that the First Amendment principle of tolerance for different voices restrain our decisions to expel a participant in that community from our midst.[15]

After the Ninth Circuit decision, the INS submitted 10,000 pages of evidence to the court—much of it FBI surveillance of the eight—and argued that this evidence showed that it was justified in targeting the respondents for deportation. Judge Wilson reviewed all of the evidence, and ruled that all of the activities revealed therein—distributing newspapers, participating in demonstrations, and organizing humanitarian aid fund-raisers—were protected by the First Amendment. (Later, Judge Wilson found that the government had withheld from plaintiffs still more documents demonstrating that defendants targeted plaintiffs for their membership and association with the PFLP. The district court characterized the withheld documents as "smoking guns.") The government appealed again, arguing that no one—citizen or noncitizen—has a First Amendment right to support the lawful activities of a foreign "terrorist organization."

In October 1996, the INS moved to dismiss the respondents' federal case against it, arguing that a "court-stripping" provision in the 1996 Illegal Immigration Reform and Immigrant Responsibility Act deprived the federal district court of jurisdiction to hear the eight immigrants' constitutional challenge to its actions. Judge Wilson denied the INS's motion to dismiss, ruling that the eight were constitutionally entitled to immediate federal district court review of their First Amendment selective prosecution claims. The Court of Appeals unanimously affirmed.[16]

Despite its many defeats in the courts, the Justice Department continued to press for deportation of the LA 8. In June 1998, the Supreme Court granted the Justice Department's request to review the case. The Court indicated that it would address only a jurisdictional question—whether the federal courts retained jurisdiction to hear the LA 8's claim in the wake of 1996 changes in the immigration law. The Court expressly rejected the government's request that it review the central First Amendment rulings of the federal trial court and the Ninth Circuit appeals court.

In February 1999, however, the Supreme Court reversed, ruling that Congress had stripped the federal courts of all power to review challenges to selective enforcement of the immigration laws.[17] Despite the fact that it had explicitly denied review of the First Amendment rulings, the Court then went on to rule that foreign nationals lack any constitutional right to object to their deportations on the ground that they were singled out for membership in an organization that engages in terrorism. The First Amendment, the Court had previously held, protects the right to join groups that engage in violence, so long as one does not specifically intend to participate in or abet such violence. The Communist Party was such a group, according to Congress, yet as discussed below in Chapter 7, the Supreme Court repeatedly held that association with the Communist Party could not be punished absent specific intent to further its illegal ends. Yet despite the fact that the activity the LA 8 were accused of would be protected by the First Amendment if engaged in by U.S. citizens, the Court held that they had no right to object to being singled out for deportation for such activity. The decision denied all immigrants the freedom to engage in political activity, for they must now fear that the government will target them for deportation in retaliation for such activity.[18]

As of this writing, the government has not ceased its efforts to deport the LA 8. After the Patriot Act became law in 2001, the government charged Hamide and Shehadeh with having violated it—despite the fact that their actions predated the Act's existence by fifteen years. When Congress amended the immigration laws again in 2005 to make deportable membership in any group that has used or threatened to use a weapon, the government added still more charges under this law—thereby bringing the case full circle to the charges of association with which it began eighteen years earlier. The government has sought to deny naturalization and permanent resident status to two others, again on political grounds. The members of the LA 8 have now been living in this country for periods ranging from twenty to thirty-five years, and not one of them has been charged with a crime, much less any act of violence. Yet the government continues to pour substantial resources into deporting persons who have never posed any threat whatsoever to the United States.

## OTHER FBI INVESTIGATIONS IN THE 1980s AND 1990s

The FBI's investigation of the LA 8 was not unique. Arabs and Arab-Americans were a particular focus of FBI intelligence gathering throughout the 1980s and 1990s, long before the attacks of 9/11. What is most striking about the investigations is how ineffectual they were in identifying any real terrorists. Their most palpable effect was to alienate the targeted communities.

### The Gulf War Visits

In January 1991, as the U.S. and its allies prepared to go to war with Iraq over its occupation of Kuwait, native Texan David Najjaab received a phone call from an FBI agent who said he was concerned about Najjaab's safety. Najjaab, an advertising photographer and co-chairman of the Arab American Institute, a bipartisan organization that encourages participation in American politics, met the FBI agent at a Denny's restaurant. The agent started the interview by saying that he was concerned about hate crimes against Arab-Americans. But he then began asking for names of the Arab American Institute's members, and asked Najjaab whether he was familiar with any dissident student groups. The agent said the FBI was trying "to get a handle on the Arab-American community." He asked Najjaab, "Do you know anyone planning to blow up a federal building?"

Najjaab's unsettling encounter was part of a nationwide effort by the FBI to question Arab-Americans and Arab nationals about terrorism.[19] Some of those interviewed were born in the U.S. Some were naturalized citizens. Others were permanent residents. Many were politically active or active in Arab-American organizations. Many were apparently selected solely on the basis of their prominence in local communities. The interviews occurred at people's workplaces and homes.

As part of the effort, agents showed up at the office of a San Gabriel Valley surgeon, a U.S. citizen who had been in the United States for twenty-three years. As the doctor's patients looked on, the agents showed their badges to the receptionist and asked to speak to the doctor. Other agents questioned customers and owners of Arab-American-operated stores and restaurants in Brooklyn, and interviewed dozens of New York City Arab-Americans in their homes.[20] The agents posed a detailed series of questions about leaders in the Arab-American community, their views on terrorism, and their knowledge of specific people. Some of those interviewed were asked questions about their support for the U.S.-allied war effort against Saddam Hussein, or about their views on Israel and U.S. policy in the Persian Gulf. In Arkansas, the state police participated in the interviews. In Los Angeles, the LAPD antiterrorist squad participated.[21]

There was some evidence that the interviews were part of a longer-term effort. In January 1991, the Arkansas state police director said that his troopers had been questioning Arabs for two to three months at the request of federal agencies. New York *Newsday* reported on January 29, 1991, that FBI agents had been interviewing Palestinian-Americans in the New York City area for the past four months, inquiring about travel plans, contacts with known Arab-American leaders, and those leaders' professional and nonprofessional activities. FBI spokesperson Joseph Valiquette said that the interviews being conducted in the New York City area were "part of long-term, ongoing investigations."[22] The head of the Arab Community Center in Youngstown, Ohio, said that he first heard from the FBI a year before the January 1991 visits.[23] Col. Tommy Goodwin, director of the Arkansas state police, when questioned about visits his troopers conducted with the FBI, candidly admitted, "They're profiling people constantly. I guess stereotyping people. It's something I would say they do unconsciously."[24]

Despite bitter protests, the FBI continued its interviews after the Gulf War ended.[25] As of March 1991, the ACLU, the Center for Constitutional Rights, and the American-Arab Anti-Discrimination Committee were reporting that the FBI was continuing to question pro-Palestinian activists and Palestinian-Americans.[26]

## GUPS—Union of Palestinian Students

The breadth of the FBI's surveillance of Arab communities is revealed in a box of documents that Hearst newspaper reporter Dan Freedman received in 1995.[27] The documents, a response to a long-forgotten Freedom of Information Act request Freedman had filed in 1989, revealed that for ten years, from 1979 to 1989, the FBI had conducted a nationwide investigation of the General Union of Palestinian Students (GUPS), a student organization loosely committed to Palestinian identity and self-determination. The specific reason for starting the investigation was unclear from the redacted material provided to Freedman, but the documents made it clear that the case was not an investigation of criminal conduct. This was another intelligence monitoring case. At the beginning of the investigation, the Detroit field office set forth "two investigative objectives: (1) Ascertain the formation of new GUPS subchapters throughout the US, and (2) Determine the identity and whereabouts of GUPS leaders." It was the group's political ideology that attracted the FBI's attention. FBI memos show that agents clearly understood that the purpose of the organization was to "provid[e] assistance to Palestinian students in their education and settlement in the United States and to report, explain, correct and spread the Palestinian cause to all people."

Agents surveilled a wide range of legitimate First Amendment activities. They trailed GUPS members. They tracked the formation of new GUPS chapters around the country and expanded the investigation to include groups with "any interest in PLO issues." Agents staked out a symposium at the University of Michigan on "Peace in the Middle East"; shot rolls of film at GUPS national conventions (at a June 1986 convention in Houston with 200 attendees, FBI agents took 256 photos) and later attempted to obtain information on those in attendance; collected flyers, literature, and articles written in student newspapers on GUPS events; reported the chants from peaceful rallies ("Reagan, Reagan, you should know, we support the PLO"); gathered biographical data on speakers at GUPS events; and surveilled places where GUPS meetings and retreats took place and recorded the license plate numbers of cars in the parking lot.

The FBI field office in Charlottesville, North Carolina, attempted to intimidate GUPS chapters at various universities in the area. Agents interviewed numerous members of GUPS. A memo explained that, based on the large number of interviews conducted, those members not personally contacted were made aware of the FBI's "interest" in the organization. Others were propositioned by the FBI to serve as informants on GUPS activities, and the agents noted where GUPS members refused to do so.

The GUPS case further illustrated the limitation of the oversight mechanisms. The congressional committees never objected to the investigation. Indeed, it is not clear that anyone in Congress ever even knew of the investigation's existence. If the intelligence committees posed any questions about the case privately, they had no impact. None of the monitoring and infiltration techniques used in the case required court approval. The Office of Intelligence Policy and Review (OIPR) in the Justice Department, which received periodic reports on the case, let it proceed *for five years* before pointing out that the FBI's summaries did not specify any facts showing that GUPS was involved in international terrorism. The FBI responded, "FBIHQ is confident that such information is available but perhaps was not properly articulated [in the report to OIPR]." Headquarters promised to submit a supplemental report. OIPR allowed the case to continue for another five years, until 1989.

# 4

# Intelligence Investigations from Amnesty International to Earth First!

The FBI investigations in the 1980s against activists in the Central American solidarity movement and persons of Arab descent were not isolated incidents. The FBI's focus on political activity and guilt by association infected its investigations across a broad spectrum, involving not only activities with a foreign nexus but also purely domestic ones.

## AMNESTY INTERNATIONAL

In 1987, Harold Pickering was at work at the Phoenix, Arizona, Fire Station No. 11 when he received a phone call from an FBI agent. The caller said he wanted to talk to Pickering about something important, but he would not say what it was over the phone. Pickering agreed to meet the caller at his home. Pickering later testified to Rep. Don Edwards's judiciary oversight subcommittee:

> On April 1st, the agents came to my house. Some of the guys at work thought that since they had decided to come over on April 1st, that this might be an April Fool's prank by a couple of fire-

fighters. I suggested this to the agents when they came to the door and they presented their badges. They came in after I invited them and they asked if I had sent or received any communication from the Soviet Union.[1]

Only then did Pickering realize that the FBI's interest had been prompted by letters he had written for Amnesty International to the Soviet embassy urging release of prisoners of conscience held behind the soon-to-crumble Iron Curtain.

From 1987 to 1989, the FBI interviewed more than two dozen Amnesty members who had written to Soviet or East Bloc embassies on behalf of political prisoners. Those interviewed included schoolteachers, doctors, business professionals, housewives, and students.[2]

The interviews lasted from a few minutes to an hour. In several cases, as with Harold Pickering, FBI agents telephoned or visited people at work. Many of those interviewed found the agents polite, but many also sensed an implication of wrongdoing. FBI agents generally conducted the interviews by asking open-ended questions and avoided disclosing how the contact came to the Bureau's attention. Instead, the Amnesty members faced vague questions such as, "Have you been in contact with any Soviets lately?"

Many of those interviewed expressed both confusion and anger that the FBI would scrutinize their human rights work. Several said that they worried about adverse effects on their employment. In one case, the FBI agent had characterized his interview as an "educational visit." In other cases, the interviewees felt that they were being lectured by the FBI agents or warned that their efforts could be exploited by the Soviets. In all cases, the visit or interview resulted in an FBI file on the Amnesty member.[3]

As part of the same effort, the FBI interviewed children doing school projects, grammar school teachers, and citizens unaffiliated with any group. One man in Ohio wrote to tell Congressman Edwards that for many years he had been writing to foreign embassies in Washington, usually to voice his opinion about what he considered to be unfair, repressive, or disagreeable policies of foreign governments. In October 1988, an FBI agent visited him at his workplace to inquire about the general purpose of such letters and to discover the type of work in which the subject was involved.

A sixth-grade elementary school student, Todd Patterson, wrote letters to 169 foreign countries in 1983 requesting information for a school project. This prompted an unannounced visit by the FBI to Todd's home in Newark in late 1983. An FBI agent questioned Todd's parents, and later the boy himself, about the school project and the international correspondence received in response to Todd's letters. After these interviews, the FBI created a file on Todd. While the FBI maintained that it conducted no further investigations after 1983, FBI documents indicate that it continued to monitor Todd's activities as late as December 1985.[4]

In May 1989, a school librarian, Phyllis Grady, returned home to Haverstown, Pennsylvania, from a weekend trip to find a handwritten note from an FBI agent left at her front door requesting a meeting. Grady had been active in Amnesty International since 1984. She often sent letters to foreign governments on behalf of prisoners of conscience and forwarded copies of the letters to the respective embassies in Washington, D.C. At the meeting, the FBI agent told Grady that her name was on a "list" at the Yugoslavian embassy. The agent asked if Grady had been recruited to spy for Yugoslavia. The agent also indicated that her phone might be tapped.[5]

The FBI argued that it was not "investigating" Amnesty International or the other letter writers. Rather, the FBI said that it was monitoring the Soviet embassy and Soviet diplomats and that, as a part of that effort, it sought to interview persons who had contact with the embassy or its officials. But the tactics of the FBI put the Amnesty International members and others in the position of having to justify to the FBI facially innocent contacts with certain foreign persons or entities. And as a result, the chilling effect on these citizens was the same as if they were being investigated: they were still being asked to explain why they were engaged in a First Amendment activity.

## THE "LIBRARY AWARENESS" PROGRAM

In 1985, the FBI launched a program of visits to public and university libraries, where agents sought to interview librarians, asking for information regarding the readers of unclassified technical and scientific journals.[6] In New York City, the visits were part of a systematic program designed to "develop counterintelligence awareness" among librarians at technical and scientific libraries. FBI agents visited other libraries around the country whenever they believed that a foreign national they suspected of being an intelligence officer may have used the library. FBI agents asked librarians to be wary of "foreigners" or persons with "East European or Russian-sounding names." Library staff were requested to report to the FBI any "suspicious activity." According to the FBI, suspicious activity included speaking a foreign language or requesting books on "underground tunneling, military installations, or technological breakthroughs."[7]

The FBI sought access to a broad range of information from library records. FBI agents asked to view library databases and search checkout records, to monitor the reading interests of those with Eastern European or Russian names, and to scrutinize books checked out through interlibrary loans. Disclosing this type of information is a violation of state library confidentiality laws in most states.

When the visits were brought to light by objecting librarians, the FBI at first tried to minimize the scope of its investigation, claiming that the "Library Awareness" program was confined to a few specialized libraries in New York, and later that it was a "very, very limited" probe of libraries in three U.S. cities. In fact, FBI agents approached libraries across the country, including university libraries in Los Angeles, California; Madison, Wisconsin; College Park, Maryland; Buffalo, New York; Houston, Texas; Arlington, Virginia; and Cincinnati, Ohio; and a public library in Broward County, Florida. An FBI agent approached one librarian at his home, and on at least one other occasion, the FBI put a wiretap on a library phone and installed hidden cameras to spy on the activities of library patrons.

The FBI underestimated librarians' attachment to the First Amendment and the privacy rights of library users. The librarians took their case to the press and to Congress, demanding that the Library Awareness program be stopped. The FBI defended the program, claiming that it had been created in response to proof that Soviet intelligence services were using American scientific and technical libraries, and that KGB agents had stolen hundreds of thousands of items of microfiche from such libraries as a means of keeping pace with American technological advances. However, the Association of Research Libraries testified at congressional hearings that it had received no reports of widespread theft of microfiche from American research libraries. As a result of the librarians' protests and the widespread press coverage and editorial criticism, the FBI largely stopped asking librarians for their assistance, although it did not stop trying to identify certain foreigners' use of libraries.

## MONITORING ASSOCIATION: LANCE LINDBLOM

In the FBI's view, virtually any association with a suspect foreign national, no matter how seemingly innocent, can trigger an FBI inquiry. Once the FBI has looked into an association, even if the contact was in fact innocent, a file is kept for potential future reference. And once a counterintelligence or international terrorism file is created, it can be kept secret indefinitely, thus shielding FBI counterintelligence practices from the public scrutiny to which criminal proceedings are subject.

Sometime in the mid-1980s, Lance Lindblom—a U.S. citizen—came to the attention of the FBI's counterintelligence division. At the time, he was the president of a major philanthropic foundation, and in that capacity he met regularly with foreign leaders and political dissidents. Apparently, one of those foreigners was of interest to the FBI, and therefore the FBI scrutinized Lindblom. The effort was short-lived. Lindblom checked out to the FBI's satisfaction. But the inquiry generated a small file. Some time later, when Lindblom filed an FOIA request, the FBI admitted it had a file on him, but refused to disclose its full contents or to say what had triggered its interest in Lindblom. It also refused to expunge the record, even though it admitted that the file consisted of reporting on Lindblom's associational activities and contained no evidence of illegal activity on Lindblom's part. The FBI claimed that it was entitled to retain a file on innocent First Amendment activity because it might be useful someday. The federal appeals court in the District of Columbia agreed.[8]

## MONITORING ACT-UP DEMONSTRATIONS

The FBI's monitoring of First Amendment activities is not limited to foreign nationals or groups with foreign ties. The AIDS Coalition to Unleash Power (ACT-UP) was highly visible in the late 1980s and early 1990s, using dramatic rhetoric and unconventional protests to call attention to the AIDS epidemic in the United States, promote greater funding for AIDS research, and advocate equal treatment of those affected by the disease. In one typical demonstration, more than 1,500 AIDS activists descended upon President George Bush's home in Kennebunkport, Maine, in September 1991, marching to within a quarter-mile of his estate and chanting "Shame!" At the beginning of the march, they held up a piñata shaped and painted in the likeness of Bush, and then proceeded to hit it with golf clubs until it broke, releasing scores of condoms. The end of the march was marked by a "die-in," during which demonstrators lay down in the street to dramatize the death toll among AIDS victims. The boisterous but nonviolent protest continued for four hours, in the presence of the Kennebunkport police force, scores of state troopers, and Portland officers.[9]

This kind of angry advocacy brought ACT-UP to the attention of the FBI, which began collecting information on the group as early as February 1988. The minimal information released under the Freedom of Information Act shows that the FBI used informers to collect information on the group and its members throughout the nation.[10] At least sixteen FBI field offices were involved.

How long the group, which advocated and practiced only nonviolence, was watched by the FBI, or for what purpose, remains unclear.[11] At one point, the FBI apparently feared that the group's members were engaged in a plot to carry out kidnappings, assaults, and assassinations during a June 1989 AIDS conference in Montreal. But the collection of information began prior to this allegation, and when nothing violent occurred in Montreal, the investigation continued for many years, until at least October 1993. As is often the case in counterintelligence investigations, the FBI exchanged information about ACT-UP with local police, often to tip them off to planned demonstrations.[12]

In 1995, after the Center for Constitutional Rights released documents it had obtained under FOIA from the FBI's ACT-UP file,

FBI Director Louis Freeh quickly promised to undertake a "complete review" of the case. Two weeks later, Freeh sent a memo to all fifty-six field offices, similar to the several memos sent during the CISPES investigation, reminding agents that activity protected by the First Amendment cannot serve as the basis for an investigation. The head of the FBI's New York field office, where half of the ACT-UP documents were found, said his office never targeted ACT-UP because "[t]hey don't even come close to the guidelines on opening up a criminal investigation."[13]

## MONITORING OTHER DEMONSTRATIONS

In the 1980s, the FBI regularly collected information about protest demonstrations by a wide range of groups across the ideological spectrum. The Senate Intelligence Committee found that the FBI had a practice of "passively receiving and disseminating information on political protest demonstrations":

> This appears to be a fairly routine practice, especially with information from local law enforcement agencies and other established FBI liaison contacts in both government and private sector institutions. The line between passive receipt and informal solicitation is hard to define and may not necessarily be reflected in FBI files. More importantly, an undetermined but substantial amount of information about protest demonstrations by a wide range of groups across the ideological spectrum is acquired, maintained and disseminated by the FBI. Many, if not most of the demonstrations reported on posed no threat to the public safety, but the information is perpetuated in the files of the FBI and other agencies.[14]

The FBI collected some of this information under specific investigations, as in the CISPES case. It obtained other information under a general case classification for investigations concerning civil disobedience and demonstrations.

## EARTH FIRST!

The summer of 1990 was supposed to be "Redwood Summer" in northern California. The militant environmental group Earth First! planned to blockade roads and engage in other civil disobedience in an effort to halt logging in 30,000 acres of virgin redwood. Earth First! had been associated with such tactics as the "spiking" of trees with steel rods that would cause chainsaws to snap, endangering loggers, but before the summer of 1990 the group had disavowed such measures. The protests planned for 1990, in which college students were to come to northern California and stay with local activists, were patterned after the Mississippi Summers of the civil rights movement. All volunteer workers were required to pledge their commitment to nonviolence.

Just before noon on May 24, 1990, Earth First! organizers Judi Bari and Darryl Cherney were driving in downtown Oakland when an explosion tore through Bari's Subaru station wagon. Local police who rushed to the scene were joined soon by FBI agents, including members of the FBI counterterrorism squad. Bari suffered a fractured pelvis and was rushed to the hospital in critical condition. Cherney received minor injuries. They and their colleagues in Earth First! assumed that the bombing was meant to interfere with their work organizing Redwood Summer. They expected the FBI to focus its attention on anti-environmentalists who had increasingly targeted Earth First! and Bari for criticism and threats.

But when Cherney was released from the hospital soon after the bombing, he was taken into police custody, and by the end of that first day, police indicated that they would charge Cherney and Bari themselves with transporting explosives. The following day, Bari was placed under arrest in her hospital bed. The authorities said that they believed that Bari and Cherney had made the bomb themselves and that it had accidentally exploded while they were carrying it to an unknown target.[15] Police and FBI agents searched houses in Oakland where Bari and Cherney had stayed and questioned their friends.

Over the next two months, the local police and the FBI continued to assert that Cherney and Bari were responsible for the bombing, claiming that nails seized in a search of Bari's house were found by the FBI lab to match the nails in the bomb. Even when a letter signed by "the Lord's Avenger" was received taking credit for the bombing, investigators continued to focus on Bari and Cherney, suggesting that the letter may have been composed on a typewriter found in Bari's house.

Finally, on July 18, the Alameda County district attorney's office announced that it would not file criminal charges against Bari and Cherney. Police and FBI officials promised to continue their investigation, but there were never any subsequent arrests or charges in the case.

Only years later did information emerge proving what Bari had long suspected: that before the bombing, the FBI had been investigating Bari and Cherney as suspected terrorists, and that immediately upon hearing of the bombing the FBI had concluded that its suspicions were confirmed.[16] Indeed, so sure was the FBI that Bari and Cherney were terrorists, based on their association with Earth First!, that the FBI failed to pursue other avenues of investigation until it was too late. Sheila O'Donnell, who investigated the case for Greenpeace U.S.A., concluded, "With the FBI, I think they had Earth First! terrorists dancing like sugarplums in their head. I don't know that they ever for a moment asked, 'Are these people victims?' . . . If you come to the scene of a crime with your own theory of who's responsible and you refuse to turn that around, you build a house of cards that will come crashing down around you." [17]

The first FBI agent who responded to the scene of the bombing was Timothy McKinley. As soon as he had determined the identity of the victims, McKinley contacted the FBI office in San Francisco, which, according to the report McKinley dictated the next day, advised him that Bari and Cherney "were the subjects of an FBI investigation in the terrorist field." McKinley conveyed this information to local police. The physical damage to the car itself, which indicated that the bomb had been hidden under the seat, was ignored. Instead, the FBI and the police reported that the bomb must have been placed on the floor behind the driver's seat, where Bari and Cherney would have seen it. Oakland Police Sergeant Mike Sitterud wrote an entry in his police log thirty minutes after the bomb went off, stating "Earth First! leaders suspected of Santa Cruz power pole sabotage, linked to federal case of attempted destruction of nuclear power plant lines in Arizona." (The latter was a reference to an FBI undercover investigation that had led to the arrest of Earth First! founder David Foreman in 1989.)

At 7:50 on the night of the bombing, the FBI agent in charge of the terrorist investigation unit in San Francisco met with Oakland police and told them that Bari and Cherney "qualified as terrorists and that there was an FBI investigation going on other incidents where these individuals were suspects." According to Oakland police officers later questioned under oath by Bari's lawyers, the FBI agent said that Bari and Cherney were involved in organizing demonstrations in the redwood region, and that Cherney had been arrested for climbing the Golden Gate Bridge to unfurl a banner with an environmental slogan. The FBI official also drew a connection between Bari and a bomb planted at a sawmill in Cloverdale,

California. And the FBI told police that Bari and Cherney were prime suspects in the sabotage of power lines in Santa Cruz earlier that year, a charge that was never substantiated.

All in all, the FBI already had a substantial dossier on Bari and Earth First!, making no distinction between violent acts and nonviolent acts of civil disobedience, and linking Earth First! to incidents for which it had not taken credit, where the only connection was the presence of logging or other environmental issues.

Author David Helvarg found that, "[a]ccording to files released under the Freedom of Information Act, the FBI's interest in Earth First! goes back . . . almost to the founding of the group in 1980." [18] In 1987, the Phoenix office of the FBI opened a domestic terrorism investigation, which came to involve FBI offices in California, Montana, and New Mexico. The investigation focused on Earth First! co-founder Dave Foreman. An FBI undercover agent befriended Earth First! members and participated in the planning of an effort to knock down a power line. Problems with the nature of the investigation were revealed by a tape the agent had inadvertently made of himself telling other agents, "This [Dave Foreman] isn't really the guy we need to pop, I mean in terms of an actual perpetrator. This is the guy we need to pop to send a message. And that's all we're really doing. . . ." [19] Evidence like this deflated the government's charge that it had broken up a dangerous terrorist group. Foreman and five others pled guilty to reduced charges. The case served as a window into Earth First! chapters nationwide. In the course of the investigation, the FBI wiretapped more than sixty people in communication with Foreman, including Judi Bari. [20]

The bombing of Judi Bari served as further reason for the FBI to look at the group. Even after the police had ruled out Bari and Cherney as suspects, the FBI obtained the telephone toll records of Earth First! activists in northern California and compiled a list of 634 out-of-town phone calls they had made. The San Francisco FBI office then sent the numbers to field offices throughout the country, asking for the name, address, physical descriptions, employment, criminal records, and other information, based only on their having received a phone call from Earth First! Helvarg reports, "More recently, the FBI has been identifying (and misidentifying) Earth First! spin-off groups to industry and other law enforcement agencies, creating problems for local environmental activists."[21]

The FBI never found out who made the bomb that wounded Bari, and may never have really tried, but the Bureau's efforts included a widespread investigation of environmental activism in northern California.[22] Cherney and Bari's estate sued federal and local law enforcement agencies for violations of constitutional rights. In June 2002, a court awarded Cherney and Bari's estate damages of $4.4 million, 80 percent of it for violations of the First Amendment. The government appealed, but ultimately settled the case in May 2004 for $4 million.[23]

## CONCLUSION

The problems identified in Part I persisted in the face of attempted reforms of the FBI. After the Church Committee documented the FBI's COINTELPRO program and related abuses, the Justice Department for the first time subjected the FBI to guidelines that purported to limit its investigations of political activities. While these reforms did curtail the FBI's activities to some extent, the FBI retained a substantial degree of uncontrolled discretion, especially in situations where the issue or group in question had a foreign component, bringing it under more lenient foreign counterintelligence guidelines. The political monitoring approach characteristic of counterintelligence investigations continued to influence the FBI's response to terrorism. The FBI's wide-ranging investigations of

Central American activists in the early 1980s revealed that the changes had not been as fundamental as many had believed. Again, after public (and internal) criticism of the CISPES probe, the Bureau claimed that it would institute new controls to prevent such investigations from recurring.[24] But the investigations of Palestinian and Islamic groups in the late 1980s and 1990s showed that again the reforms had failed to define an approach to "intelligence" investigations that would be effective in preventing terrorism and respectful of civil liberties.[25]

# PART II

# Control vs. Discretion:
# The Limits of Legal Restrictions
# on the FBI's Authority

# 5

# Mechanisms for Control of the FBI

No single constitutional provision, statute, or oversight body can, in isolation, effectively control a police and counterintelligence agency like the FBI. What is needed is a system of interlocking constraints, based on principles essential to a free and democratic society:

- Government powers should be limited constitutionally.
- The functions and authorities of agencies should be specified in binding laws adopted publicly by the legislature.
- Crimes should be narrowly defined, and citizens and noncitizens alike should be subject to arrest, detention, or punishment only under standards of fundamental fairness ("due process"), including the opportunity to know and challenge the evidence against them.
- Executive agencies should be subject to control and oversight by the legislature and by an independent judiciary committed to the protection of individual rights.
- Members of the society should have an enforceable right of access to information about the policies and practices of the government.

- Agencies and officials should be accountable to individuals harmed by their overreaching.
- The rights of association and freedom of expression should be protected, including the right to engage in peaceful opposition to government policies and to support the peaceful activities of causes and groups, foreign and domestic, that the government opposes.

## LEGAL CONTROLS/LEGAL DISCRETION

The legal system that has evolved to control the FBI incorporates all these protections. The First Amendment to the Constitution protects the freedoms of speech and association, the Fourth Amendment protects privacy against unreasonable searches and seizures, and the Fifth Amendment guarantees due process. Statutes define the offenses within the FBI's criminal investigative jurisdiction.[1] Other statutes limit the use of some intrusive techniques, requiring, for example, the approval of a judge before the government can conduct a wiretap or plant a bugging device.[2] Guidelines promulgated by the attorney general set standards for the initiation and conduct of all investigations and regulate such investigative techniques as the use of informants and undercover operations. Annual congressional statutes that authorize and appropriate funds for the FBI sometimes place conditions on the expenditure of those funds, and congressional oversight committees can inquire into the propriety of FBI activities. The Freedom of Information Act (FOIA) creates in principle an enforceable right of access to government records.[3] The courts have jurisdiction over suits against the Bureau and individual agents for violations of constitutional, statutory, and common law rights.[4]

Each of these controls, however, is limited in practice, leaving the

FBI substantial leeway to intrude on legitimate political activities. No statute or "charter" comprehensively delimits the functions and authority of the FBI: its broad "counterintelligence" mission, for example, stems only from a succession of vaguely worded presidential orders. The federal criminal code includes statutes that, if interpreted broadly, would criminalize militant rhetoric against the government.[5] Judges rarely deny requests for wiretapping.[6] Attorney general guidelines leave the FBI wide discretion, have been easily rewritten or reinterpreted, and in any event are not enforceable in court. Guidelines on counterintelligence investigations are largely classified and therefore are not even available for public scrutiny. Congressional oversight is inconsistent, often driven by partisan disputes rather than principle, and easily stymied by executive branch resistance. Indeed, the congressional oversight committees just as often serve as defenders and promoters of the agencies they are supposed to be controlling. The FOIA has exceptions sharply limiting citizen access to law enforcement and national security records, and the judiciary too often has been reluctant to exercise its intended role in reviewing executive branch decisions to withhold information.[7] And the courts have erected almost insurmountable barriers to citizens' lawsuits challenging intrusive government investigations or other abuses of power.[8]

## THE CONTEXT FOR THE 1996 AND
## 2001 ANTITERRORISM LEGISLATION

The powers under the 1996 and 2001 antiterrorism statutes were granted to an agency that, despite periodic efforts to control it, continued to enjoy considerable discretion and immunity from control. Part II summarizes the legal history of the FBI's investigative powers. It will show that the legal reforms adopted over the years to control FBI investigations were incomplete and ultimately ineffective, as the recurring FBI infringements on First Amendment rights recounted in Part I demonstrate.

This is not to suggest that the FBI today is no different than it was under J. Edgar Hoover. As far as we know, the systematic violations of law that characterized COINTELPRO are not being repeated today. There has been no proof, for example, that the FBI continues to engage in illegal break-ins or warrantless wiretaps. Nor is there evidence that the FBI is using the worst "dirty tricks" of COINTELPRO, such as sending anonymous derogatory letters to employers and family members, circulating phony pamphlets and flyers, or fomenting internal dissent and encouraging violence to disrupt activist organizations. (Then again, there are no broad protest movements today of the kind that prompted the FBI to break the law in pursuit of its vision of the national interest.) Our concern is not so much with illegal FBI conduct, but rather with how much the government can do *legally* to intrude on privacy and deprive persons of their liberty. The laws as written and interpreted grant broad latitude to investigate political activity and to interfere with First Amendment rights.

## THE ABSENCE OF STATUTORY LIMITS

The FBI has no legislative charter. As Attorney General Griffin Bell testified in 1978, "Despite its long history, the Bureau has received very little statutory guidance."[9] Efforts to enact a statute delimiting the FBI's authority foundered in the final year of the Carter administration. Today only a smattering of miscellaneous statutes define the FBI's powers and duties.[10] One authorizes the FBI to detect and prosecute offenses against the United States, to assist in the protection of the president, and to investigate "official matters" under the control of the Department of Justice and the Department of State.[11] Another authorizes the attorney general to collect crime records and exchange them with federal, state, and local agencies.[12] A third authorizes the FBI to train state and local law enforcement officers.[13] A fourth permits FBI agents to carry firearms, serve warrants, and make arrests.[14] Another limits the FBI director to a single ten-year term, a provision intended to prevent the rise of another J. Edgar Hoover (who held office for forty-eight years) but at the same time to insulate the FBI director from the normal cycle of presidential appointments.[15]

Under the criminal law, the FBI has claimed broad investigative authority over political activities—in some instances legitimately, in other instances more questionably.[16] In the past, the FBI conducted investigations of political activity under the Smith Act and the Voorhis Act, which facially punish speech and advocacy.[17] Today, the seditious conspiracy statute[18] makes it a crime to conspire to overthrow the government of the United States, and has been used to investigate persons and groups who have no chance of overthrowing the U.S. government. In June 1983, the FBI arrested four alleged members of a Puerto Rican nationalist group in Chicago and charged them with seditious conspiracy.[19] Later in the 1980s, the statute was used to investigate and arrest white supremacists and "left-wing" radicals; in both cases, juries refused to convict, but the investigations and prosecutions substantially disrupted the activities of the individuals and organizations involved. Still more significantly, the government since 1996 has pointed to the statute criminalizing "material support" of designated "foreign terrorist organizations" as a basis for wide-ranging investigations and prosecutions.[20] The government has also relied on money laundering statutes and other authorities to investigate humanitarian fundraising for foreign organizations.[21] Even though some of these investigations and prosecutions were legitimate, the critical point is that the criminal code leaves the FBI broad discretion to spy on political activity.

In addition, the FBI has long claimed the authority to investigate the lawful activities of domestic groups that oppose U.S. foreign policy or that "support" certain foreign governments or factions, even where there is no suspicion of criminal conduct.[22] On this basis, even at the end of the Cold War, the FBI examined lawful contacts between citizens of the United States and those of certain foreign nations, as illustrated by the Library Awareness program and the visits to Amnesty International members discussed in Part I. The search for foreign influence on lawful political activity was also the basis for the FBI's investigation of the nuclear freeze movement, where the Bureau claimed to be seeking to determine whether anti-nuclear activists were acting under the direction and control of the Soviet Union, even though no specific criminal violation was suspected. This same rationale also justified the investigation of CISPES for "supporting" the FMLN of El Salvador. In the 1980s, it served as the basis for wide-ranging inquiries into the activities of Arab-Americans and Muslims.

Although Congress and the president since September 2001 have created new entities with responsibilities for the collection and analysis of counterterrorism information within the United States, the FBI remains the leading domestic intelligence agency. Since 9/11, the FBI has placed greater emphasis on its intelligence mission. Yet none of the reviews of the intelligence failures associated with the 2001 attacks yielded any statutory definition of the FBI's domestic intelligence role. In the absence of meaningful statutory limits, efforts to control the FBI have for the most part come from within the agency or the executive branch. As the next chapters illustrate, these internal efforts have proven woefully inadequate.

# 6

# Reform and Retrenchment

Harlan Fiske Stone, attorney general in the 1920s, launched the first effort to control the FBI's investigation of political activity.[1] Stone was reacting in part to the domestic intelligence programs established during World War I, when the Bureau of Investigation (as the FBI was then called) investigated thousands of individuals for "un-American activities." The investigations continued even after the war ended, culminating in the notorious Palmer Raids of 1920, in which some 10,000 persons were arrested on suspicion of being "anarchist" or "revolutionary" immigrants subject to deportation.[2] Describing the Bureau's activities before he took office as "lawless, maintaining many activities which were without any authority in federal statutes,"[3] Stone pledged to limit the FBI to investigating only conduct made criminal by federal law. "The Bureau of Investigation," Stone announced, "is not concerned with political or other opinions of individuals." Upon appointing J. Edgar Hoover as acting director of the Bureau of Investigation, Stone directed that the activities of the Bureau were to be "limited strictly to investigations of violations of the law."[4]

The constraints imposed by Stone were never embodied in legislation (setting an unfortunate pattern for subsequent efforts to reform the FBI) and proved short-lived. Beginning in the mid-thirties, the FBI reinstituted and expanded its domestic intelligence activities. President Franklin D. Roosevelt, in a series of oblique orders, directed the FBI to collect intelligence about "subversive activities" and "potential crimes."[5] In the exercise of this jurisdiction, the FBI went beyond investigating crimes to searching for suspected foreign involvement in a wide swath of American life. Referring to the Roosevelt order, a special Senate committee headed by Senator Frank Church later concluded: "By using words like 'subversion'—a term which was never defined—and by permitting the investigation of 'potential' crimes, and matters 'not within the specific provisions of prevailing statutes,' the foundation was laid for excessive intelligence gathering about Americans."[6] Under the Roosevelt executive orders, the FBI once again began to investigate law-abiding domestic groups and individuals. By 1938, the FBI was investigating alleged subversive infiltration of the maritime, coal, steel, and automobile industries, educational institutions, labor unions, youth groups, political organizations, and Roosevelt's partisan critics.[7]

The FBI's intelligence programs did not cease with the end of the Second World War. "Instead," the Church Committee found, "they set a pattern for decades to come."[8] Executive directives by Presidents Truman and Eisenhower continued to direct the FBI to investigate "subversive activity," without defining what that might be.[9] "Congressional deference to the executive branch, the broad scope of investigations, the growth of the FBI's power, and the substantial immunity of the Bureau from effective outside supervision became increasingly significant features of domestic intelligence in the United States."[10] By 1960, the FBI had opened approximately 432,000 files at headquarters on individuals and groups in the "subversive" category.

## COINTELPRO—TO "DISRUPT" AND "NEUTRALIZE"

The legal regime established under Presidents Roosevelt, Truman, and Eisenhower set the stage for the worst abuses in the FBI's history, and eventually led to more comprehensive efforts at reform. Boosted by enactment of the anticommunist Internal Security Act of 1950, the FBI undertook an intensive campaign aimed at suspected Communists, working in tandem with Senator Joseph McCarthy and the House Un-American Activities Committee (HUAC). HUAC, the Senate Internal Security Subcommittee, and state-level "little HUACs" depended heavily on the FBI for information. The committees were obsessed with membership, drawing up lists of names and constructing links among organizations. Targets of the committee were confronted with information from informers, but had no opportunity to cross-examine their accusers and no access to evidence in the possession of the FBI that would assist their defense. Those who refused to testify by invoking the Fifth Amendment often lost their jobs and were ostracized from their communities. Those who refused to testify by invoking their First Amendment rights of expression and association—Frank Wilkinson was one—were punished with prison sentences for contempt of Congress.

In 1956, the FBI brought many of its domestic spying operations under the formal designation of "COINTELPRO" (COunter-INTELligence PROgrams). Their express goal was to "disrupt," "discredit," and "neutralize" domestic protest groups. As the Church Committee later explained, "The origins of COINTELPRO [were] rooted in the Bureau's jurisdiction to investigate hostile foreign intelligence activities on American soil." [11] With the opening in 1961 of a COINTELPRO program against the Socialist Workers Party, a purely domestic group, the effort lost any pretense of being directed against foreign-controlled groups. Programs against the Ku

Klux Klan, civil rights groups, and the "New Left" followed. Over the course of fifteen years between 1956 and 1971, in the words of the Church Committee, "the Bureau conducted a sophisticated vigilante operation aimed squarely at preventing the exercise of First Amendment rights of speech and association, on the theory that preventing the growth of dangerous groups and the propagation of dangerous ideas would protect the national security and deter violence." [12]

The FBI's long campaign of investigation and harassment against Frank Wilkinson exemplifies the wasteful and anti-democratic nature of the Bureau's Cold War political surveillance. The FBI began investigating Wilkinson as soon as he became interested in social reform in the 1940s. When Wilkinson was fired from the Los Angeles Housing authority, he dedicated his time to organizing public support to abolish HUAC. Even before the first meeting of the National Committee to Abolish HUAC* was held, it was smeared by accusations in the press that several of its organizers were Communist. The FBI devoted huge resources to following Wilkinson around the country. It disrupted his public speaking engagements by arranging for hecklers and by causing the cancellation of hall rentals. It planted false accusations in the press. It shared its files on Wilkinson not only with HUAC but also with private groups, such as the American Legion. It disseminated anonymous "poison pen letters," tapped phones, broke into offices, and examined bank records. The FBI even stood silent and waited after learning of an assassination plot against Wilkinson.

Wilkinson's trial for contempt of Congress illustrates, in a lesson still relevant today, the danger inherent in denying the right of cross-examination and denying defendants access to exculpatory in-

---

* The National Committee to Abolish HUAC is now the National Committee Against Repressive Legislation (NCARL). Its educational affiliate is the First Amendment Foundation, the original publisher of this book.

formation the government has about them. Wilkinson's conviction was based primarily on the testimony of a sole informant, Anita Bell Schneider, whom Wilkinson had met only once. At the trial and in the Supreme Court's decision, she was described as a "creditable witness." Over twenty-five years later, as a result of a long and hard-fought lawsuit, Wilkinson obtained previously secret documents from his FBI file. Among them was one showing that, before his trial, the FBI had concluded that Schneider "exhibited emotional instability," and that it was "not considered advisable" to use her as a witness. The government failed to disclose this evidence to Wilkinson or his lawyers at the time of his criminal trial or appeals.[13]

The investigation of the Socialist Workers Party was another typical COINTELPRO operation. From 1961 to 1976, the FBI used 1,300 informants in the investigation, who supplied the Bureau with detailed reports on SWP debates and activities, as well as at least 12,600 pilfered SWP documents. FBI agents themselves conducted 204 illegal break-ins ("black bag jobs") against the SWP, removing or copying an additional 9,864 documents. The FBI conducted 20,000 days of telephone wiretaps and maintained bugs in SWP offices for the equivalent of 12,000 days. It conducted aggressive interviews of SWP members and their relatives, neighbors, and employers, which an FBI memorandum at the time said were intended to "enhance the paranoia" of members. The explicit purpose of the investigation was the disruption of the SWP. The FBI sought to create hostility and racial discord within the organization, to frustrate its efforts to form alliances with other groups, and to cause certain members to lose their jobs.[14] The investigation was doggedly pursued even though none of the 1,300 informants ever reported a single instance of planned or actual espionage, violence, terrorism, or other illegal activities, and even though the investigation did not result in a single arrest for any federal violation. In fact, informants routinely reported that the SWP was a peaceful organization.

COINTELPRO also involved extensive surveillance of anti–Vietnam War demonstrations and campus protests, broad informant reporting, break-ins, warrantless wiretaps, infiltration of nonviolent civil rights groups and legal organizations supporting them, and efforts to get teachers fired, to prevent targets from speaking, to block the distribution of newsletters, and to disrupt peaceful demonstrations and meetings. Among the FBI's targets was Dr. Martin Luther King Jr. The techniques to achieve these goals "ranged from the trivial (mailing reprints of *Reader's Digest* articles to college administrators) to the degrading (sending anonymous poison-pen letters intended to break up marriages) and the dangerous (encouraging gang warfare and falsely leading the members of a group to believe that one of their own was a police informer)."[15] Throughout COINTELPRO, the FBI undertook activities knowing they were illegal or without legal support. In an extreme case, the FBI encouraged the violent raid by Chicago police that resulted in the killings of two Black Panthers, Fred Hampton and Mark Clark.[16]

## POST-COINTELPRO REFORMS AND THEIR LIMITATIONS

Public and congressional outrage over the abuses of COINTELPRO prompted efforts to reform FBI operations, particularly as they affected political spying. Measures specific to the FBI were accompanied by reforms directed at the entire national security apparatus. The congressional budget process was reformed to give Congress annual opportunities to use the purse strings to control executive agencies. Congressional oversight of the FBI and the foreign intelligence agencies was established. The Senate created the Select Committee on Intelligence in 1976 and the House established its counterpart in 1977.[17] President Ford issued a public executive order on intelligence activities, replacing the secret directives, orders and statements on which Hoover had based his domestic intelligence operations. Congress strengthened the Freedom of Information Act, with the intent of ensuring more effective judicial review and making information about the national security programs of the government more accessible. In the Pentagon Papers case, the Supreme Court ruled that the press could not be stopped from publishing classified national security information.[18] The Supreme Court also ruled that U.S. citizens could not be wiretapped in the name of national security without a court order,[19] and Congress responded by enacting the Foreign Intelligence Surveillance Act (FISA), requiring a court order for electronic surveillance undertaken in the name of national security.[20] Attorney General Edward Levi adopted guidelines spelling out publicly for the first time the standards for opening and conducting domestic security investigations.[21] And the Justice Department successfully prosecuted two FBI officials who had ordered black bag jobs in the course of COINTELPRO investigations.[22]

Some of these reforms had a lasting impact. Even before the attorney general guidelines were adopted, there was a sharp decline in the number of FBI domestic security investigations, and the guidelines reinforced and institutionalized the trend. The revised FOIA resulted in the public disclosure of substantial information.[23] The congressional committees established reporting requirements on the use of intrusive techniques such as undercover operations.

The reforms, however, were incomplete. Part of the problem lies in the continuing secrecy that precludes public accountability. For example, while the FBI budget is largely public, the specific funding for the Bureau's counterintelligence and counterterrorism programs is obscured in more general categories. Nor are the budgets for the CIA, the National Security Agency, or the other foreign intelligence agencies subjected to public scrutiny and debate; even the total aggregate budget for foreign intelligence remains secret.[24] The guidelines limiting counterintelligence and international terrorism investigations also are classified secret in large part.

Despite the recommendations of the Church Committee, Congress never enacted "charter" legislation that might have defined the FBI's powers and responsibilities. Consequently, the main source of the FBI's counterintelligence authority is still an executive directive without judicially enforceable standards.[25] The FBI continues to claim authority to investigate lawful, noncriminal activities of U.S. citizens.[26]

Moreover, some reforms were subsequently reversed. President Ronald Reagan, soon after taking office, pardoned two FBI agents convicted for their role in illegal COINTELPRO burglaries. President Reagan's Justice Department rewrote the attorney general domestic security guidelines to expand authority for collecting information on political activities,[27] and Attorney General John Ashcroft weakened them still further after September 11, as discussed below. Reagan issued a new Executive Order 12333 on intelligence activities, which was scarcely less ambiguous than the directives issued by Roosevelt (the concept of "subversive activities" was supplanted by "international terrorist activities," a term similarly left undefined).[28] The Reagan administration interpreted the FOIA narrowly, especially as it applied to the FBI and the intelligence agencies, and the courts in many cases deferred to executive branch decisions to withhold documents. In 1984, Congress amended the FOIA to exempt whole categories of CIA files from review, and in 1986, it amended the FOIA again to codify the Reagan administration's restrictive reading of the law.[29]

Still other reforms were not as far-reaching as expected. Thus, while national security wiretaps are no longer conducted illegally, the secretive court set up under the Foreign Intelligence Surveillance Act of 1978 to review government requests for wiretapping authority in national security cases almost always approves the applications presented to it,[30] and since 1994 this court has also had authority to issue warrants for clandestine physical searches.[31] Some argue that the mere existence of the court has constrained the use of these techniques, even if the court's orders have not done so directly, but the evidence is inconsistent with this theory: the number of wiretaps in counterintelligence and international terrorism cases has risen steadily, from 546 in 1989 to 1,724 in 2003. Under the 1968 law governing wiretaps in criminal cases, including domestic terrorism cases, there has been a similar expansion in wiretap activity, from 673 in 1987 to 1,442 in 2003. The number of federal wiretaps in criminal cases increased 145 percent from 1987 to 2003.

Congressional oversight also has proven to be limited, and the little oversight that has been conducted has not led to significant reform. For example, the well-publicized inquiry by the House Judiciary and Government Reform Committees into the fatal law enforcement assaults on the Branch Davidian compound in Waco, Texas, in 1993 produced no legislative or administrative reforms of FBI practices. After a fifty-one-day siege by the FBI's Hostage Rescue Team, an FBI assault on the compound ended in the building's burning to the ground, killing over eighty people, including twenty-two children. The committee hearings lacked a reform agenda and were riven by partisanship. A more substantive and nonpartisan Senate inquiry into the killing of the wife of white separatist Randy Weaver in Ruby Ridge, Idaho, also failed to produce any legislative reforms. Congressional inquiries into allegations of misconduct in the FBI laboratory and in the handling of FBI files for White House background checks also yielded no legislative reforms.[32]

Likewise, Congress failed to respond to documented abuses in the roundup of immigrants immediately after 9/11, the photographed torture of prisoners at Abu Ghraib, or the detentions without due process at Guantánamo. Congress adopted the Patriot Act without conducting any inquiry into the failures of the intelligence agencies before September 11. The 9/11 Commission concluded that congressional oversight of intelligence is "dysfunctional."

## ATTORNEY GENERAL GUIDELINES ON DOMESTIC SECURITY INVESTIGATIONS

The one step forward, one step back character of FBI reform can be seen in the evolution of the attorney general "guidelines" on domestic security/terrorism investigations. Domestic security investigations are those directed at homegrown groups, like the KKK and the Weather Underground, which operate only in the United States and have no foreign allegiance or support. Attorney General Edward Levi first issued public guidelines for FBI domestic security investigations in 1976.[33]

The Levi guidelines required suspicion of criminal conduct before a domestic security investigation was opened. This "criminal standard" remains in place today under the amended Ashcroft guidelines. It currently provides:

> A terrorism enterprise investigation may be initiated when facts or circumstances reasonably indicate that two or more persons are engaged in an enterprise for the purpose of: (i) furthering political or social goals wholly or in part through activities that involve force or violence and a violation of federal criminal law, (ii) engaging in terrorism as defined in 18 U.S.C. 2331(1) or (5) that involves a violation of federal criminal law or (iii) committing

any offense described in 18 U.S.C. 2332b(g)(5)(B). A terrorism enterprise investigation may also be initiated when facts or circumstances reasonably indicate that two or more persons are engaged in a pattern of racketeering activity as defined in the RICO statute, 18 U.S.C. 1961(5), that involves an offense or offenses described in 18 U.S.C. 2332b(g)(5)(B).[34]

This "reasonable indication" standard is substantially lower than the standard of probable cause required by the Fourth Amendment for searches and seizures and for arrests and indictments. It does, however, require specific facts or circumstances indicating a past, current, or impending violation before a full investigation may be conducted.

The Levi guidelines also authorized a "preliminary inquiry" on a group or individual on a much lower threshold—whenever there was an "allegation or information indicating the possibility of criminal activity." Even for a preliminary inquiry, however, the Levi guidelines required a criminal nexus. And the guidelines specifically required consideration of "the danger to privacy and free expression posed by an investigation."

Guidelines, however, are easily changed. After Ronald Reagan took office, his attorney general, William French Smith, relaxed the guidelines.[35] The guidelines were rewritten to make it clear that the FBI could open an investigation based on mere advocacy of crime. Smith's change remains in effect today. The guidelines issued by Attorney General John Ashcroft state, "When, however, statements advocate criminal activity or indicate an apparent intent to engage in crime, particularly crimes of violence, an investigation under these Guidelines may be warranted unless it is apparent, from the circumstances or the context in which the statements are made, that there is no prospect of harm."

Data provided to Rep. Don Edwards when he was chairman of

the FBI oversight subcommittee of the House Judiciary Committee show that the Smith changes resulted in investigations triggered by mere rhetoric. The FBI throughout the 1980s and early 1990s engaged in approximately two dozen full domestic terrorism investigations per year under the Smith guidelines. Through the early 1990s, nearly two-thirds of these investigations were opened on the basis of statements by members of the target group, before a crime had been committed. In many of those cases, the group never subsequently engaged in violence or any other criminal conduct.

While the Smith guidelines preserved the earlier caution against infringing on First Amendment rights, they also made it clear that such infringements were not prohibited. Thus, for example, the guidelines authorized the use of informants to infiltrate a group "in a manner that may influence the exercise of rights protected by the First Amendment," so long as approval was obtained from FBI headquarters.

The Smith guidelines also applied two expansive concepts to domestic security investigations: the "enterprise" concept perfected in organized crime investigations, and the concept of "intelligence" investigations. The Ashcroft guidelines carry over from the Smith guidelines a lengthy passage explaining the significance of these concepts:

> An intelligence investigation of an ongoing criminal enterprise must determine the size and composition of the group involved, its geographic dimensions, its past acts and intended criminal goals, and its capacity for harm. While a standard criminal investigation terminates with the decision to prosecute or not to prosecute, the investigation of a criminal enterprise does not necessarily end, even though one or more of the participants may have been prosecuted.

In addition, the organization provides a life and continuity of operation that are not normally found in a regular criminal activity. As a consequence, these investigations may continue for several years. Furthermore, the focus of such investigations "may be less precise than that directed against more conventional types of crime." . . . It often requires the fitting together of bits and pieces of information, many meaningless by themselves, to determine whether a pattern of criminal activity exists. For this reason, the investigation is broader and less discriminate than usual. . . .

The Ashcroft guidelines, again carrying forward language from the Smith guidelines, go on to warn that an "investigation of organizational activity . . . may present special problems particularly where it deals with politically motivated acts." The guidelines urge that "special care must be exercised in sorting out protected activities from those which may lead to violence or serious disruption of society." But even this warning is ambiguous, allowing investigation of activities that "*may* lead to . . . serious disruption of society." That standard would easily encompass investigations of both the civil rights and the anti–Vietnam War movements.

Another significant goal of the Smith revisions was to make it clear that the FBI could collect public material (pamphlets, flyers, newspaper clippings, reports of interest groups), including material on the exercise of First Amendment rights.[36] Soon after it revised the guidelines, the Justice Department issued an opinion concluding that the FBI may collect publicly available information if an individual or group meets the standard for either a full investigation or a preliminary inquiry. Thus, on the strength of only an "allegation or information indicating the possibility of criminal activity," the FBI may conduct a preliminary inquiry consisting of the collection of publicly available information reflecting the exercise of First

Amendment rights. This interpretation opens the door to monitoring investigations in which the FBI uses informants and local police sources to maintain a name-indexed dossier of public statements and other open political activities of domestic groups.[37]

## THE FREEH REINTERPRETATION

The Justice Department further relaxed the domestic security guidelines following the Oklahoma City bombing. The modification was accomplished by an interpretive memorandum from the Department of Justice, the language of which was negotiated by FBI Director Louis Freeh. The memorandum reminded agents that the standard of "reasonable indication" for opening a full domestic terrorism investigation is "substantially lower than probable cause." It stated that a full investigation would be justified if three factors exist: (1) statements threatening or advocating the use of violence; (2) "apparent" ability to carry out the violence; and (3) a potential federal crime. The memorandum went on to emphasize that a preliminary investigation could be opened if the FBI received "partial information" or an allegation suggesting the existence of some, but not all, of the listed factors. "Thus, a preliminary inquiry . . . would be appropriate if either the statement itself or other information suggests an ability or intent to carry out violence."

Most significantly, the memorandum stressed "that any lawful investigative technique may be used in a preliminary inquiry, with only three narrow exceptions: mail covers, mail openings, and non-consensual electronic surveillance. . . . Indeed, with appropriate approval, a preliminary inquiry may include the development and operation of new sources or informants, or even 'the planting of undercover agents in the [suspected] organization.' "

Freeh testified that the purpose of the reinterpretation was to give the FBI "a lot more confidence to conduct and begin investigations, where in the past we were clearly not encouraged and, indeed, in some ways persuaded not to conduct some of these investigations."[38] Following the reinterpretation, the number of open domestic security investigations rose from approximately 100 in 1995 to more than 800 in 1997.[39]

## ASHCROFT'S DOMESTIC TERRORISM GUIDELINES

In May 2002, Attorney General John Ashcroft further revised the guidelines on domestic security investigations. He did so without any prior consultation with the relevant committees of Congress. And he justified the changes on two misleading grounds. First, he claimed the FBI did not act to prevent the 9/11 attacks because the earlier guidelines barred the Bureau from undertaking a preventive mission. In fact, FBI guidelines from Levi onward clearly stated that preventive intelligence investigations were an FBI priority for both domestic and foreign terrorism. Second, Ashcroft stated that changes in the FBI domestic security guidelines were necessary to respond to international terrorism. In fact, organizations such as al Qaeda are generally investigated under separate foreign intelligence guidelines (discussed below). The domestic guidelines apply not only to international groups but also to domestic groups (anti-abortion groups, militias, radical environmentalists, and the like).[40]

One major element of the Ashcroft changes was to permit the FBI to collect information in the absence of any link at all to criminal conduct, severing the criminal nexus that had consistently guided FBI domestic terrorism investigations, at least on paper. Under the Ashcroft guidelines, FBI agents can attend political events of domestic groups without any suspicion of criminal or terrorist activity, with poor guidance on what can be recorded and with no time limits on the retention of data acquired. Prior to the Ashcroft changes, the FBI was not prohibited from going to mosques, political rallies, and other "public" places to observe and record what was said but, in the past, in domestic terrorism investigations, it had to be guided by the criminal nexus—in deciding what mosques to go to and what political meetings to record, it had to have some reason to believe that terrorism might be discussed. Under the new guidelines, the FBI can go to mosques and political meetings with no factual basis for suspicion whatsoever.

The Ashcroft guidelines also authorize "surfing the Internet as any member of the public might do to identify, e.g., public websites, bulletin boards, and chat rooms in which bomb making instructions, child pornography, or stolen credit card information is openly traded or disseminated." The changes also encourage "data mining" of commercial databases containing personal information about citizens and organizations, again without even a scintilla of suspicion. The guidelines provide no standards on how inferences will be drawn from such data, no limits on the actions that may be taken based on such data, no limits on FBI warehousing or sharing of such information, and no limits on retention. Preparing the way for data mining, the guidelines say that the FBI is authorized to "participate in . . . information systems . . . [that] draw on and retain pertinent information from any source . . . including . . . publicly available information, whether obtained directly or through services or resources (whether nonprofit or commercial) that compile or analyze such information. . . ." Another clause in the same new section permits acceptance and retention of information "voluntarily provided by private entities," which harkens back to the days of private intelligence gathering by right-wing groups.

Finally, the revisions decrease the internal supervision and coordination provided at various stages of FBI investigations. They expand the scope and duration of preliminary inquiries (by definition, these are cases that do not involve the reasonable indication of criminal or terrorist conduct), permit field agents to open even full investigations without headquarters approval, encourage the use of more intrusive techniques, and allow full investigations to go on for longer periods without producing results and without internal review or any independent scrutiny. On the use of intrusive techniques, the new guidelines state that "the FBI should not hesitate to use any lawful techniques . . . even if intrusive, where the intrusiveness is warranted in light of the seriousness of the possible crime." What this fails to consider is the likelihood of the crime occurring and the likelihood of the investigative technique being productive. Thus, under the new guidelines, intrusive techniques may be used when a serious crime is only remotely likely and when the techniques are not likely to produce any useful information. The prior guidelines allowed the use of highly intrusive techniques only in "compelling circumstances."

These changes could well have a negative impact on security. The criminal nexus in the Levi-Smith guidelines was designed not only to protect civil liberties but also to make the FBI's security operations more efficient by focusing inquiries and investigations on suspected criminal or terrorist activity. Headquarters supervision was intended to ensure coordination, prioritization of resources, and sharing of information. During the Hoover years, hundreds of thousands of investigations were opened and files compiled on groups and individuals engaged only in lawful speech, protest, and civil rights activities. Informants were "vacuum cleaners" of information. This massive surveillance effort proved not only intrusive but also ineffective. New authorization to surf online and utilize commercial and nonprofit data mining services absent any indication of possible criminal conduct can lead to fishing expeditions.

With the Ashcroft guidelines changes, the Department of Justice once again used the terrorism crisis as a cover for changes extending far beyond terrorism. The online surfing provisions, for example, relate not only to terrorism cases, but to all other investigations—drugs, white-collar crime, public corruption, and copyright infringement. Other changes in the Ashcroft guidelines allow the FBI to use the heavy weaponry of the racketeering and organized crime law (forfeiture, enhanced penalties) against a wider range of crimes, wholly unrelated to terrorism.

## NATIONAL SECURITY GUIDELINES

Separate attorney general guidelines govern the FBI's counterintelligence and international terrorism investigations. The FBI defines international terrorism as terrorism inside or outside the U.S. carried out by a group with ties outside the U.S.[41] In October 2003, Attorney General John Ashcroft revised these guidelines. Unlike the domestic terrorism guidelines, large portions of the foreign intelligence guidelines are classified, so it is difficult to fully assess the significance of the Ashcroft changes. However, enough of the definitions section is unclassified to appreciate their breadth both before and after Ashcroft's changes. The national security guidelines permit the investigation of Americans and others in the United States who are not suspected of breaking the law, but are engaged only in political activities. The guidelines authorize the FBI to investigate "intelligence activities," which are defined to include "any activity" undertaken for or on behalf of a foreign power "to affect political or governmental processes" in the United States. A foreign power is defined to include a foreign government or any of its components, a faction of a foreign nation, and a group engaged in international terrorism or preparatory activities. A foreign power may also be "a foreign-based political organization, not substantially composed of United States persons" (i.e., citizens and permanent resident aliens).[42] Amnesty International, the Palestinian Liberation Organization, the African National Congress, the Irish Republican Army, and opposition political parties abroad are all foreign powers under this definition, and activities undertaken in the United States for or on their behalf, even wholly nonviolent political activity, may spark a counterintelligence investigation.

Many U.S. residents have connections of kinship, ethnicity, or religion with conflicts around the globe. Our government asserts a role in many of these conflicts, sometimes supporting one side or the other in ways that do not enjoy unanimous support of the U.S. population. Unavoidably, therefore, some residents will find themselves at odds with the U.S. government's position. Such individuals often establish ties of support with foreign causes that the U.S. government opposes. For example, many Americans identified with and engaged in political activities to support the Irish Republican Army, the FMLN in El Salvador, and the African National Congress.

These activities are protected by the Constitution. The Supreme Court has held that the First Amendment protects membership in or affiliation with an organization having both legal and illegal aims, unless the individual specifically intends to further the group's illegal aims.[43] But the FBI has interpreted its guidelines as authorizing the investigation of individuals who are members of or who support a foreign organization that engages in both legal political and illegal terrorist activities. As the CISPES and LA 8 cases demonstrate, once a group is deemed terrorist, the FBI does not carefully distinguish among the activities of its members or supporters. The FBI operates on the assumption that it can investigate membership, recruitment, and fund-raising, regardless of whether the individuals investigated participate in or support the organization's illegal activity.[44]

The guidelines' definition of international terrorist is limited to any "individual or group that knowingly engages in international terrorism or activities in preparation therefore or knowingly aids, abets, or conspires with any person engaged in such activities." "International terrorism" is in turn defined as activities that "involve violent acts or acts dangerous to human life that are a violation of the criminal laws of the United States or that would be a criminal violation if committed within the jurisdiction of the United States." As the CISPES case showed, however, the FBI has stretched these concepts to cover a broad category of "support" activities for groups designated as terrorist, whether or not the support actually amounted to "aiding or abetting" violent acts. The term "support for terrorism"—the focus of the CISPES investigation—does not appear in the unclassified definitions section of the guidelines.

Even after the FBI conceded that the CISPES investigation had spun out of control, it continued to defend the practice of investigating "support for terrorism" without distinguishing between support for legal and illegal activities of a foreign group. In his testimony about the CISPES case, FBI Director William S. Sessions elided that distinction:

> The original focus and intent of the CISPES investigation were to determine the extent of monetary and other support by CISPES for terrorist movements and activities in El Salvador; . . . to identify those individuals who knowingly supported terrorist groups in El Salvador through efforts in the United States; and to determine the extent of any control over, or influence on, CISPES by the FDR or FMLN. *This focus was proper.* . . .[45]

Movements and groups that can be labeled terrorist are often engaged in both legal and illegal activities. The IRA had Sinn Fein, a legal arm engaged in legitimate political activity. The African National Congress engaged in both violent "terrorist" acts and nonviolent anti-apartheid activity. And according to Israeli security services quoted in a 1996 news article, Hamas, one of the world's most notorious terrorist groups, devoted 95 percent of its resources to nonviolent social services.[46] The focus of an FBI investigation of a terrorist group should be to determine the nature and extent of support for the group's *illegal* activities. But as Sessions's statement illustrates, the FBI has long deemed it appropriate to investigate support for the legal activities of groups labeled "terrorist" by the U.S. government, without any direct connection to illegal acts.

In the wake of the CISPES investigation, the attorney general guidelines on international terrorism were revised, but it appears that the changes did not address the question of what type of support may be investigated. To the contrary, as far as one can determine from the unclassified excerpts made available, the guidelines still failed to distinguish between support for legal activities and support for illegal activities of a foreign group.

With the 1996 law's criminalization of material support to designated terrorist organizations, discussed in Chapter 9, the line between support of lawful and unlawful activities was largely obliterated. Because it is now a federal crime to support even the wholly nonviolent, otherwise lawful activities of any group that the secretary of state has designated "terrorist," the FBI's long-standing practice of investigating political support of disfavored organizations has been given legal sanction by Congress.

In investigations of international terrorism, the FBI generally has not sought to link domestic subjects of investigations to specific terrorist acts. It has not limited the predication (or basis) of its investigations to situations where there was suspicion of criminal activity. Instead, it has focused on links or associations, sometimes several stages removed from any suspected criminal conduct. The result, as in the LA 8 case, has been the investigation of organizations and individuals whose support for foreign groups or movements is wholly limited to these groups' lawful, nonviolent activities.

The Ashcroft guidelines authorize three levels of investigative activity in national security investigations: threat assessments, preliminary investigations, and full investigations. The category of "threat assessments" is new. It is explicitly intended to allow FBI intelligence investigations when there is no evidence of activity by an international terrorist organization or other foreign power and no evidence of criminal planning or conduct. The guidelines accordingly authorize the "proactive collection of information concerning threats to the national security, including information on individuals, groups, and organizations of possible investigative interest." This is comparable to the authorization under the domestic terrorism guidelines to engage in information collection for counterterrorism or other law enforcement purposes without a specific basis of suspicion.

In addition to "national security investigations," the guidelines also address "foreign intelligence collection." They authorize assistance to foreign governments, apparently even when the matter does not directly concern U.S. national security. And they address "strategic analysis," defined as identifying, examining, assessing, and appropriately disseminating information concerning terrorist threats and national security matters. The guidelines state that, in carrying out this analytic function, the FBI may draw on information from any source permitted by law and may supplement the information in its possession through the use of methods authorized in threat assessments.

Thus, both threat assessment and strategic analysis are independent justifications for collecting and disseminating information about a group or individual without any particularized suspicion of involvement in international terrorism or foreign intelligence activities. The guidelines contain provisions on information sharing consistent with the Patriot Act—provisions that make sense in light of pre–9/11 failures to use information the government had already collected. Overall, however, even though the provisions of the guidelines specifying the actual standards and permitted investigative techniques are redacted from the unclassified version of the guidelines, it is clear that their basic trend is toward broad discretion in the conduct of investigations.

## LOCAL LIMITS ON POLITICAL SPYING AND EFFORTS TO UNDO THEM

In the 1970s, activists in a number of cities undertook litigation and other efforts to constrain political spying by the FBI and its counterparts in local "Red Squads." Lawsuits were filed in New York, Chicago, Seattle, San Francisco, and elsewhere, seeking to stop federal and local police spying and infiltration, to obtain restitution where possible, and to restrict future spying through local ordinances or court injunctions.[47] In Chicago, the litigation resulted in a court injunction against police and FBI political spying. (The case is discussed further in Chapter 7.) In 1990, San Francisco adopted a policy limiting political spying after disclosures that the police had conducted a massive intelligence gathering operation before and during the 1984 Democratic national convention. At that time, police, FBI, and other agencies had together collected intelligence on more than 100 political groups ranging from the KKK to the ACLU, "Gay Groups," and "Labor Coalitions." The 1990 policy required "reasonable suspicion" of a serious crime before permitting intelligence investigations of political or religious groups.

Almost as soon as these limits were put in place, however, the FBI began working to revoke them. In San Francisco, the FBI in 1996 proposed entering into a cooperative agreement with local police that would evade a San Francisco city policy that had limited police department collection of information on political groups, demonstrations, and other First Amendment activities.[48] The FBI proposed that SFPD members would serve on a "Bay Area Counterterrorism Task Force," and would follow the more lenient attorney general guidelines, which, as noted above, allow preliminary investigations, including the use of informants, in the absence of reasonable suspicion of a crime. In Chicago in 2001, a federal appeals court agreed with a request by the city and effectively lifted all restrictions against police spying.[49]

## THE NCARL PETITION, H.R. 50, AND THE EDWARDS AMENDMENT

The evident limitations of other avenues for controlling the FBI led three of the nation's leading legal scholars in 1985 to draft a petition to Congress, calling for enactment of statutory controls to prevent the FBI and other federal law enforcement agencies from undertaking investigations that threatened or hindered the exercise of First Amendment rights. Professors Thomas I. Emerson of Yale and Vern Countryman of Harvard, veterans of the struggles against McCarthyism, were joined by Professor Carole Goldberg of UCLA. Working with NCARL, they circulated the petition to their colleagues at other law schools. Ultimately, 590 law professors at 147 law schools signed the petition. The petition called upon Congress to enact legislation—

> limiting FBI investigations to situations where there are specific and articulable facts giving reason to believe that the person has committed, is committing, or is about to commit a specific act that violates federal criminal law, and also limiting such investigations to obtaining evidence of criminal activity; and provisions

specifically prohibiting investigations of groups because of their members' exercise of First Amendment rights.

Representatives Don Edwards (D-CA) and John Conyers, Jr. (D-MI) embraced the petition by drafting and introducing H.R. 50, the FBI First Amendment Protection Act, first introduced in 1988.[50] It went nowhere.

H.R. 50 was reintroduced in several subsequent Congresses but was never enacted. In 1994, however, Edwards succeeded in adding a small portion of H.R. 50 to the Violent Crime Control and Law Enforcement Act.[51] The opportunity arose when the Bush and later the Clinton administrations supported a provision making it a federal crime to provide material support to anyone knowing that it would be used in the commission of one of a number of federal criminal offenses relating to terrorism. Edwards amended this "material support" provision by adding the following subsection, which closely tracked a provision in the law professors' petition:

> Activities Protected by the First Amendment. —An investigation may not be initiated or continued under this section based on activities protected by the First Amendment of the Constitution, including expressions of support or provision of financial support for the nonviolent political, religious, philosophical or ideological goals or beliefs of any person or group.[52]

President Clinton signed the provision into law as part of a massive crime bill in September 1994. Less than six months later, however, the president sent to Congress proposed antiterrorism legislation. Among other things, the president's bill called for the repeal of the Edwards amendment and for the enactment of a much broader provision criminalizing support for lawful activities of "terrorist groups." The Clinton proposal drew none of the careful distinctions between support for criminal activity and support for political activity that Congress had insisted upon in 1994. Yet in 1996, Congress enacted both the repeal of the Edwards amendment and a provision criminalizing support of a terrorist group's lawful activities.

## NEW INTELLIGENCE AGENCIES

In a series of actions since September 11, Congress and the president have created additional bodies with responsibilities for collection or analysis of domestic intelligence. In the fall of 2002, Congress created the Department of Homeland Security by combining twenty-two existing agencies, including some that had their own intelligence operations. DHS's roles include integrating and analyzing law enforcement information, intelligence information, and other information from federal, state, and local government agencies and private sector entities to identify and assess the nature and scope of terrorist threats to the "homeland." The new agency is to participate in establishing collection priorities, and is authorized to utilize data mining and other advanced information analytical tools.

The president thereafter created the Terrorist Threat Integration Center (TTIC) by executive order and gave it responsibility for analyzing intelligence information from domestic and overseas sources.[53] The president also created a Terrorist Screening Center, gave it authority for consolidating information about suspected terrorists, and placed it within the FBI.

Congress later created, in the Intelligence Reform Act of 2004, a Director of National Intelligence (DNI) and a National Counter-Terrorism Center, which absorbed the TTIC. In creating these entities, neither Congress nor the president defined their powers to collect information in the United States. Congress did create a Civil Rights and Civil Liberties Officer and a Chief Privacy Officer for the Department of Homeland Security, and in creating the DNI Congress also created a Privacy and Civil Liberties Oversight Board.

## CONCLUSION

The history of the FBI has been one of an ongoing struggle between control and discretion, between efforts to limit monitoring of political dissent and efforts to preserve or extend FBI powers. Periods in which measures were adopted to control the FBI have been followed by efforts to repeal those limitations, to redefine them, or to expand powers in new areas.

In the 1940s, presidential orders gave the FBI broad powers in the name of fighting subversion. From the 1950s through the 1970s, those powers were maintained and exercised in the name of fighting Communism. Following public disclosure of the COIN-TELPRO program and the abuses documented by the Church and Pike congressional committees, the FBI came under new restrictions intended to limit its investigations of political activities. However, the reforms were limited and fragile. In the 1980s and 1990s, FBI powers were again extended. In the name of foreign counterintelligence and antiterrorism, the FBI continued to insist upon the authority to investigate legal activity that had a foreign nexus. The nationwide investigation in the early 1980s of peaceful activists opposing U.S. policy in Central America led to further criticism and reform. As Parts III and IV will show, the antiterrorism statutes of 1996 and 2001 have brought us full circle again, codifying guilt by association and making illegal the support of peaceful, nonviolent activities of certain foreign groups. As we come to the end of 2005 still engaged in a global struggle against terrorism, the FBI's powers to engage in political spying remain largely unrestricted by statute or executive regulation. New intelligence entities of uncertain authority have been created and guidelines for collecting and sharing information remain blurry. The connection between "intelligence" and "law enforcement" remains ambiguous, and that ambiguity is likely to produce more political spying without effective oversight.

7

# Constitutional Limits—
# The Role of the Judiciary

The activities of the FBI and other domestic intelligence agencies are subject, of course, to constitutional constraints. The First Amendment's free speech and association guarantees, the Fourth Amendment's protection against unreasonable searches and seizures, and the Fifth Amendment's due process guarantee and its privilege against compelled self-incrimination impose limits on the FBI and other agencies. These restrictions, however, are often difficult to enforce for a variety of reasons, from doctrines extending immunity for official misconduct to the very secrecy that surrounds intelligence activities. Moreover, while the Constitution has been interpreted to prevent prosecutions and other adverse action for First Amendment activities, the courts have been reluctant to block FBI investigations into First Amendment activities. And under the Bush administration, we have seen an aggressive assertion of presidential autonomy, coming close to the assertion that the Constitution vests the president with unlimited, unreviewable power when he acts in the name of national security.

## THE SUPREME COURT'S VIGOROUS PROTECTION OF SPEECH AND ASSOCIATION

In a series of landmark decisions over the past forty years, the Supreme Court has extended robust protection under the First Amendment to political speech and association. The Court has not always been sensitive to political freedoms, but its current doctrine is staunchly protective. Taken together, its opinions envision a vigorous clash of ideas that is at odds with the FBI's counterintelligence model and its investigations aimed at monitoring and disrupting groups that support the political activities of disfavored causes.

For example, the Court held in the 1969 case of *Brandenburg v. Ohio* that the government cannot punish statements advocating the use of force or other illegal conduct except where such advocacy is "directed to inciting or producing imminent lawless action and is likely to incite or produce such action."[1] Absent such a showing, which is difficult to make, speech advocating crime is constitutionally protected. In subsequent cases, the *Brandenburg* principle was reaffirmed and expanded, as the Court held that speech intended to stir anger and even speech that creates a climate of violence is protected under the First Amendment. The Court did not intitially protect such spech, but arrived at these rules only after experiencing years of abuse directed at political dissidents in the name of punishing advocacy of crime.[2]

The Court has provided equally strong protection for political association, holding that the First and Fifth Amendments protect association with a group engaged in legal and illegal activities so long as the individual's association is not specifically intended to further the group's unlawful aims.[3] As the Court explained in 1972:

"guilt by association alone, without [establishing] that an individual's association poses the threat feared by the Government," is an impermissible basis upon which to deny First Amendment rights. The government has the burden of establishing a knowing affiliation with an organization pursuing unlawful aims and goals, and a specific intent to further those illegal aims.[4]

These constitutional standards sharply curtail the ability of the government to punish its political opponents. Individuals cannot be punished for advocating lawbreaking, as long as they avoid imminent incitement, and they are permitted to associate with groups engaged in illegal activity, as long as they do not specifically intend to further that illegal conduct. These principles in turn require the government to focus on individual criminal acts, not mere advocacy or affiliation.[5]

## JUDICIAL BARRIERS TO RELIEF

Despite the Supreme Court's generous protections for the rights of advocacy and association, the courts have erected procedural barriers that make it difficult for the victims of political spying to obtain judicial relief. For example, under a doctrine known as "standing," the Supreme Court in 1972 ruled that anti–Vietnam War protesters could not challenge an extensive government surveillance program.[6] The Court said that the protesters had alleged only a "subjective chill." It said that in order to obtain judicial relief ordering the government to halt its surveillance, an individual must show she "has sustained or is immediately in danger of sustaining a direct injury as the result of [a governmental] action." Although the case was decided only on threshold standing grounds, and did not purport to decide whether the surveillance was legal or not, it has been read as allowing the government to investigate speech that could not constitutionally be prosecuted. On this basis, a federal appeals court refused to review a case in which Richmond police routinely surveilled demonstrations and meetings by maintaining a police presence and photographing participants, keeping the information on file, and sharing it with other law enforcement agencies, including the FBI.[7] Another appeals court rejected a challenge to undercover FBI surveillance of a convention of the Young Socialists of America.[8]

In practical terms, the standing doctrine means that much turns on the extent to which those challenging police or FBI surveillance can document the nature of the intrusion and show concrete evidence of injury. For example, while a Philadelphia court held that the mere photographing and compilation of records on political demonstrators gave rise to no First Amendment injury, it held that a tangible injury did occur when the police department publicly disclosed, in a network television broadcast, information concerning individuals and groups on whom police intelligence files were kept.[9] The court stated that disclosure of information concerning lawful First Amendment–protected activities to non–law enforcement groups chilled freedom of speech and association. Making such information generally available, the court found, could interfere with job opportunities, careers, or travel rights, and may dissuade others from joining unpopular groups under surveillance.[10]

The courts have also erected other procedural barriers to the enforcement of the First Amendment against the intelligence agencies. When twenty-one anti–Vietnam War activists sued the CIA in the 1970s for spying on them, a federal appeals court denied their requests for access to government files on the surveillance. This ruling made it impossible for the activists to demonstrate personal injury from the government's misconduct or the likelihood of future surveillance, and resulted in the dismissal of their claims for both damages and injunctive relief.[11]

On occasion, plaintiffs have succeeded in overcoming these barriers and establishing their "standing" to challenge FBI conduct. In one such case, Judge Thomas Griesa of the Southern District of New York ruled in 1986 that the FBI's COINTELPRO operations against the SWP, including the FBI's use of informants to obtain private information about political meetings and demonstrations and other lawful events of the SWP, were "patently unconstitutional and violated the SWP's First Amendment rights of free speech and assembly."[12] This victory, however, required extraordinary efforts by both plaintiffs and judge. The case lasted thirteen years. In the course of the litigation, the FBI deliberately concealed from the plaintiffs and even from the U.S. Attorney's office information about FBI break-ins against the SWP and its members. The Bureau submitted to plaintiffs (and filed with the court) answers to interrogatories that were, in the words of the judge, "grossly deceptive." And the attorney general refused to comply with the court's order to disclose information about informants.[13]

## THE COURTS' RELUCTANCE TO LIMIT FBI INVESTIGATIONS—THE CHICAGO LAWSUIT

A federal lawsuit in Chicago illustrates both the utility and the frustrations of constitutional litigation as a check upon FBI investigative activities. The case, *Alliance to End Repression v. City of Chicago*, began in 1974. Plaintiffs, including the ACLU, the Alliance to End Repression, and the Chicago Committee to Defend the Bill of Rights,[14] charged that the FBI had "conducted surveillance of, and compiled dossiers on, their lawful political and other lawful activities; gathered information about plaintiffs by unlawful means, including warrantless wiretaps and break-ins, unlawful use of infiltrators and informers, and by other unlawful means; [and] disrupted and harassed plaintiffs' lawful activities." After six years of sharply contested litigation, the parties proposed in late 1980 a settlement agreement, or consent decree, which the court approved.[15] The agreement set forth several principles the FBI was to follow while conducting domestic security investigations in Chicago. Most important, it incorporated the rules set forth in the FBI guidelines issued by Attorney General Edward Levi, giving them the force of law in Chicago.

Eighteen months later, Attorney General William French Smith issued his revisions to the guidelines, described above in Chapter 6. The plaintiffs went back to federal court and asked the judge to block implementation of the new guidelines in Chicago on the ground that they violated the settlement order. The trial judge agreed, finding that even though the introductory portion of the new guidelines included a prohibition against conducting an investigation solely on the basis of activities protected under the First Amendment, the practical effect of the revisions would be just the opposite. Specifically, the judge was concerned about the following provision in the new guidelines:

> When, however, statements advocate criminal activity . . . an investigation under these Guidelines may be warranted unless it is apparent, from the circumstances or the context in which the statements were made, that there is no prospect of harm.

The judge found the Smith guidelines deficient because they did not embody the *Brandenburg v. Ohio* test: they did not specify that the feared harm must be "imminent" and "likely" and they did not require that the speech be "directed" (i.e., intended) to cause imminent lawless action.

In 1984, the court of appeals overturned the decision of the trial judge, however, and the revised guidelines went into effect in Chicago.[16] The court of appeals stated that the FBI "has always investigated people who advocate or even threaten to commit serious violations of federal law, even if the violations are not imminent; and it always will. It 'has a right, indeed a duty, to keep itself informed with respect to the possible commission of crimes; it is not obliged to wear blinders until it may be too late for prevention.' " Accordingly, the appeals court held that the settlement order could be reasonably interpreted in a way that was consistent with the revised Smith guidelines:

This interpretation is that the FBI may not base an investigation solely on the political views of a group or an individual; it must have a basis in a genuine concern for law enforcement. Thus it may not investigate a group solely because the group advocates Puerto Rican independence . . . but it may investigate any group that advocates the commission, even if not immediately, of terrorist acts in violation of federal law. It need not wait till the bombs begin to go off, or even till the bomb factory is found.

Up to a point, the appeals court was correct: the Constitution does not require the government to ignore the threats of those who advocate violence, even when the threat is not imminent. The standard for investigation need not be as stringent as the standard for prosecution. But First Amendment concerns develop when the FBI undertakes a broad investigation of a group's political activities without a criminal predicate.

The court of appeals in the Chicago case also reversed another lower court ruling that the FBI had violated the settlement agreement during its investigation of the Chicago chapter of CISPES from March 1983 to June 1985. The trial court had found that surveillance, photographing, attendance by government agents at public meetings, reviews of financial, utility, and telephone records, and checks of law enforcement records in the CISPES investigation had violated the settlement agreement. The court of appeals overturned the lower court ruling, holding that the settlement did not bar FBI investigations of First Amendment activities if the FBI conducted the investigation "for the purpose of routing out terrorist activity only to find that the basis for thinking that the organization was engaged in terrorism was flimsy or nonexistent." The court ruled that those who would bring suit under the settlement had to prove that the FBI *intended* to interfere with First Amendment rights or that the FBI engaged in a pattern of substantial noncompliance, whether or not it was intentional.[17] Intent, almost always impossible to establish, is the wrong test. And if the CISPES investigation did not amount to substantial noncompliance, it is difficult to imagine what would. The correct test for evaluating FBI activities should be an objective one: Were the FBI's investigative activities reasonably calculated to obtain information about suspected criminal activities? Surveilling and photographing public demonstrations is generally not reasonably calculated to produce evidence of criminal conduct committed before or after the demonstrations. The CISPES investigation was never really a search for terrorism. The stated purpose was rooting out terrorism, but it was not conducted in a way likely to do so even if such terrorist activity had existed.[18]

The 1984 appeals court decision focused on the FBI, and it did not actually revise the consent decree. In 1997, the city of Chicago asked the district court to modify the consent decree to eliminate its restrictions and oversight provisions in order to give the city greater latitude in investigating First Amendment activities. The district court refused,[19] but in 2001 the court of appeals reversed and remanded the case with instructions to make the modifications in the consent decree that the city had requested.[20]

## THE FOURTH AMENDMENT

Like the First Amendment, the Fourth Amendment's prohibition against unreasonable searches and seizures imposes important limits on government conduct. As with the guarantees of the First Amendment, however, the courts have been reluctant to interpret the Fourth Amendment to rein in FBI investigations.

The courts have made it clear that wiretaps and physical searches by federal agents in criminal cases can generally be conducted only on the basis of judicial orders finding probable cause to believe that a crime has been, is being, or is about to be committed and that the search will uncover evidence of the criminal activity. Thus, for example, Judge Griesa in the SWP case held that the FBI's surreptitious and warrantless entries ("black bag jobs," i.e., burglaries) under COINTELPRO were "obvious violations of the Fourth Amendment." [21]

This principle clearly applies to investigations of domestic terrorism, although the Justice Department once tried to claim that it did not. In 1972, in the landmark *Keith* case, the Supreme Court ruled that the warrantless wiretapping of domestic activists was unlawful under the Fourth Amendment. [22] Justice Powell, writing the Court's opinion, rejected the government's argument that there was a domestic security exception to the warrant requirement of the Fourth Amendment:

> Security surveillances are especially sensitive because of the inherent vagueness of the domestic security concept, the necessarily broad and continuing nature of intelligence gathering, and the temptation to utilize such surveillances to oversee political dissent. We recognize, as we have before, the constitutional basis of the President's domestic security role, but we think it must be exercised in a manner compatible with the Fourth Amendment.

The courts, however, have divided on whether the Fourth Amendment permits warrantless searches where there is suspicion of involvement by a *foreign* government or group. (The issue has since been dealt with statutorily, as the FISA court has been granted authority over physical as well as electronic searches. The Supreme Court, however, has not yet addressed the constitutionality of FISA.) In one case arising out of the Watergate era, the courts flatly rejected the concept. The case involved two of President Nixon's assistants, who were prosecuted for conspiring to break into the office of a Los Angeles psychiatrist to steal medical records relating to one of his patients, Daniel Ellsberg, who was at the time under a federal indictment for disclosing the Pentagon Papers to the press.[23] Nixon's aides sought to defend their actions by claiming that there was a "national security" exception to the Fourth Amendment warrant requirement.[24] The district court rejected the argument, and explained that recognizing such an exception would contravene "vital privacy interests" embodied in the Fourth Amendment:

> The Court cannot find that [the recent, controversial ruling involving national security wiretaps] indicates an intention to obviate the entire Fourth Amendment whenever the President determines that an American citizen, personally innocent of wrongdoing, has in his possession information that may touch upon foreign policy concerns. Such a doctrine . . . would give the Executive a blank check to disregard the very heart and core of the Fourth Amendment and the vital privacy interests that it protects.[25]

However, other lower court rulings approved warrantless searches in cases involving foreign counterintelligence. When Morton Halperin sued his former boss, National Security Advisor Henry Kissinger, for placing a wiretap on Halperin's home telephone without judicial approval while Halperin was a staffer at the

National Security Council, the federal appeals court ruled that so long as objectively reasonable national security concerns prompted the wiretap, Kissinger was not liable.[26] And when the government sought to use information gleaned from a warrantless wiretap of an American citizen and a Soviet national to support their convictions for passing military secrets to the Soviets, the court deferred to the government's invocation of the concept of "national security."[27]

More significantly, the Supreme Court has allowed the FBI to do through informants or undercover agents what it could not do directly. Under the "invited informer" principle, the Court has reasoned that a person or political organization has no legitimate expectation of privacy in information voluntarily shared with a third party in the mistaken belief that the information will not be turned over to the government.[28] Thus, an informant can record his own phone conversations with activists who have invited him into their group or "wear a wire" to record conversations at meetings for the government, without any court order or probable cause showing. This principle was applied, for example, in a criminal case against members of a church who had provided a haven to Central American refugees fleeing civil wars in El Salvador and Guatemala. The church members were charged with violating U.S. immigration laws. The evidence against them included the testimony of an informant who had infiltrated their church. The federal appeals court in California held that infiltration into the church organization did not violate the Fourth Amendment since the defendants voluntarily and at their own risk revealed the information to the informant.[29]

## DUE PROCESS

"There are literally millions of aliens within the jurisdiction of the United States. The Fifth Amendment, as well as the Fourteenth

Amendment, protects every one of these persons from deprivations of life, liberty, or property without due process of law. Even one whose presence in this country is unlawful, involuntary, or transitory is entitled to that constitutional protection."
                                    —*Mathews v. Diaz, 426 U.S. 67, 77 (1976)*

The due process clause of the Fifth Amendment is another critical constraint on government discretion in the name of fighting terrorism. A fundamental component of due process is the right to confront one's accusers. It is founded on the premise that the truth is most likely to emerge in an adversarial proceeding, where the accused, who is in the best position to defend herself, can confront the sources of evidence against her, and can challenge their veracity, reveal their bias, and catch them in contradiction.

Thus, it is well established that in no criminal trial—even involving the most dangerous of crimes and the most secret of information—may the government rely on evidence not disclosed to the defendant. If the government wants to use an informant's testimony, the informant must take the witness stand. If the government wants to rely on classified information, it must reveal it in court. Even under the Classified Information Procedures Act, which permits the government to substitute as evidence an unclassified summary of classified evidence, the courts can accept the substitution only if it affords the defendant the same opportunity to defend herself as the classified evidence itself would.[30]

The courts have ruled that the due process clause, which protects all persons living in the United States, citizens or noncitizens, whether here lawfully or unlawfully, bars the use of secret evidence to deport noncitizens living here.[31] Accordingly, deportation proceedings throughout our history have been conducted on the basis of evidence disclosed to the person, to afford her an opportunity to defend herself.[32]

In recent years, however, the INS, in the name of fighting terrorism, has repeatedly tried to assert the power to use secret evidence in deportation hearings. The federal courts have often rejected the efforts. For example, when the INS sought to use secret evidence to expel Fouad Rafeedie, a permanent resident alien, the D.C. Circuit Court of Appeals rejected the government's effort, finding that "[i]t is difficult to imagine how even someone innocent of all wrongdoing could meet such a burden [of rebutting undisclosed evidence that he is a member of a terrorist group]."[33]

The INS sought to use secret evidence in the LA 8 case twice—first to justify detaining the eight upon their initial arrest, and later to deny permanent resident status to two of them. The first time, the immigration judge refused to consider any evidence not disclosed to the eight. The second time, the aliens had to seek relief in the federal courts, which barred the INS from relying on secret evidence because to do so would violate due process.[34] The Ninth Circuit called the risk of error inherent in the use of undisclosed information "exceptionally high." It recalled the words of Justice Jackson in *United States ex rel. Knauff v. Shaughnessy*:

> The plea that evidence of guilt must be secret is abhorrent to free men, because it provides a cloak for the malevolent, the misinformed, the meddlesome, and the corrupt to play the role of informer undetected and uncorrected.[35]

Indeed, the court concluded, "one would be hard pressed to design a procedure more likely to result in erroneous deprivations." Balancing the risk of error against the government's asserted national security interests, the appeals court held that secret evidence could not be used: "[T]he fact that a given law or procedure is efficient, convenient, and useful in facilitating functions of government, standing alone, will not save it if it is contrary to the Constitution."

Notwithstanding these courtroom defeats, the INS and DHS have continued to use secret evidence in immigration proceedings, as illustrated in Chapter 10.

Due process played a critical role in the Supreme Court's 2004 decision rejecting the Bush administration's asserted authority to detain a U.S. citizen as an enemy combatant. As discussed in more detail in Chapter 12, in *Hamdi v. Rumsfeld* the Court ruled that even when exercising the commander-in-chief power to detain an alleged enemy captured on the battlefield, due process demands that any citizen so detained must be afforded notice of the factual basis for his detention and a meaningful opportunity to respond to the charges before a neutral decision maker. Whether such requirements apply to foreign nationals held abroad, however, remains an open question. Two lower federal courts have divided on the issue and an appeal is pending.


## CONCLUSION

The First Amendment serves as the single most important safeguard against infringements on political activity, and the Fourth and Fifth Amendments also offer important protections. But enforcing those guarantees is often difficult in the face of the secrecy that impedes the uncovering of improper behavior, judicially erected barriers to recovery, and the willingness of the Justice Department to defend with tremendous resources the FBI and other law enforcement agencies against citizen lawsuits seeking to impose limits on their investigative activity. Frank Wilkinson's lawsuit lasted twelve years. The LA 8 case is in its eighteenth year.

The Chicago case shows the courts' reluctance to use the First Amendment to curb FBI surveillance even of citizens, and the Supreme Court's decision in the LA 8 case leaves noncitizens in the

United States vulnerable to politically motivated selective enforcement of the immigration laws. So long as courts refuse to acknowledge the chilling effect of investigations of protected activities, the First Amendment will provide little meaningful protection against wasteful probes of political activity. This reluctance is particularly unfortunate in light of the 1996 Antiterrorism Act's provision making "support for terrorism" a crime, for, as shown in Chapter 9, that statute literally criminalizes political activity and thereby authorizes the FBI to spend considerable resources investigating it without judicial control.

There is an obvious tension between the Supreme Court decisions carefully protecting the rights of political speech and association and those allowing the government to engage in surreptitious surveillance and use of informants without probable cause. Government spying on lawful associational activities, such as public demonstrations or meetings, can have just as real a chilling effect on the exercise of the First Amendment right to associate as the compelled disclosure of membership lists that the Supreme Court blocked in cases involving the NAACP years ago.[36] Cases denigrating the chilling effect that FBI investigations have on First Amendment rights ignore the Supreme Court's warning: "[First Amendment] freedoms are delicate and vulnerable, as well as supremely precious in our society. The threat of sanctions may deter their exercise almost as potently as the actual application of sanctions."[37]

# PART III

# The 1996 Antiterrorism Act:
# Curtailing Civil Liberties
# in the Name of Fighting Terrorism

# 8

## Prologue to the 1996 Antiterrorism Act

Curtailing civil liberties in the name of national security is often a bipartisan affair. Democrats as well as Republicans have ignored civil liberties concerns when acting in the wake of terrorist incidents. Thus, on February 10, 1995, senior Democrats introduced the Clinton administration's counterterrorism bill in the Senate and in the House of Representatives.[1] With the exception of habeas corpus "reform" provisions added subsequently, the Clinton proposal included all the critical elements of the antiterrorism law enacted one year later: it established a special court that would use secret evidence to deport noncitizens accused of association with terrorist groups; it gave the executive branch the power to criminalize fundraising for lawful activities conducted by organizations labeled "terrorist"; it repealed the Edwards amendment, which prohibited the FBI from opening investigations based on First Amendment activities; and it resurrected the discredited ideological visa denial provisions of the McCarran-Walter Act to bar aliens based on their associations rather than their acts. The bill also created a new federal crime of terrorism, carved further exceptions in the time-honored posse comitatus law barring the U.S. military from civilian law enforcement, expanded use of pretrial detention, and relaxed the rules governing federal wiretaps.[2]

The story of the Act's passage shows how easily civil liberties and constitutional principles can be cast aside under the influences of emotion and political posturing in times of crisis. The lessons of past FBI abuses from COINTELPRO through the CISPES investigation were ignored. The voices of likely victims of the statute's ideologically based approach were never heard, while those who opposed the legislation on the grounds that it was unnecessary or dangerously unconstitutional were marginalized. Instead, two incidents—the 1993 bombing of the World Trade Center and Timothy McVeigh's 1995 bombing of the federal building in Oklahoma City—overwhelmed all rational discussion, and the law was enacted as an effort to do something in response to these two crimes. The fact that suspects were arrested soon after both incidents and later convicted, and the fact that the government could point to nothing in the Act that would have prevented or made it easier to prosecute either incident, proved irrelevant.

## LONG SOUGHT AND LONG REJECTED

The most troubling provisions in the 1996 Antiterrorism Act—the resurrection of association as grounds for exclusion and deportation of noncitizens; the ban on supporting lawful activities of groups labeled "terrorist" by the executive branch; and the secret evidence provision—were developed long before the bombings that triggered their final enactment.

In the case of guilt by association, the Clinton proposal making mere membership in a terrorist group grounds for exclusion and deportation represented a return to the intolerance of the 1950s. The McCarran-Walter Act, passed in 1952, made association with communist or anarchist groups a ground for exclusion and deportation, and was used over the years to deny entry to such luminaries as Gabriel García Márquez, Graham Greene, Carlos Fuentes, Czeslaw Milosz, Yves Montand, and Charlie Chaplin. In 1990, with much fanfare, Congress repealed most of the ideological grounds for exclusion and deportation. But in the Clinton bill, they reappeared in the guise of a bar on anyone believed to be a member of a "terrorist organization."

The fund-raising ban's history went back to 1984, when the Reagan administration sent Congress a bill to make it a crime to "support" terrorism. Features of the Reagan proposal were remarkably similar to what was enacted in the 1996 Antiterrorism Act, including a provision granting effectively unreviewable discretion to the secretary of state to designate foreign groups as "terrorist." The Reagan provision was opposed on constitutional grounds and was not enacted. The first Bush administration proposed similar "support for terrorism" legislation, but again Congress rejected it. In the 1994 Clinton omnibus crime bill, a narrow support for terrorism provision was added, focused only on support for violent acts, and it was accompanied by the Edwards amendment, intended to prevent a repeat of the CISPES fiasco by precluding investigations based solely on activities protected under the First Amendment.[3] Those limits were swept aside by the 1996 Act.

Like the fund-raising ban, the secret evidence provision also had a prior record, legislatively and judicially. The Clinton provision was a slightly modified version of a proposal offered during the prior Bush administration, which Congress twice refused to enact. The INS had on several occasions sought to use secret evidence in immigration settings, but had been repeatedly rebuffed by the courts. Undeterred by these losses in the courts on constitutional grounds, the Clinton administration resurrected the Bush language in its 1995 proposal.

## ONE-SIDED HEARINGS

From the outset, congressional consideration of the legislation was largely one-sided. At the House Judiciary Committee's first hearing on the bill, in April 1995, the first six of the eight witnesses called to testify were strongly and uncritically supportive of the bill. [4] One of the other two witnesses raised questions about some aspects of the bill, but also called for repeal of the executive order banning the U.S. government from engaging in assassinations. Only one witness, Greg Nojeim of the American Civil Liberties Union, gave a consistently critical, constitutionally based analysis of the legislation.

Absent from the hearings altogether were any of the people likely to be affected personally by the bill. Yet it was their stories that Congress should have heard. Any number of people could have been called to testify, from Fouad Rafeedie, a permanent resident alien the government sought to expel using secret evidence, to the LA 8 or Frank Wilkinson. The committee could have reached a little further back into American history to consider cases like that of Ellen Knauff, a World War II "war bride" held at Ellis Island for three years on secret evidence that she could not see and therefore could not rebut. Her case went all the way to the Supreme Court, where she lost on the ground that as an alien seeking intial entry to the United States she had no constitutional rights regarding her entry. When public pressure forced Congress to give Knauff a hearing, it came out that the "secret evidence" against her was nothing more than a malevolent rumor sparked by a jilted former lover of Knauff's husband. Knauff was admitted to the United States after three years in detention on Ellis Island. Congress considered none of these stories when it took up the Clinton terrorism bill.

The House Judiciary Committee's Subcommittee on Crime held a second hearing on May 3, two weeks after the Oklahoma City bombing.[5] Not surprisingly, given the emotional reaction to the bombing, this hearing was no more balanced than the first. Once again, opponents of the legislation were relegated, as one witness stated, to the "unenviable position of testifying on the [third and] last panel."[6]

In June 1995, the full House Judiciary Committee held two additional hearings and again the majority of the witnesses, and all of those on the first panels on each day, supported the legislation. Again, Greg Nojeim of the ACLU was the sole witness who offered a comprehensive constitutional critique of the legislation.

The Senate hearings were even more one-sided. The first one was held barely one week after the Oklahoma City bombing. Not one of the ten witnesses allowed to testify criticized the legislation or warned of constitutional concerns. A second hearing, in which two witnesses would have criticized the legislation, was canceled.

Little attention was paid to whether the FBI was subject to standards that would prevent it from repeating past abuses of constitutional rights. Two exchanges between FBI Director Freeh and members of the House Judiciary Committee were particularly telling. Expressing concern that the legislation would invite a return to the days of COINTELPRO, Rep. Sheila Jackson Lee asked Director Freeh how successful he thought COINTELPRO had been. Freeh's response: "I would really have to do some research to give you an intelligent answer."[7] The director of the FBI should not have had to do "research" to discuss the worst abuses in his agency's history. Freeh should have jumped at the chance to distance himself and his organization from a program and philosophy universally condemned for violating civil liberties. He should have been able to outline concretely the principles and procedures by which agents avoid infringements on First Amendment rights. In the political climate at the time, however, Freeh felt no need to do so. When Rep. John Conyers asked Freeh to comment on the lessons of history and the difficulty of distinguishing violent rhetoric from terrorism, Freeh again declined to answer, stating, "I don't think it's appropriate for me to comment on that." Freeh sensed that he would get the expanded powers he wanted, and he saw no need even to answer these questions.

## NO IDENTIFIABLE NEED FOR
## ANTITERRORISM LEGISLATION

Despite the one-sidedness of the hearings, several members of the House Judiciary Committee, both Democrat and Republican, questioned the need for the legislation. They repeatedly asked administration witnesses to identify the specific problems that the legislation would cure. The witnesses had remarkably little to offer and at times seemed confounded by the very question. When John Conyers of Michigan, the House Judiciary Committee's senior Democrat and a veteran of many FBI scandals, specifically asked at the April 1995 hearing what lessons had been learned from the 1993 World Trade Center bombing that indicated that federal and state laws were deficient, Deputy Attorney General Jamie Gorelick at first refused to answer the question, saying only that there were a number of other cases, which she did not name, where there was inadequate federal jurisdiction. When Conyers pressed, Gorelick responded that if the facts of the World Trade Center bombing had been different, it could not have been investigated and prosecuted as a federal crime. At that, Conyers concluded: "I've never seen this much law created as a result of prosecutions that we agree worked very effectively, but you say that it may not have worked." [8]

Later, Republican George Gekas asked a similar question. Gorelick responded, "Well, speaking hypothetically . . ." Gekas asked again, "My question is . . . do we have any evidence that such things might—are brewing." Gorelick responded that she "was not at liberty" to share with the congressman at the hearing information that would respond to that question. Howard Coble, a conservative Republican from North Carolina, asked why law enforcement required new powers to combat terrorism and received equally unsatisfying answers. Congresswoman Sheila Jackson Lee asked what effect the legislation would have had on the Pan Am 103 case. Gorelick said she would have to submit an answer later. In that written answer, she admitted, "[W]e do not have examples of prosecutions that have been hampered by the lack of statutes of the type proposed in" the administration's bill.[9]

At the House Subcommittee on Crime hearings on May 3, proponents of the legislation were once again unable to explain why new legislation was needed. Members asked how the new law would change current practices, and how this would improve the fight against terrorism. Again, administration witnesses avoided answering these questions. When asked by Rep. Conyers how the proposed law would have affected the Oklahoma City bombing incident had it been in place at the time, FBI Director Freeh responded: "I really can't comment on that."[10]

## IMPACT OF THE OKLAHOMA CITY BOMBING

The antiterrorism bill drew opposition from a broad-based coalition of groups who agreed that it would unnecessarily expand government power and infringe personal liberties. Irish American and Arab American groups felt particularly threatened, but all members of the coalition came to recognize the indivisibility of civil liberties. They knew the guilt by association concept could be redirected at any time for the foreign policy or internal political purposes of the government, and they feared that the practice of using secret evidence, once established, was likely to expand.

Editorial writers questioned the need for the legislation and opposed its liberty-threatening provisions. Most significantly, perhaps, public opinion polls showed widespread reluctance to give the government more powers. The legislation languished and seemed headed for defeat.

All that changed when, on April 19, 1995, a horrifying explosion destroyed the Oklahoma City federal building, killing 168 persons, including nineteen children. Members of Congress immediately felt tremendous pressure to pass antiterrorism legislation. It did not matter that the proposals in the president's initial bill were directed largely against international terrorism, while the Oklahoma bombing was the work of homegrown criminals. Nor did it matter that, even after the bombing, polls still showed public reluctance to sacrifice liberties in an effort to purchase security. President Clinton appeared on *60 Minutes* the Sunday after the bombing to offer his condolences to the victims' families and to set a tone of reassurance for the nation. He ended up promising further antiterrorism legislation and suggesting that it might be appropriate to use the occasion to "reform" habeas corpus.

## POLITICS AND OTHER AGENDAS TAKE OVER

The antiterrorism bill soon became entangled in partisan politics. Democratic and Republican leaders introduced dueling versions of the legislation, and each party sought to blame the other for being unresponsive to terrorism.[11] Nonetheless, the House hesitated to act, in large part because of conservative opposition to expanded government wiretapping authorities and a proposal to regulate certain common explosives (seen by some as a step toward regulation of gunpowder and guns).

A different dynamic played out in the Senate, where Judiciary Committee chairman Orrin Hatch was eager to capitalize on the president's suggestion that habeas corpus reform be added to the antiterrorism package. For years, Hatch had sought to limit the right of habeas corpus, only to see his proposals dropped from every successive anticrime measure. The terrorism bill offered another chance to achieve this long-sought goal. Hatch's provisions gutting habeas corpus ended up in the Act, and are among its worst features, but they have nothing to do with terrorism. For the most part, the habeas reforms govern the standards that federal courts use in reviewing state court criminal convictions, and terrorism cases are almost never tried in state courts. What was really at issue in the habeas debate was whether state prisoners could obtain meaningful federal review of the constitutionality of the procedures by which they had been convicted and sentenced. Most of the debate centered around death penalty cases, but most of the changes sought by habeas opponents would apply to noncapital cases as well. Senator Hatch wanted to make it more difficult for federal courts to order retrials of prisoners where state courts had violated the U.S. Constitution.

The Senate acted quickly and passed the antiterrorism bill, S. 735, by a vote of 91 to 8 in June 1995, after dropping the president's wiretap proposals and adding Hatch's provisions curtailing the right of habeas corpus. The Senate bill also included Clinton's proposals to exclude and deport aliens based on their association, to criminalize fund-raising in the U.S. for designated groups, and to allow the military to assist in law enforcement efforts aimed at biological and chemical weapons.

In the House of Representatives, the legislation stalled for many months. But as 1996—a presidential election year—began, it became clear that President Clinton was going to use the terrorism issue politically. With the April 19 anniversary of the Oklahoma City bombing approaching, the House of Representatives ceded to the pressure and revived the bill. The version passed by the House omitted several troublesome provisions, reflecting the considerable opposition of a coalition of activists representing a broad spectrum of political, religious, and ethnic interests. From then on, however, the impending April 19 anniversary drove the issue. The conference committee that was appointed to reconcile the differences between the House and Senate versions was dominated by supporters of the legislation's more onerous provisions. A few objectionable provisions adopted by the Senate to expand wiretap authority were dropped, but these would have been incremental in their effect compared to the radical changes that were adopted: the prohibition on fund-raising, a provision denying entry visas to members of terrorist groups, the secret evidence provisions, provisions to facilitate the denial of political asylum benefits and to expedite deportation of aliens arriving without proper documents, and limits on habeas corpus.

Eager to get the bill on the president's desk by the April 19 anniversary of the Oklahoma City bombing, the Senate adopted the conference report on April 17 in a 91–8 vote. The next day, the House also adopted the report by a vote of 293–133. On April 24, the president signed the Antiterrorism and Effective Death Penalty Act of 1996.

# 9

# The 1996 Antiterrorism Act's
# Central Provisions

The Antiterrorism and Effective Death Penalty Act of 1996[1] contained what were, prior to the 2001 antiterrorism measures, some of the worst assaults on civil liberties in decades. The Act was wide-ranging, dealing with everything from the making of plastic explosives to trading in nuclear materials. But it also attacked basic First Amendment and due process rights. This chapter focuses on the more troublesome provisions of the Act and describes what they purported to do. These provisions were unnecessary, unwise, and unconstitutional. They were not justified by any deficiency in existing law nor, it has turned out, did they serve any legitimate purpose in deterring, investigating, or punishing acts of violence. They have been directed against disfavored groups to the detriment of the civil liberties of all.

## OVERVIEW

The Act made it a crime for citizens and noncitizens alike to provide any material support to the lawful political or humanitarian activities of any foreign group designated by the secretary of state as "terrorist."[2] Thus, the Act reintroduced to federal law the principle of "guilt by association" that had defined the McCarthy era. People can be punished, the Act says, not for crimes that they commit or abet, but for supporting wholly lawful acts of disfavored groups. If this law had been on the books in the 1980s, it would have been a crime to give money to the African National Congress during Nelson Mandela's speaking tours here, because the State Department routinely listed the ANC as a "terrorist group."

This fund-raising provision appeared to codify the focus on political ideology and association that had prompted the FBI's most intrusive investigations of political activists from COINTELPRO to CISPES. It gave the FBI reason to investigate any group or individual that supports even the wholly lawful activities of a designated foreign organization. The Act further encouraged politically focused investigations by repealing the Edwards amendment, which had barred the FBI from opening or expanding investigations solely on the basis of First Amendment–protected activities.

Reversing another reform that had been years in the making, the Act revived the practice of denying visas to foreigners based on mere membership in undesirable groups, in this case, the same groups designated "terrorist" by the secretary of state.[3] Congress repudiated such ideological exclusions (another form of guilt by association) in its 1990 reform of the immigration laws. The 1996 Act's provisions, however, allow exclusion based on membership alone, without any showing that the individual furthered any illegal acts of the group. Since an alien who was inadmissible at the time of entry is thereafter deportable, the change also gave the government grounds to deport a person who was a member of a designated organization at the time of his otherwise legal entry into the United States.[4]

The Act also created an unprecedented "alien terrorist removal procedure" designed to deny immigrants facing deportation the most basic of due process protections—the right to confront their accusers.[5] Under this provision, the government claims the authority to deport an alien alleged to be a terrorist without ever telling her the source of the evidence against her, a tactic that the courts have repeatedly ruled violates due process.[6] The provision is of such dubious constitutionality that it has never been invoked despite being on the statute books for nearly ten years.

The Act also included several provisions having nothing to do with terrorism. It sharply curtailed the right of habeas corpus, the "Great Writ" by which federal courts have granted relief to people imprisoned as a result of constitutional violations in state court criminal proceedings.[7] Other provisions limited the ability of foreign nationals to claim political asylum and deprived them of due process rights if they entered the U.S. without going through immigration inspection, even if they are not suspected of any involvement in terrorist activity.[8]

## TERRORISM IS WHATEVER THE SECRETARY OF STATE DECIDES IT IS

Perhaps the most troubling feature of the 1996 Act was its resurrection of guilt by association, criminalizing humanitarian support to any group designated as "terrorist." Under the 1996 Act, the secretary of state may designate a foreign group as a terrorist organization if she finds that the group "engages in terrorist activity" that threatens the "security of United States nationals or the national security of the United States." The Immigration and Nationality Act defines "terrorist activity" to include virtually any use of, or threat to use, a weapon, and the Antiterrorism Act defines "national security" as "the national defense, foreign relations, or economic interests of the

United States." As a result, the secretary of state can designate organizations that engage in both lawful and unlawful activity, based
on a determination that the group's activities threaten our foreign
policy or economic interests. Since courts have said that they cannot
second-guess the secretary of state on what threatens our foreign
policy, the law effectively gives the secretary of state a blank check to
blacklist disfavored foreign groups.

The Clinton administration admitted in hearings that predated
the Act that groups labeled "terrorist" may in fact engage in lawful
social, political, and humanitarian activities as well as violent activities. In 1994, the Clinton administration testified against a bill that
would have made membership in Hamas a ground for exclusion, arguing that because Hamas engages in "widespread social welfare
programs" as well as terrorism, one could not presume that a Hamas
member was a "terrorist" without indulging in guilt by association.[9]
Yet by 1995, the administration proposed to do just that for count-
less groups. The initial designations by the secretary in October
1997 fulfilled that promise, including Hamas on the list.[10] Also on
the list was the Popular Front for the Liberation of Palestine, which
the trial court in the LA 8 case found was involved in a wide range of
lawful activities, including the provision of education, day care,
health care, and social security. Notably, the list did not include any
group headed by Osama bin Laden, illustrating the limitations of
such a designation process as an antiterrorism measure.

Three consequences flow from the secretary of state's decision to
designate a foreign entity as a terrorist organization: (1) it is a crime
for anybody to contribute money or other material support or resources to a designated group, even for its social, political, or humanitarian activities;[11] (2) all members of the group are barred from
entering the United States, and are deportable if they were members
prior to entry, even if they have never been involved in illegal activi-

ties;[12] and (3) banks must freeze funds of any designated organization and its agents.

The designation authority invites selective enforcement. The secretary of state can pick and choose which groups to designate, based on the politics of the moment. There are literally hundreds if not thousands of groups worldwide that engage at least in part in violent activities. Practically speaking, the government must necessarily enforce such authority selectively. Introducing a further opportunity for politically motivated decisions, the secretary of state can remove an organization from the list whenever she decides that the national security of the United States warrants it, even if the organization is still involved in terrorist activity.

The decision of the secretary of state to designate a group as terrorist can be based on classified evidence. An organization can challenge the secretary's designation in federal court, but the scope and terms of judicial review are severely limited: a court may set aside the determination only if it finds it to be "arbitrary" or "capricious," unconstitutional, or "short of statutory right."[13] The review is to be "based solely upon the administrative record," and the statute provides no opportunity for a designated group to contribute to the administrative record. And the secretary of state can defend her decision in court with secret evidence, making it impossible to mount an effective challenge. Most importantly, because courts will not second-guess the secretary of state on what threatens our "foreign relations," the designation is effectively unreviewable. Yet the Act says that this one-sided review is the sole avenue for challenging determinations of what is and is not a terrorist organization. By the time the government brings criminal proceedings against someone for supporting such a group, it is too late to challenge the designation: the Act provides that "a defendant in a criminal action shall not be permitted to raise any question concerning the validity of the issuance of such designation as a defense or an objection at any trial or hearing." [14]


## CRIMINALIZING SUPPORT FOR HUMANITARIAN AND POLITICAL ACTIVITIES

Once a group has been designated, it is a crime to provide virtually any material support to it. [15] The law exempts medicine and religious materials, but all other humanitarian or political aid is prohibited. Congressional proponents of the measure referred to it as a ban on "terrorist fund-raising." But rather than targeting fund-raising for terrorist violence, the Act bans virtually *all* material support. This list-based approach to fighting terrorism produces some absurd results. For example, it is not a crime to raise and contribute money for violent conduct abroad that is not otherwise a crime under U.S. law, if carried out by a group that is not designated by the secretary, but it is a crime to raise money for the peaceful activities of any designated group. Moreover, if a designated group renounces violence, it remains a crime to support its peaceful activities until the secretary removes it from the list, but it is not a crime under the Act to give money to any splinter group that remains committed to terrorism, until that splinter group is designated. Increasingly, we are seeing terrorist activities for which credit is claimed by a "previously unknown group," yet it is impossible under the Act for the secretary to bar support for a group that has no name.

This provision was unnecessary. Prior to enactment of the 1996 Antiterrorism Act, it was already illegal to support the terrorist acts of any group or person if those acts were crimes under U.S. law. Aiding and abetting the commission of a crime is as illegal as the underlying crime itself. Additionally, in 1994 Congress passed a law specifically prohibiting material support of certain terrorist crimes at home or abroad (crimes against U.S. persons or interests wherever committed).[16]

The full scope of the 1996 Act prohibition is not entirely apparent. What if one knowingly gives money to an undesignated organization, but the government claims it was controlled by a designated organization? What if one gives money to an undesignated organization that has as a constituent member a designated organization? The significance of these questions lies not only in how they are answered, but also in the uncertainty that they engender. Persons legitimately concerned about conditions in other countries, and seeking to support the political and humanitarian activities of ethnic or nationalist groups, will be hesitant to exercise their First Amendment rights to support them if they fear criminal prosecution.

Furthermore, the uncertainty and ambiguity inherent in the fund-raising prohibition invites the FBI to conduct wide-ranging investigations of lawful activities. The FBI can claim that it was merely trying to determine whether contributions to a nondesignated organization were being diverted to a designated organization, or whether contributors "knew" where their contribution was ending up. On this thin reed, the FBI can try to justify wide-ranging investigations into targeted communities, repeating—with legal sanction—the abuses of its past.

Indeed, the Clinton administration was quite explicit in 1996 about its intention to investigate First Amendment activities. It simultaneously sought and obtained repeal of the seemingly modest protections of the Edwards amendment, which prohibited investigations of "material support" to terrorism based solely on activities protected by the First Amendment. The Clinton administration had agreed to the Edwards amendment in the 1994 crime bill.[17] Yet by early 1995, the administration was claiming that this provision imposed "an unprecedented and impractical burden on law enforcement concerning the initiation and continuation of criminal investigations," and in the 1996 Act the administration succeeded in obtaining its repeal, thus codifying the theory underlying the discredited CISPES and LA 8 investigations.

Simply put, the fund-raising ban of the 1996 Antiterrorism Act ignores what has long been a fundamental precept of our constitutional law—that "a blanket prohibition of association with a group having both legal and illegal aims," without a showing of specific intent to further the unlawful aims of the group, is an unconstitutional infringement on "the cherished freedom of association protected by the First Amendment."[18]

## THE 1996 ACT'S IMPACT ON IMMIGRATION LAW— IDEOLOGICAL EXCLUSION REVIVED

The First Amendment grants Americans the right to receive information and ideas, especially ideas the government finds objectionable. This right includes the receipt of information from abroad. One highly effective way of transmitting information remains the personal encounter, through speeches, conferences, and meetings. Since the immigration law sets the standards for both excluding foreign nationals from permanent admission and making them ineligible for visas for temporary visits, rendering a category of persons "excludable" on ideological grounds means that they cannot come here even temporarily to speak or engage in other activities implicating the First Amendment rights of U.S. citizens.

U.S. immigration policy for many years was dominated by the ideological exclusions of the McCarran-Walter Act. Colored by the Cold War, the McCarran-Walter Act barred from the U.S. not only suspected Communists but also critics of U.S. foreign and defense policy. Virtually every time the State Department denied a visa on ideological grounds, it was widely condemned. Ironically, the speakers' views often gained greater attention than they might have received had they entered the United States. Through the 1980s, ideological exclusion came under increasing challenge in the courts and in Congress.[19]

In the Immigration Act of 1990, Congress finally repealed the ideological exclusion provisions of the McCarran-Walter Act, repudiating guilt by association as a guiding principle in U.S. immigration law. Congress substituted a series of criteria focused largely on the criminal acts of individuals. Under the reforms, a foreigner could not be barred entry from the United States based on beliefs, advocacy, or associations that would be protected under the First Amendment if engaged in by a person within the United States. Rather, foreigners seeking to visit the United States could be barred if there was reason to believe that they had engaged in criminal or terrorist conduct abroad or would do so here. From 1990 to 1996, aliens were excludable and deportable either if they engaged in a terrorist activity themselves, or if they provided material support to an individual, organization, or government "in conducting a terrorist act at any time." Terrorist activity was defined extremely broadly, to include virtually any use of a firearm or explosive with the intent to endanger person or property. However, the law required the government to prove that the individual it sought to deport or exclude had personally engaged in such activity, or had provided material support for the conducting of such activity.

The 1996 Antiterrorism Act reversed this reform. The Act eliminated the requirement that an excluded foreign national must have any personal connection to terrorist activity per se. It substituted guilt by association, barring entry to any person who is a member or representative of a group designated by the secretary of state as terrorist, even if the individual has participated only in the group's lawful political or humanitarian activities.[20] It rendered foreign nationals excludable (and deportable if their membership predated their entry to the United States) for associational activity otherwise protected by the First Amendment. Under this test, members of the African National Congress or the IRA would have been excludable, even if they were seeking to enter the United States specifically to pursue prospects for peace.

## "ALIEN TERRORIST" REMOVAL PROCEDURES

The 1996 Antiterrorism Act also gave the Department of Justice the authority to deport noncitizens on the basis of secret evidence.[21] The secret evidence provisions apply to a specially defined category of noncitizens called "alien terrorists."[22] But according to the INS, "alien terrorists" include not only those actually engaged in terrorism, but also those who have merely supported a terrorist organization's *lawful* activities.

Under the Act, the government can invoke the secret evidence provisions whenever the attorney general determines that public disclosure of the evidence against an alleged "alien terrorist" would "pose a risk to the national security of the United States or to the security of any person."[23] It is likely that the government could make such claims whenever an informant is involved: all it needs to do is state that presenting the evidence in open court would disclose the informant's identity, and that the informant's security would be endangered. Similarly, any time any portion of the government's evidence is classified, it will be able to claim risk to the national security, since classified information is by definition information the disclosure of which would cause harm to national security. (In reality, of course, much of the information that is classified as secret would not in fact threaten national security if disclosed, but there are few checks on overclassification of information.)

The Act requires the government to provide the noncitizen with a summary of its classified information. The judge must determine that the evidence is "sufficient to enable the alien to prepare a defense." [24] It is difficult to see how a summary could ever be sufficient, however, because one cannot cross-examine a summary. If the judge determines that the summary is not sufficient, the Justice Department may immediately take an appeal to the Court of Appeals.

In a special removal proceeding, whether or not it involves the use of secret information, the foreign national is barred from seeking to suppress any evidence, even if it was unconstitutionally obtained, and has no right to discover information derived under the Foreign Intelligence Surveillance Act, which the government may use even if obtained in violation of FISA's provisions. [25] Foreign nationals in such proceedings are also barred from applying for asylum or a form of relief known as "withholding of deportation," even if it is undisputed that they will be persecuted for their political ideas upon return to their country of origin.

The Act also provides for immediate detention without bail of all persons subject to this procedure. Noncitizens here on student visas, tourist visas, or special labor visas are denied any hearing whatsoever regarding their detention. Lawful permanent resident aliens are entitled to a hearing, but the government is able to use classified information, and instead of the government having to prove that there are grounds for detention, the permanent resident bears the burden of proving a negative: that there is no basis for his detention. [26]

The secret evidence provisions are a recipe for error and a patently unconstitutional denial of fundamental due process. The courts have consistently declared unconstitutional INS attempts to use secret evidence to deport foreign nationals, even where the government claimed that national security was at stake,[27] and our nation has survived quite well for over 200 years allowing citizens and noncitizens alike to confront their accusers. Perhaps not surprisingly given the law's many constitutional flaws, the Justice Department has never invoked it, instead finding other sources of authority for using secret evidence in immigration proceedings.

# 10

# The Impact of the 1996 Act

The federal government was surprisingly slow in implementing some of the 1996 Act's central elements, calling into question the urgency with which the administration had pressed for its passage. Indeed, as noted earlier, the "Alien Terrorist Removal Court" has never been used, before or after 9/11. It took the secretary of state eighteen months to issue her first list of designated foreign terrorist organizations. And before 9/11, the government had only rarely indicted anyone for providing material support to terrorist organizations.

However, the government did aggressively pursue the use of secret evidence and guilt by association in related settings. From 1996 to 2000, it sought to use secret evidence to detain and deport about two dozen immigrants, almost all of them Muslims accused of vague associations with terrorist groups.[1] Over time, case by case, the government's evidence was revealed to be worthless, its legal theories were largely rejected, and virtually all of the accused were released. As a result, prior to September 11, the practice of using secret evidence had nearly died out, a bill to end the practice had broad bipartisan support in Congress, and President Bush himself had publicly criticized the use of secret evidence in a presidential debate.[2]

All of that progress ground to a halt, however, with the attacks of September 11. The Secret Evidence Repeal Act was shelved. The Justice Department conducted a widespread campaign of secret immigration detentions. The administration argued vigorously in court that it needs the authority to rely on secret evidence more than ever in the wake of September 11.[3] It authorized military tribunals to convict and execute enemy combatants on secret evidence. And it even went so far as to argue that it could imprison both citizens and noncitizens as enemy combatants with no process at all.

In light of the government's renewed interest in using secret evidence, the history of its reliance on this tactic in the recent past is all the more important. That history demonstrates that the desire to use undisclosed evidence cannot be reconciled with the most basic demands of fairness.


## SECRET EVIDENCE CASES

In the late 1990s, the INS selectively subjected a number of Arab and Muslim immigrants to Star Chamber treatment, arresting them on the basis of minor immigration violations and then using secret evidence of their political associations to deprive them of their liberty, deny them immigrant status to which they were otherwise entitled, and deport them. In virtually every case, the government did not charge the individuals with any violent activity, but simply with associating with the wrong group. These proceedings were not brought under the terms of the 1996 Antiterrorism Act.[4] Instead, the Justice Department claimed that the tools of guilt by association and secret evidence were available to it under other provisions of the immigration law.[5] Most of the allegations in the secret evidence cases came from the FBI, reflecting heightened FBI scrutiny of U.S. Arab and Muslim communities.[6]

## Nasser Ahmed

Most people assume that the Constitution prevents the government from arresting and jailing them without criminal charges, without bail, and without an opportunity to respond to the government's allegations. But according to the Justice Department, a foreign national does not enjoy these rights. Nasser Ahmed, an Egyptian man living in New York City with his wife and three U.S. citizen children, spent three and a half years in a U.S. prison on the basis of secret evidence that neither he nor his attorney ever saw. When Ahmed was arrested, in April 1996, he was charged with no crime. The government did not claim that he facilitated or supported any criminal activity. Instead, the INS arrested him on routine charges of overstaying his visa. But claiming that Ahmed was a "threat to national security," the INS detained him on the basis of undisclosed classified evidence. It provided no summary of the evidence, maintaining that national security would be compromised even by describing it in general terms. One year later, the INS used secret evidence again, to oppose Ahmed's applications for asylum and withholding of deportation. This time the INS gave him a one-sentence summary: it stated only that the government had evidence "concerning respondent's association with a known terrorist organization." The government would not even identify the organization. The immigration judge called the summary "largely useless."

An electrical engineer, Ahmed had lived in New York City since 1986. He worshipped at the Abu Bakr Mosque in Brooklyn, where Sheik Omar Abdel Rahman occasionally preached, and which the FBI had placed under surveillance because of some of its members' political opposition to the government of Egypt. Ahmed came under FBI scrutiny while working as a court-appointed paralegal and translator for the legal team defending Sheik Abdel Rahman during the sheik's trial for seditious conspiracy to bomb tunnels and buildings in New York City. The FBI and INS sought to convince Ahmed to join forces with them against the cleric, and threatened him with deportation if he refused to cooperate. Ahmed declined their offer. The INS carried out its threat on April 24, 1995, by arresting Ahmed for overstaying his visa. He was released on $15,000 bond three days later. Upon his release, Ahmed continued to work as a court-appointed member of the sheik's defense team.

On April 23, 1996, as Ahmed entered the federal courthouse in New York for a routine hearing on his immigration case, the INS arrested him again. This time, the INS refused to release Ahmed on bail. He remained incarcerated until November 1999.

Ahmed feared returning to Egypt because of the persecution he would face as a result of his political and religious associations. The immigration judge hearing his case, Donn Livingston, ruled that he had "no doubt" Ahmed would be imprisoned and very likely tortured if returned to Egypt, and agreed that on the public record Ahmed deserved political asylum and withholding of deportation. Ordinarily this would have been the end of the inquiry, and Ahmed would have been entitled to remain in the country. However, despite his serious reservations about the constitutionality of considering secret evidence, Judge Livingston went on to conclude, on the basis of secret evidence presented to him in a closed-door hearing, outside the presence of Ahmed and his lawyers, that Ahmed was a threat to national security, and therefore could not be released and was ineligible for asylum and withholding.

Ahmed then filed suit in federal court to challenge the constitutionality of the INS's actions. The INS responded by suddenly disclosing much of the information that it had previously claimed could not be disclosed without endangering national security. It named the group Ahmed was alleged to be associated with—al-Gama-al-Islamiya—and also charged that he was associated with Sheik Rahman. Significantly, the INS's summary contained no charge that Ahmed himself had ever engaged in any illegal activity or supported any illegal activity.

When both the federal district court judge and the Board of Immigration Appeals said that Ahmed should be given another chance to defend himself in light of the government's new disclosures, the government revealed still more of the previously classified evidence. With the newly released material in hand, Ahmed was able to rebut the charges. Judge Livingston, the same judge who earlier had found the secret evidence to be persuasive, concluded after the new hearing that Ahmed was not a danger to the national security. "Armed with a better understanding of the government's case," he wrote, Ahmed "was successful in rebutting most of the factual assertions." The remaining evidence was "double or triple hearsay," for which the FBI refused to provide any substantiation, so the judge concluded that it was not credible. The INS sought to bar Ahmed's release pending an appeal, but both the Board of Immigration Appeals and the attorney general rejected its requests, and Ahmed was released in November 1999.

Ahmed's case illustrates the dangers of relying on secret evidence. Each time the government was challenged about its use of secret evidence, it revealed a little more of the evidence. What the government ultimately disclosed could and should have been revealed the first time the evidence was used. Because it was not, Ahmed was denied the opportunity to confront any of the evidence used against him until almost three years after he was first detained. Judge Livingston specifically noted that some of the classified evidence used by the government was available from nonconfidential sources. Yet the government insisted on using the classified form, and Ahmed was not even told that the evidence existed in unclassified form. Secret evidence is almost by definition "unassailable," so short of a constitutional challenge, the government has little incentive to develop additional, public sources for its allegations.

In the end, the bulk of the evidence against Ahmed was nothing more than charges of association. In the secret hearing on Ahmed's asylum and withholding applications, the judge and the INS stated that the heart of the case was Ahmed's association with al-Gama-al-Islamiya. Yet once that was revealed, and Ahmed's lawyers were able to respond to it, both the judge and the INS admitted that association with al-Gama-al-Islamiya was not sufficient grounds to detain Ahmed or to deny him asylum and withholding.

## Mazen Al Najjar

Mazen Al Najjar, a Palestinian professor from Tampa, Florida, also spent three and a half years in prison on the basis of secret evidence. Like Ahmed, Al Najjar was not charged with engaging in or supporting any illegal acts. The only basis for his detention was his political association. Like Ahmed, Al Najjar was given only a one-sentence summary of the classified evidence used against him. The summary stated that Al Najjar was associated with the Palestinian Islamic Jihad (PIJ). He was not accused of any illegal activity on the group's behalf.[7] He was not told how he was allegedly associated, what if anything he was alleged to have done with the group, where and when the association took place, or who made the allegation.

Al Najjar had resided in the United States since 1981. He came initially to pursue graduate studies, and later settled in Florida with his wife and three U.S. citizen daughters. In 1995, the FBI began to investigate the World and Islam Studies Enterprise (WISE) in Tampa, Florida, a think tank affiliated with the University of South Florida, after its former administrator became head of the Islamic

Jihad. The FBI claimed that WISE was a front for Palestinian terror-ists. Al Najjar came under FBI scrutiny because he worked as the editor in chief of WISE's research journal.

The FBI and INS arrested Al Najjar on May 19, 1997, while he was in deportation hearings for overstaying his student visa, and de-tained him on the basis of secret evidence. Shortly thereafter, federal officials approached two people who knew Al Najjar and said that they would release him if he provided information about others in the community, suggesting that the government did not really be-lieve that Al Najjar himself posed a threat to national security.

In 1999, Al Najjar filed a constitutional challenge to his deten-tion in federal court. The court ruled that his detention violated due process because it was based on evidence that he had no meaningful opportunity to rebut, and that under immigration law, mere associ-ation with a terrorist organization, without more, was insufficient to justify detaining him. The district court ordered the INS to give Al Najjar a fair hearing on his custody status.

A two-week trial in immigration court ensued, in which the INS sought to show that Al Najjar had supported the Palestinian Islamic Jihad through his association with WISE and another Tampa-based organization, the Islamic Concern Project (ICP), which sponsored conferences on politics and Islam and raised money for indigent families in the Occupied Territories. At the close of the public por-tion of the trial, the same immigration judge who had initially or-dered Al Najjar detained ruled that the INS had failed to offer any convincing evidence to support its assertions against Al Najjar.

Specifically, the judge found that there was "no evidence before the Court that demonstrates that either [ICP or WISE] was a front for the PIJ."[8] On the contrary, he found "that WISE was a reputable and scholarly research center and the ICP was highly regarded." And he concluded that "[b]ased on the evidence presented to this Court, it appears that Respondent's involvement with WISE and

ICP amounted to cooperation with the organizations in lawful activities."

The judge also found no evidence to support the assertion that Al Najjar raised money for terrorist organizations through WISE and ICP. Indeed, the INS's principal witness "admitted that there is no open source evidence that Respondent ever sent money to a terrorist organization or that he ever advocated terrorism." Despite the fact that the INS had seized the entire contents of the WISE and ICP offices, including financial records and over 500 videotapes of the two organizations' activities, the judge found that the INS had offered "no evidence that indicates that Respondent engaged in fund-raising for the PIJ through WISE," through ICP, or, indeed, "for any organization."

The INS then sought to present secret evidence against Al Najjar once again, but the immigration judge concluded that the INS's one-page summary was insufficient to provide Al Najjar a meaningful opportunity to defend himself, and therefore refused to consider the secret evidence. He ordered Al Najjar released on bond. The INS sought a stay of Al Najjar's release before the Board of Immigration Appeals and the attorney general, but both rejected the INS's request, and in December 2000 Al Najjar was released.

In November 2001, however, after Al Najjar's deportation order became final, the INS rearrested him on immigration grounds having nothing to do with terrorism and placed him in a maximum security prison under solitary confinement and twenty-three-hour lockdown. To justify its actions, the INS issued a statement that did nothing more than repeat the very assertions that had been rejected as unfounded after a two-week hearing the previous fall. Al Najjar again challenged the constitutionality of his detention in federal court, but while that challenge was pending, Al Najjar and his family left the United States and abandoned their efforts to remain here.

In February 2003, the FBI arrested Al Najjar's brother-in-law, Sami Al-Arian, a professor at the University of South Florida, and charged him in a multi-count criminal indictment based on activities allegedly relating to the Palestine Islamic Jihad. Al Arian was not accused of engaging in, planning, or aiding or abetting any terrorist activities, but prosecutors charged that he played a leadership role in the organization. Al Najjar, long since deported, was alleged to be a co-conspirator. During Al-Arian's criminal trial, which was ongoing as of this writing, the government introduced multiple wiretap recordings that presumably had been classified as of the time of Al Najjar's hearing. It has not explained why the tapes were declassified, nor why Al Najjar was not permitted access to them while he was detained.

## Imad Salih Hamad

Imad Salih Hamad, a Palestinian born in Lebanon, has resided in the United States since 1980. He married a U.S. citizen in 1991, and sought permanent residence on that basis. The INS alleged that he was affiliated with the Popular Front for the Liberation of Palestine, and sought his deportation. In 1997, the INS claimed to have classified evidence against him. An immigration judge evaluated the secret evidence behind closed doors, but concluded that it was insufficient to establish ties to any terrorist groups. In June 1998, while the INS's appeal of the immigration judge's ruling was pending, the INS declassified the secret evidence. It turned out to be material that the government had openly confronted Hamad with at an earlier stage in his proceedings.[9] Somehow, the material had become classified, and then declassified, in the meantime.

On February 19, 1999, the Board of Immigration Appeals affirmed the immigration judge's 1997 decision granting Hamad adjustment of status. The board said that the evidence of Hamad's alleged connection with the PFLP was "vague, lacking in specificity and uncorroborated." The board stated, "The classified information provided in camera may arouse suspicion, but would require much greater detail to convince the members of this Board that the respondent is in any way a supporter of a terrorist organization."

Hamad is now a U.S. citizen. The *Detroit News* named him a Michiganian of the Year in 2003.

## Anwar Haddam

Anwar Haddam has been for most of his adult life a member of the Algerian Islamic Movement. In 1991, he was elected to the Algerian parliament. After a military coup in January 1992 canceled the election, Haddam came to the United States and was politically active in Washington, D.C., on issues relating to Algeria. The INS arrested Haddam in December 1996 for violating his immigration status and sought to deport him to Algeria. Haddam produced evidence showing that he and his family would be tortured and exe-cuted for his political affiliations and beliefs if they were forced to return to Algeria. In fact, in March 1998 Algeria condemned Haddam to death in absentia. Nonetheless, the INS pushed for his expulsion on the basis of secret evidence. Haddam's lawyers were advised that the government was relying on telephone conversations recorded under the Foreign Intelligence Surveillance Act (FISA), but they were denied access to the tapes. The transcripts of the wiretaps were never actually produced for the immigration judge's examination either. Instead, the evidence was presented to the judge in summary form by an FBI agent who testified in the judge's chambers, off the record and without even being sworn in. Haddam's lawyers, who were excluded along with Haddam from the judge's chambers, protested this procedure on the grounds that it violated procedural due process and FISA. The judge heard the evidence over these objections.

After further hearings and appeals, Haddam was granted asylum. The Board of Immigration Appeals, after considering the secret evidence, concluded that it did not support the accusation that Haddam was a terrorist. Haddam was released in December 2000, having spent four years in detention.

### Hany Kiareldeen

Hany Kiareldeen, an electronics store manager born in Gaza who has lived in the United States since 1990, was arrested in New Jersey in March 1998 and detained based on secret evidence. The summary of the evidence provided him said that he was a member of an unnamed terrorist organization, that he had relations with suspected terrorists, also unnamed, and that he had threatened Janet Reno. Kiareldeen denied all charges. From the outset, Kiareldeen suspected that one of the sources of the secret evidence against him (and perhaps the only source) was his estranged wife. Kiareldeen's lawyers made numerous unsuccessful attempts, over vigorous INS objections, to cross-examine her. She was engaged in a child custody dispute with Kiareldeen, and had on several prior occasions leveled charges against him, all of which have been dismissed as unfounded.

In April 1999, an immigration judge ordered Kiareldeen released, on the ground that the secret evidence did not establish that he was a threat to national security. The INS appealed, however, and obtained a stay of Kiareldeen's release while the appeal was pending.

Kiareldeen was finally released from jail in October 1999, after a federal judge ruled the government's use of secret evidence unconstitutional.[10] The Board of Immigration Appeals simultaneously found no basis for the government's allegations that Kiareldeen was a national security threat. It is rare for any judge—even an independent Article III judge—to reject a claim of national security by the federal government. Yet in Kiareldeen's case, seven immigration judges eventually reviewed the complete record, and all seven rejected the government's contention that he posed a threat to national security.

Although the judges were not allowed to reveal the substance of the confidential information, two judges directly discussed the quality of the government's secret evidence. Immigration Judge Daniel Meisner, who presided at the trial, stated that Kiareldeen had "raised formidable doubts about the veracity of the allegations contained in the [classified information]," and that in the face of repeated requests for more information, the INS had refused "to answer those doubts with any additional evidence, be it at the public portion of the hearing or even in camera." [11] He concluded that the classified evidence was "too meager to provide reasonable grounds to believe that [Kiareldeen] was actually involved in any terrorist activity."

BIA Judge Anthony Moscato, dissenting from a preliminary panel decision not to release Kiareldeen, wrote that the bare-bones character of the government's in camera evidence made it "impossible" for the BIA to exercise independent judgment in assessing "either the absolute truth or the relative probity of the evidence contained in the classified information." [12] Judge Moscato criticized the INS for having provided no original source material and "little in the way of specifics regarding the source or context of the classified information." He further noted that despite the immigration judge's continuing requests, the INS had provided "no witnesses, neither confidential informant nor federal agent, to explain or document the context of the actions and statements referenced in the classified information or to document the way in which the classified information became known to the source of that information." [13]

*Iraqi Detainees*

Perhaps the most unusual secret evidence case involved a group of Iraqi men who worked with the CIA in a plot to overthrow President Saddam Hussein. The men were flown to the United States by the U.S. government in March 1997 after the CIA plan fell apart. But at that point, the United States ordered six of the Iraqis excluded from the United States on the basis of secret evidence.[14] Former CIA director R. James Woolsey volunteered to represent them pro bono upon hearing of their plight, and described their situation as follows:

> Six Iraqi men are sitting in a Los Angeles prison, bewildered by the U.S. government's decision to deport them. They are all enemies of Saddam Hussein, and after the Iraqi dictator's attack on northern Iraq in late 1996 the U.S. evacuated them and their families to Guam and then to Southern California. Now the Immigration and Naturalization Service argues that the six are a threat to U.S. national security, and an immigration judge has agreed that they should be sent back to Iraq, where they face nearly certain death. Though they struggled for freedom in Iraq, these men are being deprived of their basic rights to defend themselves.
>
> Would the INS charges that these men endanger national security stand up to scrutiny? It seems unlikely, given their personal histories. But the charges against them are classified and neither the accused not their attorneys can see them.[15]

Upon their arrival in California, the men were separated from their families and placed in INS detention centers. The INS initiated exclusion proceedings against them for entering without a valid visa. Strangely, all of the family members who were transported with the men were granted political asylum. At a March 28, 1997, hearing, the INS stated that it denied the Iraqis' political asylum applications because they posed a security risk to the U.S., and the INS further indicated its intent to offer secret evidence showing the Iraqis ineligible for political asylum.

On March 9, 1998, a Los Angeles immigration judge, D.D. Sitgraves, found on the basis of the government's secret evidence that the men posed a threat to U.S. security. The judge's ruling was largely classified. As their cases proceeded through the courts, they remained in a Los Angeles detention facility. Woolsey wrote:

> Why does the INS insist on keeping them in prison facing deportation and death? A case earlier this year, involving similar charges against another Iraqi evacuee, suggests that Justice Department incompetence may be a major factor. Hasim Qadir Hawlery was singled out by the INS and imprisoned for a year after a botched interview by the FBI in Guam. Errors in translation and the interviewer's ignorance of Iraq led the INS to believe wrongly that Mr. Hawlery was lying about belonging to a particular opposition group. This mistake came to light only because the charges against Mr. Hawlery were unclassified, so the INS evidence had to be presented before both parties in an open hearing. He won his bid to stay in the U.S.
>
> Similar blunders may lie behind the charges against the six. Or disinformation may have been sown by informants among the larger group of Iraqi evacuees on Guam, some of whom may well have borne personal grudges or had other ulterior motives. Such errors will never come to light without a defense lawyer allowed to cross-examine government witnesses.[16]

As in Nasser Ahmed's case, much of the evidence initially classified and used in secret against the Iraqis was later disclosed. As that evidence was declassified, it became clear that much of it was based on unsubstantiated assertions by other Iraqis involved in the failed coup attempt.[17]

Ultimately, the government offered the men a settlement that would place them and their families in safe countries that agreed to accept them. Six of the men agreed and were released in the summer of 1999, subject to the condition that they remain in the Lincoln, Nebraska, area until countries could be found that would accept them. However, two men, Dr. Ali Yasin Mohammed Karim and his brother, declined the offer and insisted on pressing their claim for political asylum. In May 2000, immigration judge D.D. Sitgraves ruled that Dr. Karim had presented "more than sufficient evidence" to rebut the government's claim that he should be excluded as a national security threat. Finally, in August 2000, after nearly four years in jail, Dr. Karim was released. Judge Sitgraves wrote in her opinion that Karim "has sufficiently demonstrated that the government's claims were ill-founded and has rebutted the presumption that he constitutes a risk to the security of the United States."[18]

## Conclusion

The cases described above illustrate the danger of relying on secret evidence. In some cases, the government disclosed evidence that it initially said could not be disclosed, only to reveal that its charges were unfounded. In others, federal courts declared the government's use of secret evidence unconstitutional. And in others, immigration judges harshly criticized the INS for relying on insubstantial and unreliable evidence. As a result, the government eventually grew more hesitant about using secret evidence. In the last years of the Clinton administration, the Deputy Attorney General's office undertook a comprehensive review of all secret evidence cases, and in its last year the Clinton administration filed no new secret evidence cases. As noted above, President Bush publicly criticized the practice during his presidential campaign. And until 9/11, a bipartisan bill to end the practice had substantial support in Congress.

True to his campaign criticism of the practice of secret evidence, President Bush largely avoided its use, at least prior to 9/11. With the attacks of 9/11, however, the administration quickly changed its tune. As described in Chapter 12, the government rounded up hundreds of immigrants in secret and tried them in secret, closed hearings. In appeals dating from the Clinton administration in Hany Kiareldeen's and Mazen Al Najjar's cases, Justice Department lawyers argued that reliance on secret evidence in both cases was in fact constitutional. At the same time, the administration expanded reliance on secret evidence beyond the immigration setting. It successfully urged adoption of a USA PATRIOT Act provision that authorized the freezing of corporations' assets in antiterrorism cases using secret evidence, and established military tribunal rules that permit "enemy combatants" to be tried and executed on the basis of secret evidence that neither the defendant nor his chosen civilian lawyer has any opportunity to confront.

In April 2005, the administration relied on secret evidence again in an immigration case. The government arrested two sixteen-year-old girls in New York, put them in deportation hearings, and denied them bond as security threats. One of the girls was Bangladeshi, the other a Guinean. There was little evidence that the two girls even knew each other before their arrests. The government claimed that it had evidence that the girls were would-be suicide bombers, but declined to produce the evidence to the girls or their attorneys, claiming that disclosing it would jeopardize national security.[19] Thus, despite the widespread problems associated with it described above, the practice of relying on secret evidence continues.

## STATE DEPARTMENT DESIGNATION OF FOREIGN TERRORIST GROUPS

A year and a half after President Clinton signed the 1996 Antiterrorism Act, the State Department designated thirty groups as foreign terrorist organizations.[20] The list was issued in October 1997 only after political pressure was applied by private groups.[21]

Once groups were designated, anyone who provided funds or other support to the listed groups could be prosecuted. American financial institutions that have assets of these groups under their control must freeze them. Known members of such organizations are not eligible for visas. When the State Department designated the groups, its spokesperson James P. Rubin noted that "the goal of this law was more deterrence than confiscation." But in seeking deterrence, the government cast a wide net punishing individuals for constitutionally protected speech and associational activities.

The perverse quality of the material support provision is best captured by its application to the Humanitarian Law Project (HLP), a thirty-year-old human rights organization based in Los Angeles. Since 1991, the HLP has, among other things, focused on the plight of Turkey's Kurdish minority, encouraging recognition of their basic human rights, and promoting a peaceful resolution of their conflict with Turkey's government. To that end, the HLP has worked with the Kurdistan Workers Party (PKK), the principal political organization representing the Kurds in Turkey, specifically by training and assisting them in human rights advocacy. But because "training" constitutes "material support," that work became a crime when the secretary of state designated the PKK a terrorist organization.

In March 1998, HLP joined with a number of U.S. groups of Sri Lankan Tamils to challenge the material support ban. The Tamils are an abused ethnic minority in Sri Lanka. U.S.-based Tamil groups sought to provide humanitarian and political support to the Liberation Tigers of Tamil Eelam (LTTE), which represents Tamils and was engaged in a civil war against the Sri Lankan government. The LTTE provided humanitarian aid to Tamil refugees fleeing from Sri Lankan armed forces, engaged in political organizing and advocacy, provided social services and economic development through a quasi-governmental structure in Tamil Eelam, and administered a chain of orphanages. But when the secretary of state designated the LTTE a terrorist group under the Antiterrorism Act, it became a crime to support any of this work.

The HLP lawsuit argued that the ban on material support violated the First and Fifth Amendments, because providing material support to a group is a constitutionally protected form of association and the law criminalizes such association even where it is undertaken for wholly peaceful and nonviolent purposes, and because the law's prohibitions were impermissibly vague.[22]

In June 1998, the district court granted HLP a preliminary injunction, declaring that the law's bans on providing training and personnel were unconstitutionally vague. However, the court upheld the remainder of the statute, including the ban on providing any other kind of monetary support. The U.S. Court of Appeals for the Ninth Circuit affirmed the district court's order.[23] The appeals court rejected, as had the district court, the plaintiffs' argument that the process of designating foreign terrorist organizations ran afoul of the Constitution by granting the secretary of state overbroad discretion. It affirmed the district court's injunction against enforcement of two terms—"personnel" and "training"—included in the definition of material support. And it agreed with the lower court that the material support provision did not violate the First Amendment by inflicting guilt by association. Both courts acknowledged that the First Amendment protects the right to associate with "terrorist organizations," but reasoned that a ban on monetary support was justified because money is fungible. But if the right to associate does not include the right to pay dues, raise money, or provide any material support to one's group of choice, the right is an empty formalism. Associations cannot exist without the material support of their members.

In September 2001, the district court made its preliminary injunction against the "training" and "personnel" provisions final, and again refused to enjoin the rest of the statute. In 2003, the court of appeals again affirmed the lower court rulings.[24] In 2004, the district court declared unconstitutional a Patriot Act amendment to the material support law that had banned the provision of "expert advice or assistance."[25]

In response to their decisions, Congress amended the material support law yet again in the Intelligence Reform and Terrorism Prevention Act of 2004. It provided definitions of the terms the courts had found unconstitutionally vague, and added a new ban on the provision of any "services," a term left undefined. In July 2005, the district court ruled that several parts of the statute remain unconstitutionally vague, namely, the bans on providing "training," "expert advice or assistance," and "services."[26]

Meanwhile, after lying virtually dormant for its first six years of existence, the material support law has since 9/11 become the Justice Department's most popular charge in antiterrorism cases. The allure is easy to see: convictions under the law require no proof that the defendant engaged in terrorism, aided or abetted terrorism, or conspired to commit terrorism. But what makes the law attractive to prosecutors—its sweeping ambit—is precisely what makes it so dangerous to civil liberties.

## FREEZING ASSETS OF DESIGNATED "FOREIGN TERRORIST ORGANIZATIONS"

The 1996 Antiterrorism Act requires any financial institution that "becomes aware that it has possession of, or control over, any funds in which a foreign terrorist organization, or its agent, has an interest," to freeze the assets and report them to the Treasury Department. The first case to arise under this provision resulted in a court order requiring the bank to unfreeze the account of a U.S.-based distributor of *Mojahed,* a newsletter published in Europe by the People's Mojahedin Organization of Iran.

Crestar Bank of Virginia received an anonymous electronic mail message informing it that one of its accounts, held by Nasher Ltd., belonged to a designated terrorist group. Crestar promptly contacted the Office of Foreign Assets Control (OFAC) of the Department of Treasury, which, according to Crestar, informed the bank by telephone that Nasher Ltd. was a "front or conduit" for a listed terrorist group, and told Crestar to freeze the account, which had between $5,000 and $6,000, and to turn over the account holder's records.[27]

Nasher Ltd. challenged the freezing of assets on First Amendment grounds, arguing that distributors and publishers are protected by the First Amendment. Nasher also sought to prevent disclosure of any account records that would reveal the identities of subscribers to the newsletter, many of whom had already endured persecution in Iran on account of their political beliefs, and feared retribution against family members in Iran or themselves were such information shared with Iran.

Federal district court judge Leonie Brinkema granted the injunction to unblock the account, and ordered Crestar not to reveal to OFAC the names and/or addresses of any subscribers to the newsletter.[28] In doing so, Judge Brinkema held that Nasher Ltd. and its subscribers had significant First Amendment and personal security interests, and that they would suffer "irreparable injury" if the injunction was not granted. In a strange turn of events, OFAC actually denied asking the bank to freeze the account or turn over records.[29] Since both the bank and the government said that they did not oppose unfreezing the account, the judge disposed of the case without deciding the First Amendment claims. But she indicated that the evidence presented by Nasher Ltd. demonstrated a "definite indication of likelihood of success on the merits."[30]

In a still more bizarre case, the United States effectively subjected a U.S. citizen, Mohammed Salah, to a form of internal banishment. In 1998, President Clinton added Salah's name to an executive order that, like the 1996 Antiterrorism Act, bars financial transactions with terrorist organizations. The executive order, however, also designates individuals, and Salah was so designated. As such, it became a crime for anyone in the United States to have any financial dealings with Salah. He could not buy a sandwich, pay his mortgage, get a job, or go to the doctor without a special exemption issued by the Treasury Department.[31] The order even barred donations to Salah. Thus, if literally enforced, the order would have required Salah to starve to death in his own country. Yet this punishment was imposed without a trial, without a hearing, and without any provision of reasons for its imposition.

## FURTHER LEGISLATIVE DEVELOPMENTS

Several controversial provisions dropped from the 1996 terrorism bill were subsequently enacted in other legislation. Among them were changes to the posse comitatus law, which prohibits use of the U.S. military in domestic law enforcement. The posse comitatus changes were enacted later in 1996, in the Department of Defense

Authorization Act for fiscal 1997.[32] The provision authorized use of the military to assist the Department of Justice in domestic law enforcement investigations "during an emergency situation involving a biological or chemical weapon of mass destruction." (Similar authority had previously been granted for situations involving nuclear materials, and major changes to the posse comitatus law had been enacted in the 1980s, allowing use of the military in drug interdiction and other anti-narcotics activities.) The 1996 changes allow the military to carry out arrests, conduct searches and seizures, and collect intelligence for law enforcement purposes, if the action "is considered necessary for the immediate protection of human life, and civilian law enforcement officials are not capable of taking the actions."

The Clinton administration had also offered with its antiterrorism package a proposal to weaken the standards for government use of so-called roving wiretaps, potentially very wide-ranging wiretaps that follow a target as he moves from phone to phone. Congress eventually enacted a broadened roving tap authority in October 1998, in the Intelligence Authorization Act for Fiscal Year 1999.[33] In what was basically a legislative sneak attack, the provision was added behind closed doors by the conference committee after it had been left out of the bills passed by both the House and the Senate. The change adopted in 1998 was even broader than the one Congress had rejected two years earlier. Under prior law, investigators had been able to obtain a roving tap only when they could show to a judge that the target of surveillance was changing telephones (e.g., by using different pay phones) with the purpose of avoiding interception. Under the 1998 law, it became sufficient to show merely that any of the person's actions could have the effect of thwarting interception. Moreover, the roving tap may remain "for such time as it is reasonable to presume that the person [identified in the order] is or was reasonably proximate to the instrument through which such communications will be or was transmitted." This authority, expanded still further in the USA PATRIOT Act, means the government can tap phones in the homes and offices of friends, relatives, and business associates visited by a suspect, despite the Fourth Amendment's requirement that the government specify with particularity the person or place to be searched.

The fiscal 1999 intelligence authorization act also included other enhancements of FBI authority, creating explicit authority to use pen register and trap and trace devices in counterintelligence and international terrorism investigations and granting the government access to hotel, car rental, bus, airline, and other business records.[34] Interestingly, the changes were not as discretionary as the FBI had wanted. The pen register and trap and trace authority adopted in 1998 required the approval of a federal judge. And the standard was in some ways more stringent than the standard for pen registers and trap and trace devices in a criminal case, requiring investigators to provide information that "demonstrates" that the surveilled line has been or is about to be used in communication about activities that "involve or may involve a violation of the criminal laws." As to accessing business records concerning hotels, transportation, car rental, and similar services, the FBI had originally sought authority to issue so-called administrative subpoenas, a piece of paper signed by an FBI official, without any judicial oversight, compelling a business to turn over records on its customers. Instead, Congress required the issuance of an order by a judge. In some respects, this standard, too, was tougher than the standard for access in criminal cases, where a grand jury subpoena can be issued without any effective judicial control. (Those limitations, however, were abandoned in the 2001 Patriot Act, as we explain in Chapter 13.)

## NO POSITIVE RESULTS

In February 1998, a Senate subcommittee examined the status of counterterrorism efforts in the United States.[35] Dale L. Watson, section chief for International Terrorism Operations at the FBI, admitted that the fund-raising ban had produced no tangible results. The fact is that, with the exception of the material support provision, the government has not made much use of the antiterrorism authorities in the Antiterrorism and Effective Death Penalty Act of 1996 discussed here, despite the urgency with which the administration said they were needed. The much-touted expansion of law enforcement powers from the Antiterrorism Act of 1996 produced no visible concrete results in the fight against terrorism. Yet the principles they established—especially reliance on secret evidence and guilt by association—imposed serious constitutional restrictions on civil liberties. There was and is little evidence that these sacrifices were warranted, or that they resulted in any increased security. But, as the next chapters illustrate, these measures were harbingers of what was to come in the wake of 9/11.

PART IV

After 9/11:
Fighting a War on Terror,
at Home and Abroad

# 11

# New Challenges, Old Dilemmas

When terrorists hijacked four airplanes on a crisp Tuesday morning in September 2001, turning them into devastating explosives directed at the World Trade Center and the Pentagon, they not only killed thousands of innocent civilians in the most brutal act of terrorism ever perpetrated, but they also threatened to change the fabric of American life. Before September 11, we had been relatively free of foreign attacks on our soil, at least since Pearl Harbor. Before September 11, terrorists had done many unspeakable things, but never had they committed an act so heinous or so devastating. After September 11, Americans confronted a new vulnerability. The attacks of that day made the unthinkable gruesomely real.

In the wake of those attacks, new security measures were undoubtedly warranted. In light of the ongoing threats that the country faces, we must improve our defenses against terrorism, including intelligence and law enforcement capabilities. The fact that U.S. intelligence agencies were unable to prevent the September 11 attacks despite various warning signs reflected a failure that justifiably prompted a reevaluation of traditional structures and procedures.

That reevaluation continues to this day. In this chapter and those that follow, we review the post–9/11 response and assess it from the standpoint of balancing liberty and security.

Three principles in particular guide our assessment. First, we should recognize the tendency to overreact in a time of fear, a mistake our nation has made all too often in the past. Second, we should not countenance infringements on the bedrock foundations of our constitutional democracy—political freedom, due process, accountability, governmental transparency, individual privacy, and equal treatment—absent compelling showings of necessity. And third, in balancing liberty and security, we should not selectively sacrifice the liberties of a vulnerable minority—whether it be foreign nationals in general or Arabs and Muslims in particular—in a misguided effort to obtain security for the majority. Failure to adhere to these principles not only results in unwarranted intrusions on liberties, but is likely to undermine security as well.

Unfortunately, the government's response to the events of September 11 has violated all three principles. Many antiterrorism measures, including some provisions in the USA PATRIOT Act, hastily enacted in October 2001, were undoubtedly justified. But in several critical areas, Congress gave the executive branch broad new powers that went far beyond the fight against terrorism and infringed unnecessarily on fundamental liberties. And in many other areas outside the Patriot Act, the administration simply appropriated power to itself, issuing presidential orders and regulations and exploiting existing laws—especially immigration laws—for ends they were never designed to serve.

As we will show, the government overreacted in harmful ways, intruding on the liberties of thousands of people who had no terrorist ties whatsoever. It failed to show that many of the new powers it asserted were in fact necessary to fight terrorism. It often failed to narrowly tailor these powers to the threat of terrorism. And it targeted the lion's share of its infringements at the most vulnerable among us, namely foreign nationals, and particularly Muslim immigrants.

At the same time, there have been encouraging signs c to these sacrifices of constitutional rights. Most notably, the Supreme Court ruled in the summer of 2004 that the president does not have a "blank check" in the war on terror. The Court rejected the president's claims of unreviewable discretion to hold citizens and noncitizens as enemy combatants. Congress denied funding to the Total Information Awareness program and placed tight limits on an airline passenger screening system that would use government and commercial data to rate the terrorism risk of individual air travelers.[1] Grassroots activists, coordinated by the Bill of Rights Defense Committee, organized local initiatives against police cooperation with some of the federal government's anti-immigrant measures. The American Civil Liberties Union, the Center for Constitutional Rights, and other human rights groups made effective use of the Freedom of Information Act to document prisoner abuse, and at the close of 2004, the Justice Department responded to a storm of criticism by revoking an August 2002 legal memorandum that had condoned brutal interrogation tactics and had argued that the president could order torture in wartime.


## REPEATING HISTORY

Before turning to the specifics of the post–9/11 response, it is worth recalling that this is not the first time our nation has responded to fear by asserting unchecked power, trampling rights, targeting immigrants, and treating individuals as suspect because of their group identities rather than their personal conduct. In World War I, we imprisoned dissidents, most of them immigrants, for merely speaking out against the war. In 1919, the federal government responded to a series of terrorist bombings by rounding up thousands of immigrants in thirty-three cities across the country—not for their part in the bombings, but for their political affiliations. In World War II, we interned 110,000 persons, over two-thirds of whom were citizens of the United States, not because of individualized determinations that they posed a threat to national security or the war effort, but solely for their Japanese ancestry. And in the fight against communism, Congress made it a crime to espouse communist ideas or to be a member of the Communist Party, and passed the McCarran-Walter Act, which authorized the government to keep out and expel noncitizens who advocated communism or other proscribed ideas, or who belonged to the Communist Party or other groups that advocated proscribed ideas.

All of these measures are now seen as mistakes. Yet the post–9/11 response at home features many of the same mistakes of principle—in particular, targeting vulnerable groups not for illegal conduct but for speech, political activity, or group identity; relying on broad investigatory sweeps rather than focusing investigations where there is objective individualized suspicion of wrongdoing; and eschewing the safeguards of the rule of law for unchecked executive power.

At the same time that we face new threats to our security, we also confront new threats to our liberties. Information technology is an important tool in fighting terrorism, but the combination of the vast aggregations of personal data generated by daily life in the digital age and the government's largely unchecked access to that information threatens privacy as never before.

For the rest of Part IV, we will review—and find wanting—the government's efforts since 9/11 to strike a proper balance between liberty and security in light of the new vulnerability we all feel.

# 12

# Detention and Interrogation

The Bush administration's "war on terrorism" has put a premium on two tactics: detention and interrogation. The administration has been quite candid about its intention to detain suspected terrorists in order to prevent another terrorist attack. But as with prior periods in our history, such initiatives inevitably round up many people who pose no threat whatsoever. Having swept broadly, the challenge then is to distinguish the innocent from the guilty, the harmless from the dangerous. But when officials detain suspects preemptively, they cannot develop the intelligence they might otherwise obtain through surveillance and more traditional forms of investigation. Accordingly, interrogation of detained persons becomes a major investigative priority. And as the photographs from Abu Ghraib illustrate, that road easily leads to humiliation, abuse, and torture. In this chapter, we will show how the policy of preventive detention led to the practice of coercive interrogation, and how both policies have ill-served us from a security and liberty standpoint.

## PREVENTIVE DETENTION AT HOME

One of the touchstones of the "war on terrorism" has been preventive detention, both at home and abroad. In the weeks immediately after the September 11 attacks, Attorney General John Ashcroft announced a sweeping campaign of preventive detention. Everyone wants to prevent the next terrorist attack, of course, but the preventive detention program has been spectacularly unsuccessful in identifying actual terrorists.

To this day, the government has refused to issue a cumulative total of the "suspected terrorists" it has detained, but by piecing together official disclosures in several different forums, it is clear that over 5,000 foreign nationals were detained in antiterrorism preventive detention measures in the two years after September 11.[1] Some were detained for only a matter of days; others for months; still others for more than a year. But of the more than 5,000 detained, not one stands convicted of any terrorist crime.[2] After four years, Ashcroft's preventive detention campaign was 0 for 5,000.

Many of those detained were initially arrested and held without any charges at all. Many of the initial detainees were also locked up in secret. Their arrests were not disclosed to the public, to the press, to lawyers, or even to family members.[3] The detainees were initially placed under a "communications blackout" during which they were permitted no contact whatsoever with the outside world. Thereafter contact was severely limited, so that most of the detainees were never able to get the assistance of a lawyer.[4]

When criticized about this massive preventive detention campaign, government officials often responded that most of those detained were "illegal aliens." Many of those initially rounded up were eventually charged with some sort of immigration infraction. But immigration violations are generally civil, not criminal, and do not justify detention of the individual charged unless the government can also show that he poses a danger to the community or a risk of flight. Yet under a blanket policy that made no provision for individual circumstances, the government denied bond to all of the immigration detainees picked up in the weeks after September 11, even where it had no evidence to show that they were either dangerous or a flight risk, or in any way connected to terrorism.

Those ultimately charged with an immigration violation were tried in secret, closed proceedings. By order of the attorney general, their cases were not listed on the public docket, and immigration judges were directed to refuse to confirm or deny that such cases existed. This unprecedented use of secret proceedings raised fundamental questions of fairness, because the rule of law, to be effective, requires public scrutiny. Two district courts and one court of appeals ruled the secret trials unconstitutional, as violating both the public's First Amendment right of access to the trials and the detainees' due process rights to a fair and open deportation proceeding. Another court of appeals, however, upheld the practice by a divided vote, and the government successfully urged the Supreme Court not to review the issue.[5]

In June 2003, the Justice Department's own Inspector General issued a lengthy report strongly condemning the government's treatment of immigration detainees in connection with the September 11 investigation. The Inspector General's report found that guards engaged in harassment and physical abuse. In New York, where many detainees were held, guards had a practice of walking through the cell block asking detainees if they were "doing all right." The guards then treated any affirmative response as a waiver of that individual's right to make a weekly phone call to try to find a lawyer. The Inspector General found that the "vast majority" of detainees were never accused of terrorism-related offenses but only of civil violations of federal immigration law. Most significantly, the report found that at the time of arrest the link between many of the detainees and the attacks of 9/11 was "extremely attenuated." In one instance, for example, the government arrested several foreign nationals solely on the basis of a tip that there were "too many" Middle Eastern men working at a convenience store. The government had no evidence whatsoever that the men were terrorists, or in any way violent, but because it could not immediately rule out the possibility that they might be terrorists, they were listed as "of interest" to the September 11 investigation, treated as "suspected terrorists," and locked up without bond. The Inspector General said the government's "of interest" designation of detainees was "indiscriminate and haphazard."[6]

Some of the detainees had overstayed their visas or committed some other deportable offense. Many admitted that they had done so, and agreed to leave the country. Ordinarily, that would have been the end of the case, because the only legitimate purpose of an immigration proceeding is to remove someone who is in the country unlawfully. But when the government's purpose is not the legitimate one of enforcing immigration law, but the illegitimate one of using immigration infractions as an excuse to lock up "suspected terrorists" without any evidence that they were in fact engaged in terrorism, a detainee's agreement to leave the country constitutes a problem. The government "solved" the problem by adopting a policy called "hold until cleared," which barred foreign nationals from leaving even when they had agreed to leave, and kept them locked up, often for months, simply so that the FBI could continue to investigate them. In other words, the detainees were treated as guilty until proven innocent, even when there was no affirmative evidence linking them to terrorism. This policy was patently illegal, because detention is permissible in the immigration setting only where necessary to effectuate removal from the country. In these cases detention was used not to facilitate but to *block* removal.

Some immigration judges ordered "of interest" detainees released on bond when the government was unable to offer any evidence to support their detention. So John Ashcroft changed the rules. In October 2001, he gave immigration prosecutors (district directors) the power to keep foreign nationals locked up for months even after an immigration judge had ruled that there was no basis for detention and had ordered their release. The regulation, still in effect, provides for an "automatic stay" of release whenever the immigration prosecutor files an appeal to the Board of Immigration Appeals. The stay lasts as long as it takes to resolve the appeal. Appeals typically take months, and often well over a year, to decide. Thus, this regulation gives immigration prosecutors the authority to ignore an immigration judge's ruling that a foreign national should be released and to keep him locked up for months, without any showing that the government is likely to succeed on appeal. Several federal judges have declared this regulation unconstitutional, because it gives the government the power to lock up individuals where there is no objective basis for doing so, but the government continues to invoke the authority.[7]

When the government could not detain suspects on pretextual immigration or criminal charges, it often declared them to be "material witnesses." The "material witness" law permits the government to lock up a person if it can be shown that he or she has information material to a trial or grand jury proceeding but would flee before testifying.[8] Before September 11, the "material witness" authority, which allows incarceration without even a charge of wrongdoing, was used only rarely. Prosecutors are generally disinclined to lock up potential witnesses, because such treatment is likely to render the witness hostile to the prosecutor who seeks to use his testimony. The material witness law is designed solely to ensure that a witness be available for testimony. The government may not detain someone without probable cause while it searches for more evidence, or detain someone it thinks might be dangerous on less than probable cause of illegal conduct. Yet that appears to be the only justification for many of the "material witness" detentions imposed by the government since September 11. The *Washington Post* reported in November 2002, for example, that about half those detained as "material witnesses" were never brought forward to testify.[9] And there were numerous stories of witnesses who were not resistant in any way nonetheless being locked up as "material witnesses."[10]

Detainees were also subjected to increased restrictions on their rights to consult with attorneys. In October 2001, the administration adopted a rule permitting it to listen in on attorney-client conversations of any federal prisoner, without a warrant, on the attorney general's unilateral determination that there is "reasonable suspicion"—a standard substantially lower than probable cause—that the communications might further terrorism.[11] Attorney-client conversations have long been subject to a strong presumption of confidentiality, but the government has always had the authority to listen in on attorney-client communications where a judge issues a warrant based on probable cause that the relationship is being used to further a crime. Under the Ashcroft regulation the government need obtain no warrant, nor have probable cause of criminal wrongdoing, in order to listen in.

In sum, in the war on terrorism at home, the Justice Department detained thousands of people not charged with terrorism or association with al Qaeda, refused to reveal even the names of the vast majority of those detained, held them without bond even where there was no evidence that they posed a threat to anyone, kept them locked up even after immigration judges ordered their release or the foreign national agreed to depart the country, interfered with their access to lawyers, conducted immigration trials in secret, and asserted the authority to listen in on attorney-client communications without a warrant or probable cause. The government never showed that these measures were necessary to deter terrorism or to find terrorists. And it consistently reserved its most harsh treatment for those with the least voice in our political process: noncitizens.

## PREVENTIVE DETENTION—AND TORTURE—ABROAD

Despite the abuses detailed above, the more than 5,000 men detained in the United States were fortunate compared to those the United States has detained beyond our borders. The United States is holding several thousand prisoners outside the country, some traditional prisoners of war in Iraq, but many others anything but traditional prisoners in the war on terrorism. Many of the war on terrorism prisoners have been held in a military prison at Guantánamo Bay, formally part of Cuba but subject since 1903 to total U.S. jurisdiction and control under a lease that cannot be terminated without U.S. consent. Until the Supreme Court stepped in and ruled against the Bush administration, the Guantánamo detainees were held incommunicado for over two and a half years, without trial, charges, or even a hearing to assess their status. Only the International Committee of the Red Cross had any regular access to them. Meanwhile, the United States is holding an undisclosed number of other prisoners in secret locations around the globe, to which the Red Cross and all others have been denied any access.

## GUANTÁNAMO: THE BLACK HOLE OF LEGAL LIMBO

For much of the world, Guantánamo Bay has become a symbol of the Bush administration's dismissive attitude toward the rule of law. The administration chose to hold prisoners at Guantánamo precisely to avoid the limits of law. The administration claimed that it could warehouse there any person it labeled an "enemy combatant," or as President Bush put it, "a bad guy." It maintained that it could hold them until the war on terrorism ends, or as U.S. Defense Secretary Donald Rumsfeld elaborated, until there are no more terrorist organizations of global reach left in the world. Since everyone has global reach these days, and political violence shows no signs of disappearing from the face of the earth, the power the administration claimed is literally unlimited.

Who are the Guantánamo detainees? Relatively little is known, because the United States has kept their identities secret. U.S. military officials initially described them as "the worst of the worst," and assured the public that prisoners were sent to Guantánamo only after an extensive internal review process involving multiple layers of input from military officials, intelligence experts, and even behavioral psychologists. Yet we now know that there have been captives as young as thirteen years old, and as old as ninety, held at Guantánamo.[12] Government officials have admitted to reporters that there are few if any "big fish" there. A CIA report found that the Guantánamo detainees posed little danger and had provided little information of value in the war on terrorism.[13] And the military has released between 100 and 200 detainees, suggesting that they were not "the worst of the worst" after all.[14] Five men returned to Great Britain from Guantánamo in the spring of 2004 were promptly released by that country, the United States' closest ally in the war on terrorism.[15] Despite having been detained and interrogated for over two years by U.S. officials, these men could not be charged with committing a single crime by British authorities.

When the Center for Constitutional Rights and a private law firm, Shearman and Sterling, filed lawsuits challenging the legality of the Guantánamo detentions, the government argued that the courts could not even hear the cases. The government maintained that as "enemy" foreign nationals held outside the United States, the detainees were not entitled to seek any relief in federal court, or indeed in any court at all. The lower federal courts unanimously sided with the government, but the Supreme Court agreed to hear the cases, and reversed the lower courts.

In an historic ruling in June 2004, the Supreme Court ruled that the federal courts are indeed open to the Guantánamo detainees to challenge the legality of their detention.[16] It noted that the habeas corpus statute, which generally authorizes detainees to seek court review of the basis for their detention, does not distinguish between citizens and foreign nationals, and applies at least to any detention in a location under U.S. jurisdiction and control. The Court rejected the government's arguments that foreign nationals have no right to seek judicial review of their detention and that Guantánamo was beyond the reach of our law merely because it was technically part of Cuba.

That decision forced the military to provide hearings for the Guantánamo detainees to determine their status—the very hearings that the detainees' lawyers, and the world at large, had been seeking from the outset. But the government provided these hearings years too late, and with inadequate procedures. Under the Geneva Conventions, a country at war may detain those fighting for the other side for the duration of the conflict. But the Conventions require that where there is any doubt regarding an individual's status, the country must provide a hearing to determine that status definitively before prolonged detention.[17] The Bush administration argued from the beginning that it did not need to provide any hearings, because President Bush had categorically determined that anyone fighting for al Qaeda or the Taliban was an "unlawful combatant." But this contention ignored the possibility that some of those detained might not have been fighting for al Qaeda or the Taliban at all, but were simply innocent civilians turned in by bounty hunters to collect a reward.

It is unlikely that the world would have objected to the United States' detaining those fighting against it on behalf of al Qaeda had they been afforded any sort of fair process and treated with elemental dignity while detained. But the world could not accept the Bush administration's assertion that it had sole discretion to determine who would be detained without any hearing and without any legal limitation whatsoever. The Supreme Court's decision did much to reassert the rule of law, but the damage in terms of America's claim to represent democratic values had already been done.

## ENEMY COMBATANTS AT HOME—JOSÉ PADILLA AND YASER HAMDI

While the Bush administration initially justified the detention of the Guantánamo detainees by emphasizing their status as foreign nationals lacking constitutional rights, it ultimately extended the same treatment to U.S. citizens held here in the United States. It insisted that it had the untrammeled right to detain even U.S. citizens whom the president had labeled "bad guys." And it did not matter whether the citizens were captured on the battlefield of Afghanistan, as the administration alleged with respect to Yaser Hamdi, or were arrested getting off a plane at Chicago's O'Hare International Airport, as was the case with José Padilla. Both men were labeled "enemy combatants" and placed in indefinite incommunicado military custody.

Initially, the government argued that, as with the foreign "enemy combatants," these U.S. citizens had no right whatsoever to seek court review. When the U.S. Court of Appeals for the Fourth Circuit, the most conservative court in the country, rejected that proposition, the Justice Department retreated slightly.[18] It conceded that courts could review citizens' challenges, but argued no more than rubber-stamp review. In its view, all the government had to do was to submit a short affidavit explaining why it had designated the individual an enemy combatant. At that point, the government argued, the courts were compelled to defer to the government's allegations, and could not even hear from the detainee on whether the allegations were true or false. In short, much as it argued in the Guantánamo cases, the government's position was that the courts would simply have to accept the government's word, and that there was no need for any kind of adversarial process to determine the truth.

On the same day that it ruled on the Guantánamo cases, the Supreme Court rejected the government's position in the Hamdi case by a vote of 8 to 1.[19] The Court ruled that while the government had a right to hold U.S. citizens captured on a foreign battlefield fighting for the enemy, due process demanded that the individual be afforded notice of the charges against him and a meaningful opportunity to confront the charges before a neutral decision maker—exactly what the United States had denied Hamdi.

The Supreme Court dismissed the case of José Padilla, the U.S. citizen arrested at O'Hare airport, on jurisdictional grounds—his lawyers filed their challenge in the wrong court. But the Court's opinion suggested that had it reached the merits, it would have ruled that the United States had no authority to hold Padilla as an enemy combatant.[20] Now that he has refiled in the correct court, Padilla is entitled to at least as much process as Hamdi, and perhaps more.[21] In February 2005, a district court ruled that the government had no authority to hold Padilla as an enemy combatant, because the authority to detain U.S. citizens on the battlefield abroad does not extend to domestic arrests.[22] In September 2005, the court of appeals reversed, maintaining that because Padilla allegedly fought with al Qaeda against the United States in Afghanistan, he was in essentially the same shoes as Hamdi; the fact that he was captured here rather than there, the court said, was immaterial.[23] Padilla's lawyers are seeking Supreme Court review.

From a Supreme Court that has historically deferred to the president during wartime and is today predominantly conservative, the enemy combatant decisions of June 2004 were a resounding defeat, for which the administration was totally unprepared. It had reportedly drafted "talking points" for a complete victory and for a partial victory, but had no talking points for a loss.[24] The Court left many questions unanswered—what type of process would be required for the Guantánamo detainees, how long could the government hold detainees who were found to be fighting for the enemy, were lawyers required for all enemy combatants or only for those whose cases made it to court without a military hearing? Lower courts are beginning to answer those questions, but their ultimate resolution will probably require a return trip to the Supreme Court. Most importantly, however, the Supreme Court's decisions reaffirmed that the rule of law must survive, even in the face of a terrorist threat. As Justice Sandra Day O'Connor wrote in the *Hamdi* decision, "a state of war is not a blank check for the President."[25]

## MILITARY TRIBUNALS

Some of the Guantánamo detainees may ultimately be tried for war crimes, in military tribunals that more closely resemble criminal trials, and in settings where they are allowed legal representation. These tribunals, however, also raise serious concerns from the standpoint of basic human rights and fundamental fairness.

In those proceedings, the military acts as prosecutor, judge, jury, and executioner. The president authorizes charges to be brought, the case is heard by military officials subject to his command, and the final level of review is the defense secretary, with no independent court oversight. The presidential order setting out procedures for these tribunals provides that no court may review a determination of guilt, but the Supreme Court's ruling in the Guantánamo case suggests that habeas corpus review may be available to test the legality of the conviction. Under the procedures, the government is not obligated to share with the defendant any classified information that shows the defendant is innocent. And it may use against the defendant classified information that neither the defendant nor his chosen lawyer has any opportunity to see or confront. If a defendant were by some miracle acquitted under these one-sided procedures, he would not be released, but would continue to be held as long as the United States says the war on terror continues.

The military tribunals have, like Guantánamo itself, come under harsh international criticism, and the government has been very slow to bring anyone to trial. President Bush issued the order creating the tribunals in November 2001, yet as of October 2005, no military trials had been held. In November 2004, U.S. District Judge James Robertson ruled that the tribunals were illegal, both because they are being applied to persons who have not been properly determined "unlawful combatants" under the Geneva Conventions and because the tribunal rules permit defendants to be convicted on secret evidence that they cannot confront.[26] In July 2005, a unanimous panel of the D.C. Circuit, including John G. Roberts Jr., now Chief Justice of the United States, reversed Judge Robertson, and allowed the military tribunals to proceed.[27] Effectively granting the president the very "blank check" that the Supreme Court had warned against, the court ruled that the Geneva Conventions do not limit the president at all in his treatment of al Qaeda detainees. Even if U.S. courts permit the tribunals to go forward, the world will be watching. If the proceedings are seen as unfair "show trials," they will likely do more harm than good in the war on terrorism, as they will only reinforce the image of a United States unwilling to be constrained by the rule of law.


## ABU GHRAIB AND THE TORTURE MEMOS

Almost from the beginning of the war on terrorism, newspapers reported that the administration had decided to use coercive tactics to obtain information from detainees. In a series of articles, unidentified government officials admitted that they had "taken the gloves off" in the interest of encouraging detainees to talk.[28] It was also reported that the administration was employing its harshest tactics against a group of high-level al Qaeda leaders detained in undisclosed foreign locations run by the CIA.[29] These disclosures led to the usual objections from human rights groups but did not generate substantial public interest.

All of that changed in April 2004, when the first photos from Abu Ghraib prison near Baghdad were released. They depicted a man, hooded, standing on a box, with electrical wires attached; naked prisoners forced to masturbate or to lie on top of each other; a naked man being held on a leash by a U.S. servicewoman; and unmuzzled dogs lunging at prisoners. These images, which sped around the globe on the Internet and were emblazoned across the front pages of the world's newspapers, made the unspeakable undeniable. They transformed euphemisms about "gathering intelligence" into harsh realities of cruel and inhuman behavior.

The Bush administration quickly sought to contain the damage. It condemned the acts as "un-American," and minimized them as isolated actions of rogue agents. And it pointed to ongoing military investigations. The Justice Department brought a criminal charge against a civilian employee accused of killing a man in the course of an interrogation in Afghanistan. The official message was that this was not a systemic problem, and not a problem of policy, but the actions of a few untrained and unprepared individuals.

From the outset, however, there were reasons to question that account. The abuses at Abu Ghraib followed a visit there by Major General Geoffrey Miller, then in charge of Guantánamo. He was sent to Iraq out of concern that the military was not getting sufficient information from its detainees. Moreover, the government's tactic of widespread detention, followed by interrogation, placed tremendous pressure on investigators to obtain information from interrogations. If one investigates first, and detains only when one has developed evidence of culpability, confessions are not so critical. But where one locks up first and then begins to investigate, a premium is placed on confessions, as there is little other way to find out who actually poses a threat.

If there was ever any doubt, it became clear in June 2004 that the torture at Abu Ghraib could not be dismissed as the responsibility of a few bad actors. Two leaked memos, one dated August 2002 to White House Counsel Alberto Gonzales from the head of the Justice Department's Office of Legal Counsel, and the other dated March 2003 to Defense Secretary Rumsfeld from a "Working Group on Detainee Interrogations in the Global War on Terrorism," made crystal clear that the Bush administration consciously sought out every loophole it could construct in order to justify inflicting physical and psychological pain on captives for intelligence purposes.[30] The August 2002 memo was reportedly sought by the CIA out of concern that the tactics it was employing against high-level al Qaeda detainees might expose its agents to criminal liability for torture. The Defense Department memo, drafted some seven months later, adopted the Justice Department's analysis wholesale.

The Office of Legal Counsel is often referred to as the "constitutional conscience" of the executive branch. It interprets the Constitution for the executive branch, and has the power to resolve disputes between various agencies of the administration. But its memo, and the working group memo that later adopted its analysis, read not like the work of public servants bound by the Constitution, but rather like the efforts of a tax lawyer to exploit every last loophole. The criminal ban on torture requires "specific intent," the OLC memo reasoned, so if the interrogator knows that his actions will inflict severe harm, but he doesn't "specifically intend" them to do so, he's off the hook. Threats of death are permissible as long as they are not threats of "imminent death." Drugs designed to disrupt a suspect's personality may be administered, so long as they do not "penetrate to the core of an individual's ability to perceive the world around him." Mental harm is perfectly fine as long as it's not "prolonged." Physical pain is not torture unless it rises to the level of pain associated with death or organ failure.[31]

If an interrogator fails to follow this road map and commits what is, even in the Bush administration's eyes, torture, the OLC memo went on to offer a series of creative defenses. The interrogator can claim it was "necessary" to torture, that he was torturing "in self-defense," or that he was following "superior orders." All of this is directly contrary to established federal and international law on torture, which holds that under no circumstances is torture ever "justified" or "excused."

As if these loopholes were not enough, the OLC memo argues further that the president is simply not bound by law in interrogations in the war on terrorism, and is therefore free to order outright torture. Neither international law nor federal law can bind the president, the memo argues, when he is exercising his "Commander-in-Chief authority." Indeed, were Congress to ban torture in the war on terrorism, the memo contends, it would "violate the Constitution's sole vesting of the Commander-in-Chief authority in the President." [32]

At a news conference on June 10, 2004, following the release of the memos, President Bush said that he instructed his troops to adhere to the law, and "that ought to comfort you." But he repeatedly refused to answer whether he understood the law to ban torture. And he said he "can't remember" whether he read the memo that argues that "the law" does not bind him as commander in chief.[33] The administration has now officially replaced the August 2002 torture memo, but notably did so only after the memo had become public, and on the eve of Alberto Gonzales's confirmation hearing for attorney general. If the memo had remained inside the administration, there is no sign that it would have been repudiated.

## COMMON THEMES

What unites the torture memos, the detention of enemy combatants, and the military tribunals is a resistance to checks and balances and the rule of law. In each setting, the Bush administration has essentially argued that it is above the law and that its actions cannot be tested by the other branches. It argued that no court could question the legality of its "enemy combatant" detentions. It contended that neither Congress nor international law could bar the president from authorizing torture when he is acting as commander in chief. And its military tribunal rules contemplate executing individuals on the basis of secret evidence without independent judicial review.

The Supreme Court's rejection of the government's position in the enemy combatant cases, and the administration's repudiation of the torture memos—after they became public—illustrate that the rule of law may be strong enough to resist such naked assertions of unchecked power. But the fact that the administration was willing to take these positions in the first place shows that it has utterly failed to adopt a narrow and calibrated response to the threat of terrorism. These practices have in all likelihood made us less safe, by fueling anti-Americanism, which in turn makes it less likely that we will get the cooperation we need to keep ourselves secure, and much more likely that al Qaeda and other enemies will find willing recruits to their cause against us.

# 13

# The Patriot Act—Unleashing Government Spying, Reducing Oversight

In its enemy combatant decisions, the Supreme Court stood up to the president's assertion of unchecked power. Congress, by contrast, has done relatively little to check the president in the "war on terror." Since the attacks of September 11, Congress has passed the USA PATRIOT Act, a statute that gave the executive branch new forms of unchecked authority; the Homeland Security Act of 2002, which created a vast new bureaucracy directed toward surveillance and security; and the 2004 Intelligence Reform Act, which established a new set of intelligence organizations with ill-defined responsibilities.

The USA PATRIOT Act (abbreviated from United and Strengthening America by Providing Appropriate Tools Required to Intercept and Obstruct Terrorism Act of 2001)[1] was passed just six weeks after 9/11. Congress acted under extraordinary pressure from Attorney General John Ashcroft, who essentially threatened Congress that the blood of the victims of future terrorist attacks would be on its hands if it did not swiftly adopt the administration's proposals. The bill was never the subject of a committee debate or markup in the Senate. There was a truncated process in the House, which heard no official testimony from opponents of the bill but at least held a full committee markup. But the results of even that minimal process were thrust aside by the administration and the House leadership and never brought to a vote in the full House. Instead, after three weeks of behind-the-scenes discussions between a few senators and the administration, a bill was introduced in the Senate on October 5 that included the vast majority of the administration's proposals. That bill passed the Senate on October 11 by a vote of 98 to 1, following a brief debate that made it clear that even supporters of the legislation had not read it and did not understand its provisions. The next day, a slightly different bill was introduced in the House, and was taken up and passed the same day under a procedure barring the offering of any amendments. Given its 342-page heft, it is virtually certain that not a single member of the House read the bill before voting for it. The president signed the bill into law on October 26.

Some measures in the Patriot Act make sense. These include provisions ensuring adequate personnel on the northern border, strengthening the laws on money laundering, eliminating some institutional barriers to the sharing of information between law enforcement agencies and intelligence agencies, and improving the processing of visas. Some of the expanded electronic surveillance provisions would also have made sense had they included appropriate limitations and judicial controls. Over the administration's objections, Congress sensibly included sunsets for some of the most controversial surveillance provisions, requiring Congress to reapprove these measures by the end of 2005 or they would expire. Congress is likely to make most of these provisions permanent, but the sunsets both ensured that the measures would be debated and imposed a check on executive abuses in the meantime, because officials knew that if they abused the powers, the likelihood of reenactment would be reduced.

But in many respects, the Patriot Act reflected an overreaction all too typical in American history. It cast a cloak of secrecy over the exercise of government power by removing limitations and judicial controls on investigative authorities and short-circuited procedures designed to protect the innocent and punish the guilty. It violated core constitutional principles, rendering immigrants deportable for their political association and excludable for pure speech. It authorized the government to freeze property on the basis of secret evidence, without any findings of wrongdoing by the property owner. It fundamentally altered the power of the FBI and the role of the CIA within the United States, without imposing adequate checks to protect against abuses. And by reserving its harshest measures for immigrants, measures directed predominantly at Arab and Muslim immigrants, it sacrificed commitments to equality by trading a minority group's liberty for the majority's purported security—a trade that has from all objective measures proven ineffective.

In brief, the most significant provisions of the Patriot Act: (1) impose guilt by association on immigrants, extending that philosophy far beyond the 1996 Antiterrorism Act; (2) authorize executive detention on mere suspicion that an immigrant has at some point provided humanitarian aid to a proscribed organization; (3) empower the government to deny entry to aliens for pure speech, resurrecting yet another long-interred relic of the McCarthy era; (4) expand the government's authority to conduct criminal searches and wiretaps without first showing probable cause that the subject is engaged in criminal activity; (5) authorize secret searches in cases having nothing to do with terrorism; (6) give the CIA access to the awesome power of criminal grand juries; (7) reduce judicial oversight of intrusive information-gathering powers and expand the scope of FBI access to a wide range of business records on innocent citizens, essentially sanctioning fishing expeditions without probable cause of any criminal activity; and (8) give the Treasury Department power to freeze property based only on a claim that an entity or person is under "investigation," and then permit that freeze order to be defended on secret evidence.

## GUILT BY ASSOCIATION

Building on the 1996 Antiterrorism Act, the Patriot Act expanded guilt by association, a McCarthy-era philosophy that the Supreme Court has condemned as "alien to the traditions of a free society and the First Amendment itself."[2] Under the immigration law that existed before September 11, foreign nationals were deportable for engaging in or supporting terrorist activity. The Patriot Act made aliens deportable for material support of a "terrorist organization," irrespective of any nexus between the individual's support and any act of violence, much less terrorism.[3] The new law defines "terrorist organization" as any group of two or more persons that has used or threatened to use violence, and makes material support a deportable offense. Thus, the Act's proscription on associational activity potentially encompasses every organization that has ever been involved in a civil war or a crime of violence, from a pro-life group that once threatened workers at a clinic that provides abortions to the African National Congress, the Irish Republican Army, or the Northern Alliance in Afghanistan.

Like the criminal "material support" provisions of the 1996 Antiterrorism Act, the new law contains no requirement that the support have any connection whatsoever to a designated organization's violent activity. Thus, a foreign national who sent coloring books to a day-care center run by a designated organization would apparently be deportable as a terrorist, even if she could show that the coloring books were used only by three-year-olds. Indeed, the law apparently extends even to those who seek to support a group in the interest of countering terrorism. Thus, an immigrant who offered his services in peace negotiating to the Irish Republican Army (IRA) in the hope of furthering the peace process in Great Britain and forestalling further violence could be deported as a terrorist if the secretary of state chose to designate the IRA as a terrorist organization.

The Patriot Act expanded the "guilt by association" provisions of the 1996 Antiterrorism Act in several ways. Unlike the 1996 Act, the Patriot Act immigration provisions make no exception for the donation of medicine or religious materials. They expand the government's authority to blacklist groups by permitting the designation of wholly domestic groups, requiring no notice to Congress and providing no opportunity for groups to challenge their designation. And the immigration provisions extend their prohibitions retroactively, making it a deportable offense to have provided support to organizations long before they were in any way "proscribed," at a time when it was fully lawful to provide such support. Invoking this provision, the government has charged Khader Hamide and Michel Shehadeh, two of the LA 8 discussed in Chapter 3, are deportable under the Patriot Act for activities dating back to the mid-1980s, including the distribution of magazines and the provision of humanitarian aid.

Some argue that the threat from terrorist organizations abroad, and the fungibility of money and support, require us to compromise the constitutional principle that prohibits guilt by association. But that principle was developed in the crucible of a battle against what appeared to be an even more formidable foe—the Communist Party, an organization that Congress found to be, and the Supreme Court accepted as, a foreign-dominated organization that used sabotage and terrorism for the purpose of overthrowing the United States by force and violence.[4] If association with the Communist Party deserves protection, surely association with much less powerful groups deserves similar protection.

For groups that engage in substantial political or social activity, the fungibility theory rests on a faulty factual assumption. It maintains that because money is fungible, even a donation of blankets to a hospital will free up resources that will then be devoted to terrorism. But this argument assumes that a group engaged in a political struggle that uses both legal and illegal means will devote every marginal dollar to its illegal means. On this assumption, every dollar donated to the African National Congress (ANC) for its nonviolent opposition to apartheid translated to a dollar that the ANC then spent on violent terrorist ends. While some groups may be so committed to violence that everything else they do is only a front for terrorism, that is not likely true for most political organizations that use violence. For most such groups, violence is not an end in itself, but one means to a political end. This is not to excuse the violence in any way, but to suggest that one must distinguish between a group's lawful and unlawful activities.

If it could be shown in a particular case that a group's "legitimate" activities were a cover for its illegal activities, action against its legitimate enterprises would be justified, just as federal law allows the government to seize legitimate businesses if it can show that they are fronts for organized crime. But short of such a showing, we can and should distinguish between lawful and unlawful activities.

Supreme Court decisions are fundamentally at odds with the fungibility argument. During the McCarthy era, the Supreme Court repeatedly struck down or narrowly construed laws that penalized association with the Communist Party. It consistently ruled that in order to avoid imposing guilt by association, the government had to prove that the individual specifically intended to further the group's illegal ends. If fungibility made the provision of material support to a group legally different from membership itself, then all of the anticommunist measures declared invalid by the Supreme

Court could have simply been rewritten to hinge punishment on the payment of dues, the volunteering of time, or any of the other material manifestations of political association. Unless the right of association is to become a meaningless formality, it must include the right to support lawful activities of an organization one has a right to join.

## DETENTION VS. DUE PROCESS

The Patriot Act gives the attorney general unprecedented power to lock up any foreign national he certifies as a "suspected terrorist."[5] Such persons may be initially detained without charge for seven days, and are subject to potentially indefinite detention thereafter. The attorney general must have "reasonable grounds to believe" that an individual has committed any of a wide range of immigration violations, but the attorney general need not provide a hearing to determine whether the individual actually poses any real threat. And the legislation defines "terrorist activity" so expansively that it literally includes virtually every immigrant who is suspected of being involved in a barroom brawl or domestic dispute, as well as aliens who have never committed an act of violence and whose only "crime" is to have provided humanitarian aid to an organization disfavored by the government. Such persons may be detained indefinitely, even if they are "granted relief from removal" and therefore have a legal right to remain here permanently. That is akin to allowing the state to keep a man in prison after the governor has granted him a pardon.

Under preexisting law, the INS already had authority to detain any alien in deportation or exclusion proceedings who presented either a threat to national security or a risk of flight. What the new legislation adds is the authority to detain persons who do not pose a current danger or flight risk, and who are not removable because they are entitled to asylum or some other form of relief.

This measure raises several constitutional concerns. First, it permits preventive detention of persons who pose no threat to national security or risk of flight. The Supreme Court has upheld preventive detention of accused criminals, but only where there is a specific reason for the detention—namely, that they pose a danger to others or a risk of flight.[6] Under the Patriot Act, however, if the attorney general says that he has reasonable grounds to believe that an alien has threatened to use a weapon, the alien is presumptively detained, whether or not he poses any continuing threat to anyone. Preventive detention without a showing that the detainee needs to be incarcerated violates due process.

Second, the legislation allows the government to detain foreign nationals indefinitely, even where they have prevailed in their removal proceedings. Once a foreign national has been granted relief from removal, he has a legal right to remain here. At that point, immigration authorities have no legitimate reason to keep him in jail. The immigration bureau's authority to detain has always been incidental to its authority to deport, yet under this provision, the government would have freestanding authority to detain indefinitely persons never convicted of a crime and legally residing here.[7]

Third, the evidentiary threshold for detention is too low. The provision authorizes potentially indefinite detention, a far more severe deprivation of liberty than holding a person for interrogation or trial. Yet, in other contexts, the government has argued that the "reasonable grounds to believe" standard used in this statute is essentially equivalent to the "reasonable suspicion" required for a brief stop and frisk under the Fourth Amendment. Such "reasonable suspicion" does not even authorize a full arrest in criminal law enforcement. It surely cannot authorize indefinite detention in immigration law enforcement.

Fourth, it is critical to the constitutionality of any detention provision that the government bear the burden of justifying any preventive detention promptly in a scrupulously fair proceeding. Few intrusions on liberty are more severe than being locked up. Yet the Patriot Act imposes no affirmative burden of proof on the government, provides for no hearing, and authorizes detention on the attorney general's say-so. The only "process" the alien is afforded is the right to go to federal court and sue the government for its actions. But due process requires that the agency seeking to deprive a person of his liberty afford him a fair procedure in which to be heard; the availability of a lawsuit after the fact is not sufficient.

Finally, the provision permits detention of certified aliens for up to seven days without the filing of any charges. Yet the Supreme Court has ruled in the criminal setting that charges must be filed within forty-eight hours except in the most extraordinary circumstances.[8] The new law extends blanket authority to detain for seven days on mere certification that the attorney general suspects that an alien was at one time involved in a barroom brawl. Such overbroad authority does not meet the Supreme Court's requirement that preventive detention authority must be accompanied by heightened procedural protections and narrowly drawn laws.[9]

The administration strongly insisted on the need for this provision in the Patriot Act negotiations with Congress. Yet in the more than four years that the new authority has been on the books, the government has never invoked it. Instead, as described above, it found other ways to lock up thousands of individuals without showing that they posed a risk of flight or danger to the community. The failure to invoke this provision even once suggests that it was not in fact as necessary as the administration claimed when the Patriot Act was under consideration. However, this provision, like all of the Act's immigration provisions, has no sunset, and Congress has shown no inclination to revisit it.


## IDEOLOGICAL EXCLUSION

The Patriot Act also expanded ideological exclusion, authorizing the government to deny entry to aliens for pure speech.[10] It excludes aliens who "endorse or espouse terrorist activity" or who "persuade others to support terrorist activity or a terrorist organization," if the secretary of state determines that such speech undermines U.S. efforts to combat terrorism. It also excludes aliens who are representatives of groups that "endorse acts of terrorist activity" in ways that similarly undermine U.S. efforts to combat terrorism.

In the summer of 2004, the administration reportedly relied on the Patriot Act to revoke a visa that had previously been granted to Tariq Ramadan, a Swiss-born Islamic scholar who had been hired for a prestigious chair at Notre Dame's Institute for International Peace Studies. Ramadan, author of over twenty books and one of the world's most highly regarded Islamic scholars, is no extremist. Two days after the attacks of September 11 he called on Muslims to condemn the attacks. He argues that Islam needs to be modernized. Yet the administration relied on the Patriot Act to deny him admission to the country, without ever identifying his offending words or ideas.

While the Supreme Court has long ruled that foreign nationals outside our borders—in contrast to those living among us—have no constitutional right to enter the country, such ideological exclusions nonetheless raise constitutional concerns. The First Amendment is designed to protect a wide-open and robust public debate, and if our government can keep out persons who espouse disfavored ideas, our ability as Americans to hear and consider those ideas will be diminished. More broadly, excluding people for their ideas is contrary to the spirit of freedom for which the United States stands. It was for that reason that Congress repealed all such grounds in the Immigration and Nationality Act in 1990, after years of politically motivated visa denials. We are a strong enough country, and our resolve against terrorism is strong enough, to make such censorship wholly unnecessary. Yet we have now returned to the much-criticized ways of the McCarran-Walter Act, targeting people not for their acts but for their words.

In 2005, Congress went still further, amending the immigration law to make foreign nationals living here deportable for speech and pure association. In the REAL ID Act, passed as part of an Iraq supplemental appropriations bill, Congress made endorsement of terrorist activity and membership in any organization that has used violence deportable offenses.[11] In July 2005, the DHS invoked the new law against Khader Hamide and Michel Shehadeh, claiming that their alleged association with a PLO faction in the 1980s made them deportable more than twenty years later.

## SECRET SEARCHES AND WIRETAPS WITHOUT CRIMINAL PROBABLE CAUSE

The Patriot Act also made substantial and controversial changes in the rules that govern the collection and sharing of information by law enforcement and intelligence agencies. The administration argued that it needed more expansive search and seizure authority and needed to be able to share the information it gained through criminal investigations more broadly with intelligence agencies. While some of the administration's criticisms about the strictures that had grown up before September 11 were valid, some key changes went far beyond what was needed to respond to terrorism. Some changes were not limited to terrorist investigations at all, but applied across the board to all criminal investigations. And while Congress imposed a four-year sunset on some of the surveillance provisions, permitting reevaluation in light of their implementation, most of these provisions are likely to be made permanent by the end of 2005, and other troublesome surveillance and information gathering provisions were permanent from the beginning.

One of the most significant changes allowed prosecutors and investigators to invoke in criminal investigations the looser rules previously reserved for collection of foreign intelligence, thus authorizing warrants for secret searches (so-called black bag jobs) and wiretaps in criminal investigations without probable cause of criminal conduct and without other protections applicable to searches and wiretaps in criminal cases.[12] The Fourth Amendment generally permits the government to conduct searches or wiretaps only where it has probable cause to believe that an individual is engaged in criminal activity or that evidence of a crime will be found. But the Patriot Act allows the government to evade that requirement wherever it says that its investigation also has a significant foreign intelligence purpose.

The Patriot Act did this by amending the Foreign Intelligence Surveillance Act (FISA).[13] FISA authorizes the FBI to obtain court orders to conduct electronic surveillance and secret physical searches without a criminal predicate, on the theory that foreign intelligence gathering is not designed to detect crimes but to gather information about foreign agents. Accordingly, FISA requires not a showing of probable criminal conduct, but a showing that the target of the intrusion is an "agent of a foreign power." "Foreign power" is defined to include not only foreign governments and international terrorism organizations, but any "foreign-based political organization" comprised principally of foreign nationals, regardless of any involvement in terrorism or other illegal activities. Under this definition, the Likud Party of Israel and Amnesty International could both be treated as foreign powers. "Agent" is defined so broadly that it includes any employee of such a group. Noncitizens can be "agents" subject to surveillance under this standard without regard to whether the individual or the group has ever engaged in any illegal, much less terrorist, activities. If the suspected agent of a foreign power is a U.S. citizen or permanent resident alien, the government is not allowed to base its warrant on First Amendment–protected activities, but even as to citizens the standard is looser than that applicable to ordinary wiretaps in criminal cases, requiring only probable cause to believe that the person's activities "may be" illegal. The statute's First Amendment limitation does not apply to foreign nationals here on temporary visas.

FISA searches and wiretaps are exempt from other important protections as well. While targets of searches are normally entitled to notice at the time of the search, and while targets of ordinary wiretaps must be notified as soon as the investigation is closed, searches and wiretaps under FISA may be kept secret forever. Under FISA, a person is notified of surveillance only if he or she is later prosecuted using the evidence seized. Even then, defendants have little opportunity to challenge the validity of the search, for they are not provided the affidavit that served as the basis for the surveillance. Nor are they permitted access to any portions of the wiretap transcripts to use in their defense, other than those introduced by the government or deemed by the government to be exculpatory. Where individuals are not prosecuted—those cases where the likelihood of government overreaching is greatest—notice is never provided, and therefore the search cannot be challenged.

When FISA was adopted, this extraordinary authority was justified on the ground that intelligence gathering is different from criminal law enforcement, and that the FISA authority would not be used for the purpose of investigating crime. Congress recognized that evidence of crimes might nonetheless sometimes be obtained during foreign intelligence gathering—espionage, for example, is a crime—and the law always allowed the use of FISA evidence in criminal cases. But in order to obtain a FISA warrant, the "primary purpose" of the investigation had to be the collection of foreign intelligence, not criminal law enforcement. Otherwise, the statute would serve as an end run around the strict requirements of the criminal wiretap statute.

In the Patriot Act, Congress eliminated the primary purpose test, amending FISA to allow wiretaps and physical searches without probable cause in criminal investigations so long as "a significant purpose" of the intrusion is to collect foreign intelligence. The express justification for this amendment was to permit the government to initiate wiretaps under FISA's lower standards where the investigation's primary purpose was to collect criminal evidence. The scope of this loophole remains uncertain. But in an extraordinary case in 2002, a special panel of appellate judges heard a secret, one-sided appeal by the government and then upheld the constitutionality of the Patriot Act changes.[14] In a surprise ruling, the court held that the "primary purpose" test had never actually been part of FISA, and that FISA had always been available to prosecutors investigating national security crimes. It may be important, however, that the court stressed that the special powers available under FISA were available only in response to threats to the national security from foreign powers, which suggests that the government cannot use FISA to investigate ordinary crimes even if they involve a "foreign power." Moreover, the court's emphasis on national security crimes suggests that FISA's use by prosecutors may have to meet something very close to the probable cause standard applicable to other criminal investigations. But if, as appears likely, FISA warrants will be used more frequently for collecting evidence for use in criminal trials, it would be advisable to ensure full adversarial testing of the legality of the warrant when the government attempts to introduce FISA-obtained evidence in criminal court. At present, FISA operates almost completely in the dark, even when its results are relied upon in criminal trials.

## "SNEAK AND PEEK" SEARCHES

Another provision of the Patriot Act expands the settings in which government agents can search a home without providing notice at the time of the search. Criminal searches have long been subject to the "knock and announce" rule, under which law enforcement officers executing a search warrant must generally knock on the door of the place to be searched and give notice to the owner that the search is to be conducted. The purpose of this long-standing requirement has been to allow owners to ensure that the warrant is being executed at the proper address, to monitor the scope of the search to ensure that it does not extend beyond the terms of the warrant, and, in the case of a prolonged search, to seek judicial intervention to narrow the scope of the search. Under a "sneak and peek" warrant, FBI agents can secretly enter an apartment or home while the owner is asleep or away, take, alter, or copy things, and not tell the owner that they were there for a "reasonable period thereafter." The Justice Department has stated in its Field Guidance on the Patriot Act that ninety days could be a "reasonable period." [15] Prior to the Patriot Act, courts had permitted so-called sneak and peek searches in extraordinary circumstances, such as where someone's life would be endangered or evidence would likely be destroyed if simultaneous notice of the search were given. But the Patriot Act provision transformed a narrow exception to the rule of advance notification into a new rule, permitting delayed notification any time notice might "seriously jeopardize" the investigation.[16] Government officials will almost always be able to claim that notice would seriously jeopardize a criminal investigation, and thus this exception threatens to swallow the rule.

The "sneak and peek" provision is not limited to terrorism cases but applies to any federal crime, from drug cases to giving false information on a student loan application. Moreover, it is not subject to the "sunset" provision, but marks a permanent change. The Justice Department has acknowledged that it has used this provision in nonviolent cases unrelated to terrorism.

## ELIMINATING BARRIERS BETWEEN LAW ENFORCEMENT AND INTELLIGENCE

One of the purposes of the Patriot Act was to promote the sharing of information between law enforcement agencies and intelligence agencies. That goal is legitimate. Many experts, including the 9/11 Commission, have concluded that one of the reasons for our failure to learn about the September 11 plot before the damage was done was that the many federal agencies that engage in intelligence and law enforcement did not communicate among themselves very effectively. But the obstacles to information sharing were more bureaucratic than legal. Some barriers may be inevitable—such as the need to maintain the confidentiality of sources. Other barriers, much less inevitable, stemmed from turf wars that divided the FBI, the CIA, and other intelligence and law enforcement agencies. These need to be addressed, but are unlikely to be solved by anything in the Patriot Act.

Still another reason for the failure to share information, however, was that Congress had imposed legal barriers out of concern that intelligence investigations are broad and secretive and therefore more easily intrude on constitutional freedoms. The Patriot Act sought to promote information sharing, for example, by authorizing criminal prosecutors to share grand jury information and other criminal investigative information with the CIA where it constitutes "foreign intelligence." This reform was not flawed in its basic thrust. However, Congress appears to have overcompensated, creating the risk that intelligence agencies such as the CIA will now have substantial access to domestic criminal law investigatory tools, even where international terrorism is not involved. This change could result in the CIA and other intelligence agencies assuming a much greater domestic role, while leaving them shrouded in secrecy and largely immune to judicial or public oversight. At the same time, as shown above, the Patriot Act also gave criminal prosecutors expanded authority to employ foreign intelligence tools in criminal investigations, bypassing the constitutional safeguards that ordinarily apply to criminal investigations.

When the Central Intelligence Agency was created in 1947, Congress explicitly said that the agency was to have no domestic police powers.[17] The CIA's operations were to be directed overseas, focused on foreign nationals, in the world of spy-versus-spy and relations between states, where criminal law was largely inapplicable. The information the CIA secretly collected was intended to inform the president in carrying out foreign affairs and national defense, not to be used to arrest people or prosecute crimes. The secrecy with which the CIA operated—collection activities could go on for years, even decades, without being publicly revealed—was fundamentally incompatible with the criminal justice system, where investigations must have a clear criminal objective, and the information collected and the means by which it is acquired must in most cases ultimately be shared with the accused and tested in open court.

Since the CIA was not supposed to engage in law enforcement, and since its agents were not supposed to appear in court, the CIA was not granted law enforcement powers. Law enforcement powers, including the power to search, arrest, prosecute, and incarcerate, are in some ways more awesome than the powers of the intelligence agencies, but they are subject to checks and balances unknown to the world of foreign espionage.

One of the most powerful tools of the criminal justice system is the grand jury—an institution originally designed to protect against prosecutorial abuse but since turned into an investigative tool. Through the grand jury, prosecutors can compel anyone to testify under oath. Anyone who refuses to testify can be sent to jail. A witness who lies can be prosecuted for perjury. The grand jury can also compel anyone with any record or tangible thing to produce it, irrespective of probable cause, again with the threat of jail time for those who refuse. Neither the Fourth nor Fifth Amendments generally protect against the compelled disclosure of records. Witnesses before a grand jury are not entitled to have a lawyer with them in the room while they testify. In practice, the grand jury operates as the arm of the prosecutor who convenes it. While technically subject to the oversight of a judge, the prosecutor issues subpoenas without the prior approval of the judge. In fact, the subpoenas are often issued in blank to FBI agents, who fill them in, serve them, and collect the records. The judge usually never sees what is turned over. Much of it is never even shown to the grand jurors.

These powers are subject, however, to two important controls: anything from the grand jury that the government uses in a criminal case becomes subject to the full panoply of due process protections, while anything not used in open court can be disclosed only for law enforcement purposes and otherwise must be kept secret.[18] The rules of due process ensure that evidence collected by the grand jury cannot be used against a person without the full vetting guaranteed by the confrontation clause of the Constitution, and must ultimately satisfy the government's burden of proof beyond a reasonable doubt. The rule of grand jury secrecy protects the innocent: much of what the grand jury collects turns out to be about innocent conduct. Some of the testimony is wrong, honestly or intentionally so, some is misleading, some irrelevant. If disclosed, especially if taken out of context, it could lead to wrong conclusions and harm reputations.

The Patriot Act created an exception to grand jury secrecy, giving the CIA the benefit of the grand jury's powers with none of the protections of the criminal justice system.[19] Section 203 of the Act amended Rule 6(e) of the Federal Rules of Criminal Procedure to allow information collected by grand juries to be shared with the CIA and other intelligence agencies, as well as any national defense or national security official, without the prior approval of a judge. In effect, CIA agents working with law enforcement officers can now jointly draw up subpoenas, obtain the fruits of the grand jury's power, and never have to appear in open court or explain how they used the information.

At its core, this provision addresses a real problem. The grand jury that investigated the role of Osama bin Laden and al Qaeda in the bombing of the U.S. embassies in Africa, for example, collected some of the most comprehensive information available at the time anywhere in the U.S. government on the operations of al Qaeda. The CIA could have used such information to pursue leads overseas beyond the scope of the criminal case. Thus, sharing information obtained in grand juries is undoubtedly justified in certain settings.

But Section 203 has no oversight and accountability mechanism. A better solution would have required judicial approval for the sharing of grand jury information, but Congress acceded to the Bush administration's insistence that law enforcement agencies should be free to act without judicial approval. In addition, the sharing of information should have been limited to cases of terrorism. The Patriot Act allows the government to share any grand jury information that "involves" foreign intelligence or counterintelligence. And foreign intelligence is expansively defined to include any "information relating to the capabilities, intentions, or activities of foreign governments or elements thereof, foreign organizations, or foreign persons."[20] Thus, while the sharing of information regarding international terrorism makes sense, Congress essentially removed any checks on the mixing of intelligence and law enforcement functions, failing to address the very real concerns that the foreign intelligence approach may lead to serious invasions of liberty of people residing here.

## INTELLIGENCE ACCESS TO RECORDS—THE DRAGNET APPROACH

The Patriot Act also expanded the government's ability to collect information under the rubric of investigating terrorism or clandestine intelligence activities—without convening a criminal grand jury. Section 215 of the Act, which has come to be popularly known as the "libraries provision," authorizes the government to secretly seize "any tangible things (including books, records, papers, documents, and other items)" where those items are sought for an investigation "to protect against international terrorism or clandestine intelligence activities."[21] Separate Patriot Act provisions authorize the government to issue special demands, called "national security letters" (NSLs), to require disclosure without court approval of financial records, credit reports, and transactional records regarding telephone calls, e-mail, and Internet usage (but not the content of communications). Section 215 orders and NSLs can be issued even if the person whose records are being sought is not suspected of any criminal wrongdoing whatsoever; indeed, the provisions are written so broadly that they seem to authorize orders that are not limited to the records of a particular person but that encompass entire collections of data related to many individuals.

Prior to the Patriot Act, Congress had given the FBI power to compel disclosure of bank records, telephone long-distance records, and other categories of data for intelligence and counterintelligence investigations, using either a court order or a national security letter. But in each instance, Congress applied two simple rules: the government had to specify the person whose records were being sought, and it had to have some factual basis giving it reason to believe that the person targeted was a terrorist or an agent of a foreign power.

The Patriot Act eliminated the requirement that the government articulate any factual basis for its demand, and it eliminated the requirement of a particular nexus between the records sought and a suspected agent. And Section 215 expanded the universe of information subject to such demands, giving the FBI the ability to compel any entity of any kind to disclose any record or tangible thing that the FBI claims is relevant to an investigation to prevent international terrorism or "clandestine intelligence activities."

The implications of these changes are enormous. Previously, the FBI could get the credit card records of anyone suspected of being an international terrorist or other foreign agent. Under the Patriot Act, the FBI can get the entire database of the credit card company. Under prior law, the FBI could get library borrowing records only by complying with state law and always had to ask for the records of a specific patron or concerning a specific book. Under the Patriot Act, the FBI can get an order for the records on everybody who ever used the library, or who used it on a certain day, or who checked out certain kinds of books. It can do the same at any bank, telephone company, hotel or motel, hospital, or university—merely upon the claim that the information is "sought for" an investigation to protect against international terrorism or clandestine intelligence activities.

Defenders of the Patriot Act often dismiss criticism of the Section 215 and NSL provisions by claiming that even before the Patriot Act, prosecutors could obtain such records through grand jury subpoenas. Such subpoenas, they currently note, do not require independent judicial approval but need only be filled out by the prosecutor. But this argument ignores two salient differences between traditional grand jury subpoenas and the new authorities. In order to issue a grand jury subpoena, the prosecutor must be willing to empanel a grand jury of citizens for a criminal investigation—a process not likely to be triggered lightly. In addition, the grand jury subpoena is subject to two possible oversight mechanisms—the grand jury itself and the press. The recipient of a grand jury subpoena is generally free to make the subpoena public. Thus, if a prosecutor subpoenas a library or bookstore, he must risk the possibility that the subpoena will appear on the front pages of the newspaper—a significant check in itself. Section 215 orders and NSLs, by contrast, require no grand jury to be empaneled, and are subject to a gag order barring the recipient from disclosing the existence of the order or letter in public. In fact, in September 2004, a federal court ruled the NSL provision for telephone and Internet records unconstitutional, because the gag order that accompanies it is so draconian as to effectively bar recipients of such requests from challenging them in court without first violating the order.[22] Thus, like so much else in the Patriot Act, these authorities expand surveillance power while removing critical oversight.

## FREEZING PROPERTY ON SECRET EVIDENCE

Finally, the Patriot Act expanded the government's already capacious authority to freeze assets of individuals, organizations, or corporations that it labels as "terrorists." The Clinton administration first adapted the tools of the International Emergency Economic Powers Act (IEEPA) to target individuals and political groups in 1995. As employed by President Clinton, that law, intended to authorize financial sanctions against foreign nations, was used for the first time to target politically disfavored groups and individuals, freezing their assets and criminalizing financial transactions with them without notice or a hearing. The Bush administration, with the encouragement of the Patriot Act, has gone still further.

Under the Patriot Act, the Treasury Department can now freeze all assets of any organization or individual simply by stating that it is investigating possible violations of IEEPA. It need not designate the entity or person as a "terrorist," nor even allege that the entity has violated any laws; it need only say that the entity is under investigation. In addition, the Patriot Act provides that if an individual or entity challenges a freeze order in court, the government may defend it using classified evidence presented to the judge behind closed doors and not disclosed to the challenger.

The Bush administration has employed these authorities to designate hundreds of individuals and organizations worldwide as "specially designated global terrorists." This term is nowhere defined by statute. Thus, a "specially designated global terrorist" is whatever the administration says it is. Most of those designated are based abroad, but some are here in the United States, including three of this country's largest Muslim charities: the Holy Land Foundation, Global Relief Development Corporation, and Benevolence International Foundation. The administration froze the assets of all three charities, two based only on a claim that they were under investigation, ultimately designated all three as "specially designated terrorists," and then defended the freeze orders with secret evidence in court. None of the charities ever had a meaningful opportunity to confront the evidence that apparently led to its being closed down.

## CONCLUSION

The Patriot Act radically transformed the landscape of government power in ways that virtually guarantee repetition of some of the government's worst abuses of the past. By criminalizing speech and association, targeting foreign nationals for their political affiliations, and expanding surveillance powers while diluting or eliminating oversight, these changes permit the FBI to cast its net far wider than ever before. Many have argued that such changes are needed to reorient the FBI to a more intelligence-based approach. But, as we have shown above, the FBI has historically focused far too much of its counterterrorism effort on the monitoring of political activity. The issue is not whether the FBI can investigate people who say that they want to kill Americans—they clearly can and should be investigated, and could legally be investigated long before the Patriot Act was passed. The issue is whether the FBI can investigate people who merely say that they support a Palestinian state, make a donation to a charitable organization, or are employed by a political group composed principally of foreign nationals. What was striking about the September 11 attackers is that they appear to have engaged in none of the kinds of overt political activities that the FBI has traditionally made the focus of its counterterrorism efforts. Yet the new powers in the Patriot Act will almost certainly result in broader collection of data on persons suspected of no wrongdoing and engaged only in political activity. The FBI and the other intelligence agencies are already awash in information that they cannot digest. Drawing in even more information on more innocent people is unlikely to make the picture any clearer.

# 14

# Casting a Broad Net,
# Catching Few Big Fish

One of the most common features of the Bush administration's post–9/11 security measures is that they sweep broadly in the name of preventing future terrorist attacks. No one can predict where the next terrorist attack will come from, but the administration has targeted what it considers "likely suspects" for special attention and treatment in the hope that it might net a terrorist by doing so. Thus far, these efforts have led to widespread ethnic profiling and the development of massive data collection and analysis programs, but have netted few if any actual terrorists.

## ETHNIC PROFILING

One of the most dramatic responses to the attacks of September 11 was a swift reversal in public attitudes about racial and ethnic profiling as a law enforcement tool. Before September 11, about 80 percent of the American public considered racial profiling wrong.[1] State legislatures, local police departments, and the president had all ordered data collection on the racial patterns of stops and searches. The U.S. Customs Service, sued for racial profiling, had instituted measures to counter racial and ethnic profiling at the borders. Even Attorney General John Ashcroft spoke out against racial profiling.[2] A federal law banning racial profiling seemed likely.

After September 11, however, polls reported that 60 percent of the American public favored ethnic profiling, at least as long as it was directed at Arabs and Muslims.[3] The fact that the perpetrators of the September 11 attacks were all Arab Muslim men, and that the attacks were orchestrated by a group espousing a radical form of Islam, led many to believe that it is only common sense to pay closer attention to Arab-looking men boarding airplanes and elsewhere. And for many, the high stakes made the case for engaging in profiling stronger here than in routine drug interdiction stops on highways.[4]

The federal government publicly professed to be opposed to ethnic profiling, but conducted the most extensive nationwide campaign of ethnic profiling that this country has seen since World War II. It called in 80,000 men for "special registration" with the Department of Homeland Security, simply because they were foreign nationals from Arab and Muslim countries. Registration consisted of fingerprinting, interviews, and photographs. Nearly 3,000 of those who registered were detained, though none of the 80,000 was charged with any terrorist crime. The FBI sought to interview 8,000 men, again simply because they were young and had come from Arab and Muslim countries. The government targeted its "Absconder Apprehension Initiative" not at *all* immigration absconders (persons with final deportation orders who have not left the country) but at those absconders who came from Arab and Muslim countries. And virtually all of the more than 5,000 foreign nationals who were subjected to antiterrorism preventive detention after September 11 were Arab or Muslim. Each of these initiatives was justified on the ground that it was aimed at finding terrorists, yet not one of the thousands of individuals ensnared in these programs stands convicted of a terrorist crime.

There is no question that the immediate aftermath of September 11 called for greater urgency than the ongoing "war on drugs," or that the immediate threat posed to our national security was greater. But that does not answer whether ethnic profiling is a legal, much less an effective, response. The argument that we cannot afford to rely on something other than racial or ethnic proxies for suspicion, after all, is precisely the rationale used to intern 110,000 persons of Japanese ancestry during World War II. While subjecting individuals to closer inspection, interviews, registration, or even searches is less extreme than detaining them, the rationale—that we should rely on ethnic background as a proxy for suspicion—is the same.

Precisely because of the history of racial discrimination in this country, the equal protection clause of the Fourteenth Amendment to the Constitution presumptively forbids government authorities from relying on explicit racial or ethnic distinctions. Such actions trigger "strict scrutiny," a stringent form of court review that requires the government to justify its distinctions by showing that they are "narrowly tailored," or "necessary," to further a "compelling government interest." There is no question that protecting citizens from terrorism is a compelling government interest, but so too is drug interdiction—in fact, all criminal law enforcement would likely be viewed as a compelling state interest.

The critical question from a constitutional perspective is whether the means adopted are necessary to further that interest. It is highly unlikely that profiling could satisfy that scrutiny. First, the vast majority of persons who appear Arab and Muslim—probably well over 99.9 percent—have no involvement with terrorism. Arab and Muslim identity or appearance, in other words, is a terribly inaccurate proxy for terrorism, as the results described above show. In the sex discrimination context, where the Supreme Court applies less stringent scrutiny than it does to ethnic or racial discrimination, the Court held that statistics showing that 2 percent of young men between the ages of eighteen and twenty-one had been arrested for drunk driving did not justify denying men of that age the right to purchase an alcoholic beverage.[5] By that measure, ethnic profiling since 9/11 certainly cannot be justified.

Second, the use of ethnic stereotypes is certainly not "necessary" to effective antiterrorism law enforcement. In fact, it is likely to produce bad law enforcement. When agents treat a whole group of people as presumptively suspicious, they are more likely to miss dangerous persons who do not fit the profile. Profiling, in other words, can lead to lazy policing. In addition, the fact that the vast majority of those suspected on the basis of their Arab or Muslim appearance will be innocent will inevitably induce agents to let their guard down.[6] Overbroad generalizations, in other words, are problematic not only because they constitute an unjustified imposition on innocents, but because they are poor law enforcement tools.

Profiling undermines effective law enforcement in still another way. It is virtually certain to alienate members of the targeted communities. Studies of policing have shown that it is far more effective to work with communities than against them. Where a community trusts law enforcement, people are more likely to obey the law, and more likely to cooperate with the police in identifying and bringing to justice wrongdoers in their midst. If the government has reason to believe that there are potential terrorist threats within Arab and Muslim communities in the United States, it should be seeking ways to work with the millions of law-abiding members of those communities to help identify the true threats, not treating entire communities as suspect. Moreover, the effects of alienation extend beyond our borders. The foreign press, especially in the Arab and Muslim world, is highly sensitive to U.S. initiatives that appear to target Arabs and Muslims unfairly, and reporting on such initiatives receives widespread attention outside the United States, throughout the Arab and Muslim world. That in turn contributes to the unprecedented levels of anti-Americanism now evident worldwide, making it less likely that we will get the cooperation we need on the international front and more likely that al Qaeda and others will find willing recruits to their cause against us. So the costs of ethnic profiling are substantial, and the gains, at least thus far, are minimal at best.

The government's defense to charges of ethnic profiling has been to claim that it is relying on nationality, not ethnicity. It did not call in all Arabs and Muslims, regardless of nationality, but only foreign nationals from countries whose populations are predominantly Arab and Muslim. Thus, American citizens of Arab descent or Muslim faith were not required to register, and some of the foreign nationals from predominantly Arab and Muslim countries who were required to register were not Arab or Muslim. In the immigration area, the courts have long permitted the government to treat people differently based on their nationality, without requiring any special justification or defense. Here, however, the use of nationality seemed but a pretext for targeting as many Arabs and Muslims as could be targeted without triggering a constitutional challenge. A more candid defense would have acknowledged this fact and sought to justify ethnic profiling on the merits. But that defense never came.

The ethnic profiling issue is complicated further by the fact that some reliance on ethnicity was probably permissible in the immediate wake of the September 11 attacks. When a bank reports a robbery, and describes the robbers as three white men wearing blue shirts, the police can rely on race in seeking to identify and catch the suspects. In that setting, the use of race does not derive from negative stereotypes, but is simply an identifying marker, like the fact that the robbers were wearing blue shirts. Moreover, as one of the few identifying characteristics, reliance on race in that setting is narrowly tailored to the compelling interest of catching the robbers.

Ethnic or racial profiling, by contrast, consists of reliance on race as a generalization about future behavior—the assumption that because an individual is black, he is more likely to rob a bank. Such reliance on generalizations is generally impermissible, whereas reliance on race as an identifying criterion for a specific crime that has occurred is usually allowed.

In the aftermath of September 11, it was often difficult to separate out these two uses of ethnicity. If law enforcement agents had reason to believe that there were others involved in the planning and carrying out of the attacks or that the hijackers' associates might have been planning further attacks, and that these others were likely to be Arab or Muslim men given the makeup of al Qaeda and the hijackers themselves, then relying on ethnic criteria to seek to identify the guilty parties may have been warranted.

However, to the extent that law enforcement agents rely on ethnicity as a predictor of future behavior, they are using impermissible generalizations. Where the perpetrators are thought to be planning future attacks, the distinction between an identifying criterion and a prospective generalization is particularly difficult to draw. Therefore, where ethnicity is being accorded a dominant role in investigative activities, two other factors become very important. First, the use of an ethnic identifying factor becomes more objectionable when it is applied on a nationwide basis over an extended period of time. It is one thing to say that the police, having only the information that three white men robbed a bank, can stop and question all white men *in the vicinity of the bank* immediately after the robbery. It would be another matter for the police to stop and interview white males nationwide for months or years afterward. Yet the latter is much closer to what this administration has done.

Second, when the government relies on ethnic identifying characteristics, it is critical that it act quickly to resolve its suspicions and to determine whether other nonethnic factors justify or disprove its selection of certain people for scrutiny. What is particularly trou-bling about the government's response to September 11 is that gov-ernment officials have seemed determined to apply ethnic profiling on a nationwide, seemingly arbitrary basis, and have failed to re-solve promptly their selection of certain individuals for the worst form of ethnicity-based action: detention without serious criminal charges.

Facing substantial protest and little positive results, the govern-ment eventually suspended its special registration program. But it continues to engage in a less formal but no less real campaign of tar-geting Arabs and Muslims. And when the Bush administration is-sued a policy memorandum in 2003 barring federal officials from engaging in racial profiling for ordinary law enforcement purposes, it crafted an explicit exception, maintaining that ethnic profiling was permissible for border control and national security purposes.[7] So despite its initial disclaimers, the federal government has contin-ued to engage in a widespread campaign of ethnic profiling.


## DATA MINING

A second tactic for sweeping broadly in the interest of prevention involves the use of computers to collect, collate, and analyze infor-mation in search of patterns of suspicious behavior. Technological developments have made such efforts more feasible, and post–9/11 security demands have created incentives for private companies and government agencies to develop and implement such programs. These developments pose new and important questions about the proper balance between privacy and security.

There is no question that information technology offers impor-tant tools to the government in fighting terrorism. One of the salient failures of the intelligence agencies in the months leading up to the September 11 attacks was their inability to analyze and share information they had collected about the intentions and operations of al Qaeda. The challenge is to adapt the power of computer technologies to improve intelligence collection, sharing, and analysis without creating a surveillance state. The preservation of privacy is especially difficult in the digital age, when the innocent activities of everyday life generate digital records that can easily be recorded, collected, and "mined" for meaning.

Even before September 11, the federal government was researching, and in some cases already implementing, new ways to use the vast databases of personal information routinely maintained in public and private domains. Since 2001, this process has accelerated. The information available in private databases ranges from insurance, travel, and financial data, to records of retail purchases, to information compiled from disparate governmental records such as court papers, licenses, and property records. Computers have vastly expanded the depth and breadth of personally identifiable information available in government and commercial databases, and have simultaneously provided the tools to analyze such data and draw from them patterns, inferences, and knowledge. By and large, the rules for the government's use of databases for counterterrorism purposes are fragmentary and unresponsive to the new kinds of screening applications that are being developed.[8]

Some of the issues surrounding database analysis were brought to the fore in late 2002 and early 2003, thanks to news reports and commentary about the Total Information Awareness (TIA) program, conducted under the auspices of the Pentagon.[9] According to John Poindexter, head of TIA, the technological capabilities being developed by TIA were intended to search "for indications of terrorist activities in vast quantities of transaction data" generated in everyday life. In the fall of 2003, after substantial public objections were voiced, Congress cut off funding for TIA research, giving the impression that the government had retreated from the use of commercial data.[10] To the contrary, various other government agencies continue to explore the use of commercial sector data for counterterrorism and other law enforcement and intelligence purposes, and the private sector continues to develop and offer the government services and systems based upon the aggregation and analysis of personally identifiable information.[11] For example, through the Computer Assisted Passenger Prescreening System II (CAPPS II) project, the Transportation Security Administration (TSA) proposed to rely on commercial databases as well as intelligence, law enforcement, immigration, and other governmental databases to assign airline passengers a risk score to determine whether to permit them to board their flights or to subject them to more intensive screening.[12] Facing substantial popular and congressional criticism, TSA replaced CAPPS II with a narrower program known as Secure Flight, the details of which were still being developed in October 2005.[13]

The Justice Department's Foreign Terrorism Tracking Task Force has announced that it is employing "risk modeling algorithms, link analysis, historic review of past patterns of behavior, and other factors to distinguish persons who may pose a risk of terrorism from those who do not."[14] Changes to the attorney general guidelines in 2002 expressly gave the Federal Bureau of Investigation authority to engage in "data mining."[15] The FBI and other government agencies have entered into contracts with data warehousing companies.[16] The Information Analysis and Infrastructure Protection directorate at the Department of Homeland Security received congressional authorization to use "data mining" technology.[17] In May 2003, the Terrorist Threat Integration Center commenced operations with a mandate to analyze the full breadth of intelligence information, making it an almost certain candidate for the use of pattern-analysis technology. Other preexisting data mining efforts have expanded. The Financial Crimes Enforcement Network (FinCEN) relies on pattern-based searches to try to identify from among all large money transfers the few that involve wrongdoing, whether terrorist financing or ordinary money laundering.[18] And state and local governments explored the use of aggregated commercial and governmental data in a DHS- and DOJ-funded system known as the Multistate Anti-Terrorism Regional Information Exchange System (MATRIX).

There are few existing legal constraints on government access to commercial databases for counterterrorism purposes.[19] The Supreme Court has interpreted the Fourth Amendment right of privacy not to apply to information shared with a third party, such as a credit card company or Internet service provider, so long as the government obtains that information from the third party. Accordingly, there are few meaningful constitutional limits on government access to and use of such data. Thus, if there is to be protection it must be found in federal statutes. But the United States has no comprehensive privacy law for commercial data, so a great deal of information is available to law enforcement and intelligence agencies through voluntary disclosure or for purchase from data aggregators. The privacy laws that do exist for specific categories of records (credit, medical, financial) are riddled with exceptions of varying breadth that allow access to and sharing of data for law enforcement or intelligence purposes. All the privacy laws include exceptions for access pursuant to grand jury subpoena.[20] And under the Patriot Act, as explained in Chapter 13, the FBI acquired broad authority to issue national security letters (NSLs) or obtain court orders compelling the disclosure of data from commercial entities for intelligence investigations of international terrorism. Once the government obtains commercial data for counterterrorism purposes, there are no effective constraints on further disclosure to other agencies for counterterrorism purposes.

Government use of personally identifiable data poses a range of significant risks. Some risks involve unintentional mistakes, such as may arise in the case of mistaken identity. Sometimes when information is used to make judgments about people, a person will be misidentified as a criminal or a suspected terrorist when in fact he is innocent but shares some identifiers with someone who is of interest to the government. Thus, in 2004, as a result of the program to match airline passenger lists with a terrorist watch list, Senator Edward Kennedy was informed that he was on a no-fly list, presumably because he shared a name with an Irish suspected terrorist on the list. This has proved to be a recurring problem with watch lists.[21] Even when identity itself is not mistaken, mistakes may be made in the inferences drawn from the data, leading to the targeting of many people who pose no real security threat.[22]

A second kind of risk involves intentional abuse. Government employees have used authorized access to personal information for unauthorized purposes—for example, an employee of an intelligence or law enforcement agency may perform checks for a fee for private investigators, transferring the information to an unauthorized and possibly uncontrolled use.[23] But potential abuse need not be limited to acts of unscrupulous government agents—through poor security practices, information in the hands of government agencies or their contractors can be stolen or carelessly disclosed.[24]

A third risk is mission creep. Government information systems justified in the name of fighting international terrorism may be turned to more ordinary criminal justice or administrative purposes, further expanding the government's control over individuals. Data mining may seem warranted for particularly serious crimes, but once such practices are in place, there will likely be considerable pressure to extend their application to all law enforcement.

Finally, data mining poses a substantial risk of chilling innocent citizens' lawful behavior. Citizens who feel that they are or may be under generalized surveillance are likely to have reduced trust in government and less willingness to participate even in lawful activities, whether it be attending political demonstrations, joining political groups, taking firearms training, or enrolling in pilot school.

All of these dangers are to some degree inherent in police and intelligence work, but it is necessary to give them extra attention in light of the power of computer technology. The potential today for abuse far exceeds anything that was possible in the era of paper records.[25] The data revolution is taking us into uncharted territory. How will the government use intelligence generated by computerized analysis of commercial and governmental data? Could the data analysis trigger a criminal or intelligence investigation? Will it be used to build a criminal case? (Once a criminal investigation proceeds to the stage of search and seizure or arrest, traditional probable cause protections come into play.) Will it be used to place someone on a watch list? Will it be used for screening purposes—to trigger a more intensive search of someone seeking to board an airplane, to keep a person off an airplane, to deny a person access to a government building, to deny a person a job?

Even the sharing of information collected for law enforcement and antiterrorism purposes poses challenges. In December 2004, Congress adopted and the president signed the Intelligence Reform and Terrorism Prevention Act of 2004, implementing many of the recommendations of the National Commission on Terrorist Attacks upon the United States (the "9/11 Commission"). Section 1016 of the Act requires the president to create an "information sharing environment" for the sharing of terrorism information among all appropriate federal, state, local, and tribal entities, and the private sector. The ISE, as the information sharing environment is known, is supposed to emerge from a combination of policy guidelines and technologies. The Act requires the president to designate the organizational and management structures that will be used to operate and manage the ISE, and to determine and enforce the policies, directives, and rules that will govern the content and usage of the ISE. The ISE is intended to: (1) provide the functional equivalent of a decentralized, distributed, and coordinated environment that connects existing systems and allows users to share information among agencies, between levels of government, and, as appropriate, with the private sector; (2) ensure direct and continuous online electronic access to information; and (3) facilitate the availability of information for use in analysis, investigations, and operations. The Act requires the ISE to incorporate mechanisms to protect privacy and civil liberties and to enhance accountability, including audits, authentication, and access controls. The president must appoint a Privacy and Civil Liberties Oversight Board and, in consultation with that board, issue guidelines that protect privacy and civil liberties in the development and use of the ISE. The requirements in Section 1016 of the intelligence reform law overlap with a series of executive orders and homeland security directives that the president issued in August 2004.

Much remains to be developed in the area of information sharing, and nowhere is it more true that the devil is in the details. What is clear is that the government is entering a new phase in the collection, sharing, and analysis of personally identifiable information. As of October 2005, the rules for this environment were largely unwritten. In the absence of clear-cut privacy rules, Congress did create some potentially important oversight mechanisms. The legislation creating the Department of Homeland Security established both a Privacy Officer and a Civil Rights and Civil Liberties Officer for the new department, charged with helping set policy and investigating complaints of abuse. Privacy officers can force attention to privacy issues internally before those issues escalate into scandals, and they can help ensure that existing laws are followed. The intelligence reform law also included a sense of Congress provision stating that other agencies with law enforcement or counterterrorism responsibilities should designate privacy officers. And the FY 2005 omnibus appropriations act included a provision requiring privacy officers in all departments and agencies.[26] The intelligence reform bill also required the Transportation Security Administration to create redress procedures for airline passenger screening. The E-Government Act of 2002 included provisions requiring government agencies to conduct privacy impact assessments whenever they initiate new collections of data; notably, the provision applies to national security and intelligence systems. Taken together, these measures could help mitigate privacy invasions, although important questions of enforcement and individual redress remain unanswered.

## ASSESSING EFFECTIVENESS

Have the administration's initiatives—from preventive detention to ethnic profiling to data mining—made the nation safer? This is not an easy question to answer, for it is possible that some of these initiatives have deterred would-be terrorists from even attempting attacks, and it is possible that other initiatives have incapacitated would-be terrorists on nonterrorist grounds before they were able to act. But those "results" are essentially unknowable. The tangible record, meanwhile, raises serious questions about the effectiveness of many of the measures adopted in the wake of 9/11. Thankfully, there has not been a terrorist attack on U.S. soil in the nearly four years since September 11, 2001. But the record offers little basis to give credit to the domestic war on terrorism.

As noted above, the administration's record with respect to its preventive detention campaign directed at foreign nationals is 0 for 5,000. The Justice Department boasts that its terrorism investigations have led to more than 300 criminal indictments, over 100 convictions, and over 500 deportation orders. But the convictions are virtually all for minor charges, *not* terrorism. The Transactional Records Access Clearinghouse of Syracuse University found that the median sentence actually handed down in cases labeled "terrorist" by the Justice Department in the first two years after 9/11 was fourteen days. And under the department's policy of not deporting individuals until they were cleared of any connection to terrorism, the 500 deportations are misses, not hits, in terms of identifying actual terrorists.

The government has brought a number of terrorism prosecutions since 9/11, each one generally announced with much fanfare in a national news conference, often featuring the attorney general himself. But few of the government's indictments charge actual terrorism. The vast majority charge only "material support" to a group the government has labeled terrorist, under a statute that criminalizes such support whether or not it has any connection to furthering a terrorist act. While the government has obtained convictions or guilty pleas in several such cases, none of the defendants has been charged with engaging in terrorist activity.

Some of the government's most prominent cases have disintegrated under close scrutiny. Captain James Yee, a Muslim chaplain at Guantánamo, was charged with taking classified information off base—but all charges were dismissed when it could not be established that any of the information was indeed classified. The government was also compelled to drop most of its charges against Ahmad Al Halabi, a translator from Guantánamo whom the government also initially charged as a spy. The government prosecuted Sami al-Hussayen, a Saudi Arabian student at the University of Idaho, for material support to a terrorist group, but when the evidence showed that all he had done was run a website with links to other websites—pure speech—a jury acquitted him of all terrorism charges. Brandon Mayfield, a Muslim lawyer, was arrested on assertions that his fingerprints had been found at the scene of the March 2004 Madrid bombing, only to be released a month later when the FBI admitted the fingerprints were not Mayfield's after all.

The government declared Yaser Hamdi a dangerous "enemy," and claimed that even allowing him access to a lawyer would undermine national security. But when the Supreme Court ruled against the government and required that it give Hamdi a fair hearing, the government quickly folded and let Hamdi go, subject only to the conditions that he give up his U.S. citizenship and make a wholly unenforceable promise that he never leave Saudi Arabia.[27]

The government charged Seattle-based black activist James Ujaama with conspiring to run a terrorist training camp in Nevada but ended up dropping all terrorism charges for a plea that Ujaama had made a humanitarian donation to the Taliban in violation of an economic embargo. And the government's first conviction for terrorism in a post–9/11 case was thrown out on a showing that the prosecutor had failed to disclose that its principal witness had lied on the stand.[28]

Much of this strategy was predicated on the supposition that there were al Qaeda terror cells in the United States. But three and a half years later, the Justice Department has not identified a single such cell. ABC News reported that a secret FBI memo from February 2005 admitted that the FBI had yet to identify a single al Qaeda sleeper cell in the United States.[29]

The only criminal conviction involving an actual terrorist incident since September 11 is that of shoe bomber Richard Reid, and he was captured not through any investigative work by the FBI, DHS, or Justice Department, but simply because an alert airline employee noticed a strange-looking man trying to light his shoe on fire.

So at the end of the day, the war on terrorism, at least at home, has netted almost no actual terrorists. At the same time, these policies have contributed to widespread distrust of law enforcement within the Arab and Muslim communities here, and unprecedented anti-Americanism abroad. The perception and reality that the administration has unfairly targeted innocent Arabs and Muslims, and has disregarded fundamental principles of the rule of law in doing so, has fueled resentment here and abroad. In the long run, that resentment is the gravest threat to our national security.


## CONCLUSION

We must respond vigorously to the new terrorist threat, but in doing so we must ensure that our responses are measured, balanced, and effective. Judged by these standards, is the quality of our intelligence improved by abusing and humiliating detainees hastily arrested at home or abroad? Is our antiterrorism effort improved by making deportable anyone who provides humanitarian aid to any organization engaged in a civil war? Is it effective or balanced to enact laws that allow the attorney general to label every domestic dispute or barroom fight with a weapon by an immigrant an act of terrorism? Are we made more secure by subjecting anyone suspected of such activity to mandatory detention, without any showing that he poses any current danger? Is it necessary to try immigrants in secret, and to hold them in detention even after judges have ordered their release? Is it measured to deny visas for the mere expression of ideas we dislike? Is it balanced to authorize wiretaps and searches in criminal investigations without probable cause of a crime, or to allow evidence acquired that way to be admitted into a criminal case without offering the defendant the normal right to challenge its legality? Have we taken a measured approach to the threats we face when we allow secret searches in cases having nothing to do with terrorism? Is it effective to authorize the government to engage in fishing expeditions with no particularized suspicion that the vast quantities of data being swept in have any connection to persons suspected of engaging in terrorism? Is it appropriate to engage in profiling based on the color of one's skin? Is it fair to detain haphazardly thousands of people in the name of terrorism when none can be convicted of a terrorist crime? And is it measured, balanced, and effective to assert unilateral presidential authority to lock up any human being anywhere in the world on the president's say-so, while rebuffing all attempts to provide meaningful judicial review?

We agree that the government needs strong tools to fight the war on terrorism, but such powers should be subject to strong safeguards. The FBI should be able to carry out roving taps during intelligence investigations of terrorism, just as it has long been able to do in criminal investigations of terrorism. But the Patriot Act standard for roving taps in intelligence cases lacks important procedural protections applicable in criminal cases. The law should allow the government to intercept transactional data about Internet communications (something the government was doing before the Patriot Act). But the standard for pen registers and trap-and-trace devices for both Internet communications and telephones is so low that judges are reduced to mere rubber stamps, with no authority even to consider the factual basis for a surveillance application. Prosecutors should be allowed to use FISA evidence in criminal cases (they did so on many occasions before the Patriot Act) and to coordinate intelligence and criminal investigations (there was no legal bar to doing so before the Patriot Act). But FISA evidence in criminal cases should be subject to the same due process protections that apply to other evidence.

Prior to 9/11, the government had awesome powers, but failed to use them well. The intelligence failures leading up to 9/11 had little to do with the rules protecting privacy or due process, but since 9/11 the executive branch has proceeded as if the elimination of checks and balances would make its efforts more effective. The lessons of history and the experience of the past four years show that law enforcement and intelligence agencies without clear standards to guide them and without oversight and accountability are more likely to engage in unfocused, unproductive activity and more likely to make mistakes.

It is too early to judge how the United States as a country will in the long run react to the new threat of terrorism. The real test may come after the next round of attacks, and after the attacks that follow that. But our early responses unfortunately reflect the pattern of overreaction that we have so often seen in the past. Many of the expansive authorities that have been granted or assumed are neither necessary nor likely to make us more safe. To the contrary, by penalizing even wholly lawful and nonviolent associational activity, sacrificing fundamental commitments to the rule of law, and unjustly targeting Arabs and Muslims who have no connection to terrorism, we have wasted valuable resources, encouraged extremists, and made the communities targeted by such broad-brush measures less likely to cooperate with law enforcement. As Justice Louis Brandeis wrote more than seventy-five years ago, the framers of our Constitution knew that "fear breeds repression; that repression breeds hate; and that hate menaces stable government."[30] Never have those words had more salience than today, as the world has turned from widespread sympathy for the United States to unprecedented anti-Americanism, largely in reaction to the repressive measures that our government has adopted in the war on terrorism.

# 15

# Conclusion

In times of crisis, the Government will exercise its power to conduct domestic intelligence activities to the fullest extent. The distinction between legal dissent and criminal conduct is easily forgotten. Our job is to recommend means to help ensure that the distinction will always be observed.[1]

As September 11 dramatically demonstrated, the United States faces a real terrorist threat from abroad. At the same time, however, the United States itself has not been a fertile breeding ground for homegrown terrorism. This may well be because values central to our system of democratic governance make it difficult to nurture within this country the ideological, ethnic, or religious hatred that fuels much terrorism. These values include appreciation of diversity and religious and ethnic tolerance, reflected in our repeated absorption of large influxes of immigrants. They also include constitutional limits on government powers, checks and balances, access to government information, accountability of public officials, and due process accorded in judicial proceedings open to public scrutiny, all of which increase public confidence in government. Perhaps most important is our strong protection for political freedoms of speech and association, with a nearly unlimited right to criticize government and government officials, and a nearly insurmountable presumption against prior censorship, assuring the disaffected that their concerns can be heard without violence.

Unfortunately, much of our official response to the threat of terrorism is incompatible with these core civil liberties values. The 1996 Antiterrorism Act, for example, deems people guilty not on the basis of what they have done, but on the basis of the groups with which they are associated. It denies one of the most fundamental elements of due process—the right to confront one's accusers in open court. And measures taken after September 11 have similarly threatened basic values—criminalizing speech, imposing guilt by association, conducting trials in secret, engaging in ethnic profiling, and intruding on the privacy of innocent persons. The question is whether we can respond effectively to the new threat of terrorism without jeopardizing the very freedoms that have contributed to our security at home.


## THE FALSE TRADE-OFF—CURTAILING LIBERTY WILL NOT NECESSARILY ENHANCE SECURITY

In the ongoing debate over responding to terrorism, many argue that civil liberties must be sacrificed in order to ensure the safety of our democratic way of life. Something unique about the threat of terrorism, it is argued, requires us to alter the constitutional balance we have long struck between government power and personal freedoms. The premise of this argument—so unquestioningly accepted that it often goes unstated—is that antiterrorism measures infringing civil liberties will work. While there are often difficult trade-offs to be made between liberty and security, it does not follow that sacrificing liberties will always, or even generally, promote security.

Efficacy, of course, does not determine the outcome of the constitutional debate. Even if a police state were efficient, it would not reflect our fundamental values. But many of the rights we have discussed in this book actually promote governmental efficacy in defending the common good. We guarantee the right to confront one's accusers, for example, not only as an element of human dignity but also because we know that cross-examination is an effective engine of truth. Relying on untested evidence not only risks convicting the innocent, but it also means that the search for the truly guilty party may be called off prematurely. We subject executive decisions to judicial review not only because the judicial system gives a voice to individuals but also because we know that the adversarial process can produce a fuller factual record, exposing faulty assumptions, and because deliberative review by life-tenured judges can protect against the rash decisions resulting from the pressures felt by elected officials. We reject guilt by association not only to protect political freedom, but also because a system that holds individuals responsible for their own actions is more closely tailored to deterring crime. We protect freedom of speech not only because it allows room for personal self-expression, but also because the availability of channels for peaceful change promotes stability. We have more to fear from the pressure cooker of repressed dissatisfaction than from the cacophony of dissent. For these reasons, many of the counterterrorism measures that we have criticized are not only unconstitutional, but are also likely to be counterproductive.

Curtailing civil liberties does not necessarily promote national security. In COINTELPRO, the FBI experimented with the massive monitoring of political dissent. It failed to produce any substantial evidence of violent conduct, suggesting that politics is a poor guide and extensive monitoring an ineffective strategy for counterterrorism investigations. Other more recent examples here and abroad have shown that racial and ethnic stereotyping is also a poor basis for security policy. The assassin of Yitzhak Rabin escaped detection because the prime minister's bodyguards were on the lookout for Arab assailants. If police had listened only to those who claimed that the Oklahoma City bombing bore the trademarks of

Muslim fundamentalists, they might not have captured Timothy McVeigh as he fled from the crime.

Violations of civil liberties often "work" only in a narrow sense: random or door-to-door searches will uncover contraband in some houses, and torture of arrestees will induce some to provide truthful evidence of wrongdoing, including evidence that may allow the prevention of violent attacks. But these "successes" must be balanced against the wasted resources consumed by fruitless random searches and generalized monitoring of groups or movements, the mistakes caused by reliance on faulty coerced confessions, and, most importantly, the tremendous loss of trust in government (and the consequent shutting off of voluntary cooperation) generated by unfocused investigations and the harassment of communities on the basis of stereotypes. On balance, even measured only in terms of effectiveness, there is little evidence that curtailing civil liberties will do more good than harm.[2]

## IMPLICATIONS OF A NEW, MORE DANGEROUS TERRORISM

In every age, dangers can be cited that make limitations on intelligence operations seem imprudent—threats of such an urgent and unique nature that it seems necessary to expand government powers, at least long enough to turn back the new threat. Today's proponents of expanding government power to fight terrorism argue that the terrorist threat now is qualitatively different than in the past. September 11 certainly gave these arguments added weight.

But the heightened risk of terrorism simply means that the consequences of failing to adopt a sound antiterrorism policy are more serious than ever before. It does not tell us what policy to adopt.

Indeed, aspects of the new threat of terrorism point in quite different directions. Before adopting measures that curtail personal freedom, it might be more effective to address the highly destructive products that pose such serious risk to life. The United States and its allies have not done nearly enough to gain control of the nuclear materials of the former Soviet Union, a project that probably would mean far more to national security than curtailing civil liberties. Lethal biological and chemical materials are widely produced and are subject to inadequate controls. A program of stringent federal regulation of anthrax would have no civil liberties implications, but could meaningfully restrict access to such products by both the malevolent and the merely careless.

It is also clear that not nearly enough was done with investigative and protective authorities that existed before the 1996 and 2001 Acts and that had little to do with intrusions on political freedoms. For example, prior to September 11 there were repeated warnings about poor airport security. Documents disclosed by the *New York Times* in January 1999 showed that explosives and guns avoided detection in government tests of airline security, due largely to lax practices on the part of screening personnel.[3] Similarly, it became clear following the embassy bombings in Africa that Washington officials were largely unresponsive to the intense, well-founded, and forcefully expressed concerns of the American ambassador to Kenya, who warned repeatedly that the embassy was insufficiently protected against terrorist attack. Indeed, the CIA repeatedly told the State Department that there was an active terrorist group in Kenya connected to Osama bin Laden, since accused of masterminding the bombings there and in Tanzania.[4]

Despite the wartime rhetoric of stamping out terrorism everywhere, the terrorist threat will never be eliminated. We must develop sound responses. But in doing so, we should be careful not to sacrifice the fundamental principles that characterize our democratic identity. The better course is to adhere to our liberal principles, to use the criminal laws to punish those who plan or carry out violent acts, and to invite critics of our government into the practice of democracy and tolerance.

## REFORMING FBI COUNTERTERRORISM ACTIVITIES

The principles guiding FBI counterterrorism activities were laid down more than fifty years ago, before World War II, and were codified more than twenty-five years ago, while the Cold War was still under way. At that time, the main national security threat was the Soviet Union, which was understood to be conducting a worldwide campaign against the United States through clandestine means and covert proxies.

At the beginning of the Cold War, the criminal law was thought to be of little relevance to this struggle. The foreign agents conducting or directing hostile actions against the United States were often operating under diplomatic immunity. It was assumed that criminal prosecution would reveal too much classified information, compromising continued counterintelligence efforts. Even with respect to United States citizens suspected of spying in the United States, the presumption was against criminal prosecution. Clandestine disruptive actions and double agent operations were justified as the best means of preventing damage to U.S. interests, on the ground that the criminal law was not available.

Major changes over the last two decades have upset many of the assumptions on which FBI national security activities were founded. The Soviet Union has disintegrated. Human rights protection has emerged as a leading principle of U.S. foreign policy (at least in theory). International law has undergone revolutionary change, to the point where the United States now has at its disposal a range of international sanctions to punish state sponsors of terrorism.

Most importantly, criminal law has assumed a primacy in national security policy. It is now routine to arrest and prosecute suspected spies, through trials in which all of the government's evidence is presented publicly and subject to cross-examination. The Classified Information Procedures Act makes such public prosecutions less risky to ongoing operations, while preserving defendants' rights to confront the evidence against them. U.S. criminal law has been given wide extraterritorial effect, reaching almost any attack anywhere in the world against an American citizen, U.S. government property, or property owned by U.S. corporations. International cooperation in the field of criminal law makes it more likely than ever that terrorism can be dealt with through arrest and prosecution in U.S. courts.

A revised view of intelligence is also demanded by another change: The United States, always a diverse society, has become even more so. Consider just religious diversity. There are 3,000 religious denominations and sects in the United States today. Not only are there more Muslims than Episcopalians in the United States, but there is a diversity within this diversity that defies common assumptions. For example, contrary to popular perception, most Muslims in the United States are not of Arab origin and most persons of Arab descent in the United States are not Muslims.

In the face of such diversity, principles of pluralism, tolerance of dissent, and individual rather than group culpability should guide the development of national security, intelligence, and counterterrorism policy. The alternative is a stereotyping that can ossify or mislead the investigative focus. While the FBI was conducting an intensive investigation of the PLO-affiliated PFLP in the 1980s and 1990s, the U.S. government was promoting the signing of an

Israeli-PLO peace accord, and the focus of terrorism concern in the Middle East shifted to anti-PLO Muslim fundamentalists. As soon as the FBI launched a massive campaign against Muslim fundamentalists in the wake of the World Trade Center bombing, the Murrah building in Oklahoma City was blown up by white, native-born ex-GIs. And while the FBI and the INS pursued innocent Arab and Muslim political activists, terrorists careful to avoid any showing of religious or political orientation planned and carried out the September 11 attacks.

## INTELLIGENCE IN A DEMOCRATIC SOCIETY

Improving "intelligence" is obviously a critical factor in preventing future terrorist attacks. Some advocate the clandestine collection, without particular suspicion of wrongdoing, of large quantities of information, the immediate relevance of which may not be clear, in order to piece together a mosaic that might help policy makers anticipate actions of potential adversaries. The tools of this type of intelligence include monitoring of political, ethnic, or religious groups, electronic surveillance without focus on illegal conduct, and the sifting without individualized suspicion of vast databases of information on innocuous transactions. Much of the information generated by these means is inconclusive or unreliable; rarely is it ever subjected to the testing of the adversarial process; and all too often the collection of it intrudes on privacy, due process, or protected political activity.

Inside the United States, we favor another vision of intelligence, one rooted in the concepts of the criminal law. "Intelligence" in this context means the collection and analysis of information about a criminal enterprise that goes beyond what is necessary to solve a particular crime. Intelligence of this type is intended to aid law enforcement agencies in drawing a fuller picture of the enterprise. It allows the government to identify the silent partners, those who provide money for violent attacks or issue the commands. Intelligence allows investigators to link seemingly disparate crimes into a pattern. At its best, intelligence allows the government to anticipate and prevent a group's next dangerous crime, thereby saving lives.

The FBI routinely conducts "intelligence" operations of this second type against organized crime families and drug cartels. It does so subject to the ordinary rules of criminal procedure. The goal of such investigations is to arrest the leaders and to put them on trial for specific crimes. And one of the most important constraints on such criminal intelligence is the public trial—everything done in the name of criminal intelligence must ultimately bear scrutiny in a court of law.

The concept of criminal intelligence can be fully compatible with the Constitution. The First Amendment does not require the FBI to be deaf when someone advocates violence. The Constitution does not require the government to wait until a bomb goes off or even to wait until a bomb factory is brought to its attention—it does, however, require the FBI to focus its investigations on the interdiction of violence and other criminal conduct. Too often, the FBI has not limited itself to uncovering evidence of a crime, but instead has conducted lengthy investigations that consist of routine monitoring and disrupting of lawful political activities.

We live in a world of political, ethnic, and religious violence. There will undoubtedly be more acts of terrorism both here and overseas against U.S. targets. It is incumbent on those who criticize current counterterrorism policies to say how they would go about addressing the threat of terrorism. We believe that an effective counterterrorism policy can be implemented in this country based on traditional criminal procedures directed at crimes of violence, including intelligence gathering aimed at preventing terrorist acts before they occur.[5]

The FBI is at its best when it does criminal investigations. It is at its worst when it acts in a counterintelligence, monitoring mode, secretly pursuing an ethnically, religiously, or ideologically defined target without the constraints and focus of the criminal code and without the expectation that its actions will be subjected to scrutiny in the adversarial context of a public criminal trial.

Counterterrorism investigations should investigate terrorist acts as crimes, regardless of their political motivation. Murder, kidnapping, or bank robbery by terrorists, even murder on a mass scale, is most effectively investigated using the same techniques that are applied to murder, kidnapping, and bank robbery by nonterrorists. By and large, this was the FBI's focus under the Levi domestic security guidelines. The focus on criminal activity was also for some years a central feature of U.S. policy against terrorism abroad. In the 1980s, a major component of the policy was the extension of extraterritorial jurisdiction over crimes of violence committed by terrorists against Americans abroad, so that terrorists could be extradited to the United States to be tried here.

Indeed, the United States has continued to pursue this approach, in tandem with the broader monitoring approach reflected in the 1996 and 2001 antiterrorism laws. Federal prosecutors in New York sucessfully prosecuted al Qaeda members who carried out the African embassy bombings. If a criminal trial is possible against the hierarchy of entire organized crime families, it is also possible against those members of terrorist organizations who are engaged in carrying out or directly supporting violent activities, at least in situations short of war. In the case of a group having both legitimate and illegitimate activities, the focus should be on identifying and prosecuting all those responsible for the illegal activities, not penalizing innocent support of lawful conduct.

To reform FBI counterterrorism policies and avoid repetitions of CISPES-type cases, it is necessary to redraw the lines between criminal investigations and foreign counterintelligence investigations. Overbroad intelligence monitoring is a diversion from the harder work of identifying real terrorists. The CISPES case after it closed was seen inside and outside the FBI as a waste of resources. Counterintelligence monitoring displaced the search for evidence of crimes. Even though the FBI had an allegation that CISPES was planning terrorist attacks in Dallas, the investigation never actually had as its goal a resolution of that allegation. In the few instances in which the FBI received information concerning other possible violent activity by specific CISPES chapters, agents failed to pursue those allegations. Instead, agents devoted their efforts to identifying all CISPES chapters throughout the United States and monitoring clearly legal activities. If members of CISPES had actually been planning terrorist activity, the investigation conducted by the FBI was not likely to have uncovered it. In the case of those convicted of the first World Trade Center bombing, some of whom were the subject of a counterintelligence investigation prior to the bombing, a similar adherence to the monitoring approach may have contributed to the FBI's failure to pursue the case to an earlier resolution, which could have prevented the 1993 attack.

All antiterrorism investigations in the United States, whether of foreign or domestic groups, should be conducted pursuant to criminal rules, with the goal of arresting people who are planning, supporting, or carrying out violent activities and convicting them in a court of law. Law enforcement must stop framing terrorism investigations in political, religious, or ethnic terms. The FBI still classifies its investigations as "environmental terrorism" ("eco-terrorism") or

"Islamic fundamentalist terrorism" or "Puerto Rican terrorism." This only reinforces the notion that the Bureau's role is to monitor politics or to target its efforts based on religion or ethnicity rather than to investigate crime. Instead, once a politically motivated group advocating violence is identified, the goal of the investigation should be to identify those engaged in the criminal enterprise, not to identify those who merely share the ideology.

Such a counterterrorism program would, in many respects, be the exact opposite of what was reflected in the Antiterrorism Act of 1996 and the Patriot Act of 2001. Where those Acts empowered the FBI to investigate a new, broadly defined offense of "support for terrorism," we would propose express legislative limits on the government's discretion to investigate and prosecute First Amendment activities. Where those Acts expanded the concept of support for terrorism to include support for the political and humanitarian activities of groups that also engage in violence, we advocate limiting the crime of support for terrorism, like any crime of aiding and abetting, to support for activities that are themselves crimes. Where those Acts endorsed guilt by association, we would require the FBI to focus its investigations on collecting evidence of individual culpability. Where those Acts allowed the use of secret evidence, we maintain that the government should subject its evidence to the test of cross-examination. And where those Acts adopted a political approach to terrorism, we insist that the FBI must get out of the business of monitoring political activity and associations, foreign and domestic, and instead dedicate itself to the urgent task of identifying those planning violent activities. Only such a transformation can successfully meet the threat of terrorism without sacrificing our political freedoms.

# Notes

## 1. Introduction

1. *United States v. United States District Court*, 407 U.S. 297, 314 (1972).
2. *United States v. Robel*, 389 U.S. 258, 264 (1967).
3. The FBI is not the only federal agency involved in counterterrorism. The Department of Homeland Security, for example, enforces laws excluding and removing aliens for engaging in terrorist activity. The Bureau of Alcohol, Tobacco and Firearms has used its jurisdiction over firearms offenses to target radical domestic groups, and was responsible for launching the disastrous raid on a religious compound at Waco, Texas, in 1993. The State Department denies visas to persons seeking to enter the U.S. to engage in terrorism. The Central Intelligence Agency has made collection of foreign intelligence on terrorism one of its priorities.
4. Antiterrorism and Effective Death Penalty Act of 1996, Pub. L. 104-132, 110 Stat. 1214.
5. *Reno v. American-Arab Anti-Discrimination Comm.*, 525 U.S. 471 (1999).
6. Carol D. Leonnig, "Further Detainee Abuse Alleged—Guantanamo Prison Cited in FBI Memos," *Washington Post*, Dec. 26, 2004, A1; Neil A. Lewis and David Johnston, "New F.B.I. Memos Describe Abuse of Iraq Inmates," *New York Times*, Dec. 21, 2004, A1; Thomas E. Ricks, "Detainees Abuse by Marines Is Detailed," *Washington Post*, Dec. 15, 2004, A1; Barton Gelman and R. Jeffrey Smith, "Report to Defense Alleged Abuse by Prison Interrogation Teams," *Washington Post*, Dec. 8, 2004, A1; Neil A. Lewis, "Red Cross Finds Detainee Abuse in Guantánamo," *New York Times*, Nov. 30, 2004, A1; Dana Priest and Barton

Gellman, "U.S. Decries Abuse but Defends Interrogation; 'Stress and Duress' Tactics Used on Terrorism Suspects Held in Secret Overseas Facilities," *Washington Post*, Dec. 26, 2002.

7. Many of these abuses are detailed in the reports of the Lawyers Committee for Human Rights, "Assessing the New Normal: Liberty and Security for the Post–September 11 United States," Sept. 2003, and "Imbalance of Powers: How Changes to U.S. Law & Policy Since 9/11 Erode Human Rights and Civil Liberties," March 11, 2003.

8. Steve Fainaru and Margot Williams, "Material Witness Law Has Many in Limbo: Nearly Half Held in War on Terror Haven't Testified," *Washington Post*, Nov. 4, 2002, A1.

9. See discussion in Chapter 6.

10. See generally, Robert O'Harrow, *No Place to Hide* (Free Press, 2005); James X. Dempsey and Lara M. Flint, "Commercial Data and National Security," 72 *George Washington Law Review* 1459 (2004), available online at http://www.cdt.org/publications/.

11. For an account in Frank Wilkinson's own words, see Griffin Fariello, *Red Scare: Memories of the American Inquisition* (W. W. Norton, 1995), 530–36.

12. *Wilkinson v. United States*, 365 U.S. 399 (1961).

13. David Helvarg, *The War Against the Greens* (Sierra Club Books, 1997), 393.

14. Ibid., 392.

15. Ibid., 393–94.

16. The official name of the Church Committee was the "Select Committee to Study Governmental Operations with Respect to Intelligence Activities." Its final report was published in six volumes, accompanied by seven volumes of hearings and supporting documents. "Intelligence Activities and the Rights of Americans, Final Report of the Senate Select Committee to Study Governmental Operations with Respect to Intelligence Activities," 94th Cong., 2d Sess. (1976).

The initial evidence about the breadth and depth of FBI spying on dissenters became public not through congressional oversight but as a result of a burglary at an FBI satellite office in Media, Pennsylvania, in March 1971. Domestic counterintelligence documents were stolen, then released to the press and published widely.

17. See "FBI Oversight: Hearings before the Subcomm. on Civil and Constitutional Rights of the House Comm. on the Judiciary, Part 2," 94th Cong. (1975), 2, 12 (testimony of Elmer B. Staats, Comptroller General, reporting on GAO review of FBI domestic intelligence operations).

18. "FBI Authorization Request for Fiscal Year 1986: Hearings before the

Subcomm. on Civil and Constitutional Rights of the House Comm. on
the Judiciary," 99th Cong., 1st Sess. (1985), 15.

19. Ibid., 29.

20. "The FBI and CISPES: Report of the Senate Select Comm. on Intelligence," 101st Cong., 1st Sess. (1989), 2 [hereinafter "Senate Intelligence Report"]. Other agencies participated in the intelligence gathering. Customs agents questioned travelers returning from Nicaragua about their activities, seizing and copying from people's luggage personal written materials and turning them over to the FBI. *Heidy v. U.S. Customs Service*, 681 F. Supp. 1445 (C.D. CA 1988). See generally "Break-ins at Sanctuary Churches and Organizations Opposed to Administration Policy in Central America," Hearings before the Subcomm. on Civil and Constitutional Rights of the House Comm. on the Judiciary, 100th Cong., 1st Sess. (1987), 200–204 (testimony of the Center for Constitutional Rights).

21. See Frank Tejo, "Lives on Hold: Palestinians Accused of Terrorism Fight to Stay in US," *Dallas Morning News*, Dec. 29, 1992, 1A. For the legal history of the case, see *Reno v. American-Arab Anti-Discrimination Comm.*, 525 U.S. 471 (1999), *vacating and remanding* 119 F.3d 1367 (9th Cir. 1997); *American-Arab Anti-Discrimination Comm. v. Reno*, 70 F.3d 1045 (9th Cir. 1995); *American-Arab Anti-Discrimination Comm. v. Meese*, 714 F. Supp. 1060 (C.D. Cal. 1989), *aff'd in part, rev'd in part, American-Arab Anti-Discrimination Comm. v. Thornburgh*, 970 F.2d 501 (9th Cir. 1991).

22. See Maureen O'Hagan, "A Terrorism Case That Went Awry," *Seattle Times*, Nov. 22, 2004; Timothy Egan, "Sensing the Eyes of Big Brother, and Pushing Back," *New York Times*, Aug. 8, 2004, §1, 20: Associated Press, "No Conviction for Student in Terror Case," *New York Times*, June 11, 2004, A14.

23. See Dan Eggen, "Protesters Subjected to 'Pretext Interviews'—FBI Memo Shows No Specific Threats," *Washington Post*, May 18, 2005, A04; Eric Lichtblau, "F.B.I. Goes Knocking for Political Troublemakers," *New York Times*, Aug. 16, 2004, A4.

24. See *Socialist Workers' Party v. Attorney Gen.*, 642 F. Supp. 1357, 1389 (S.D.N.Y. 1986) (quoting FBI memorandum).

25. Janine Anderson, "War: Probes and Profits; FBI Questions OC Residents from Mideast," *Orange County Register*, Feb. 8, 1991, A5.

26. Kenneth Reich, "Arab-Americans Upset over Questioning by FBI," *Los Angeles Times*, Jan. 12, 1991, A1.

27. U.S. Department of Justice, Office of the Inspector General, "The September 11 Detainees: A Review of the Treatment of Aliens Held on Immigration Charges in Connection with the Investigation of the September 11 Attacks" (April 2003) (released June 2, 2003).

28. Allan Turner and Dale Lezon, "Our Changed World; Remembering Sept. 11; Nothing to Hide; A Year Later, Many Muslims Still Shackled by 9/11 Stigma," *Houston Chronicle*, Sept. 8, 2002.
29. Thomas I. Emerson, "National Security and Civil Liberties," 9 *The Yale Journal of World Public Order* 83, 99 (1982). See also Thomas I. Emerson, *The System of Freedom of Expression* (Random House, 1970).
30. Emerson, "National Security and Civil Liberties," 98.
31. See, e.g., Neil A. Lewis, "Terror in Oklahoma," *New York Times*, April 25, 1995, 19 (quoting a former senior official as saying, "The problem is that these rules require we have a criminal predicate before we investigate. . . . That means we have to wait until you have blood on the street before the bureau can act.").
32. E.g., John Deutch, "Terrorism," *Foreign Policy*, Fall 1997, 10, 18–19 (arguing that "some loss of civil liberty inevitably accompanies measures to combat terrorism").

## 2. The FBI's Investigation of Central American Activists, 1981–1985

1. FBI CISPES document, 199-8848-128x1 (Nov. 10, 1983), reprinted in "CISPES and FBI Counterterrorism Investigations: Hearings before the Subcomm. on Civil and Constitutional Rights of the House Comm. on the Judiciary," 100th Cong. (1988), 230–31 [hereinafter "CISPES Hearings"].
2. FBI CISPES document, 199-8848-1 (March 30, 1983), reprinted in CISPES Hearings, 203.
3. "The FBI and CISPES: Report of the Senate Select Comm. on Intelligence," 101st Cong., 1st Sess. (1989), 12, 20–22, 88–89 [hereinafter "Senate Intelligence Report"]; CISPES Hearings, 129 (testimony of FBI Director William S. Sessions). The Foreign Agents Registration Act is at 22 U.S.C. §§ 611 *et seq.*
4. "Break-ins at Sanctuary Churches and Organizations Opposed to Administration Policy in Central America: Hearings before the Subcomm. on Civil and Constitutional Rights of the House Comm. on the Judiciary," 100th Cong. (1987), 435–42 (testimony of Frank Varelli); Senate Intelligence Report, 58–59; Ross Gelbspan, *Break-ins, Death Threats and the FBI: The Covert War Against the Central America Movement* (South End Press, 1991).
5. CISPES Hearings, 117, 139 (statement of William Sessions, Director, FBI).
6. Senate Intelligence Report, 28.
7. FBI CISPES document, 199-8848-24 (May 23, 1983), reprinted in CISPES Hearings, 207.

8. FBI CISPES document, 199-8848-103 (Oct. 7, 1983), reprinted in CISPES Hearings, 218–19.

9. Senate Intelligence Report, 36.

10. Ibid., 2.

11. Ibid., 5–7, 81–85.

12. In April 1985, when the case was still open and its existence and scope were not yet publicly known, FBI Director Webster appeared before Edwards's subcommittee. Webster was asked about reports of FBI interviews of CISPES members. Characterizing the interviews as scattered and claiming that each had an independent counterintelligence purpose, he testified, "We are not keeping track of the membership of CISPES as such." "FBI Authorization Request for Fiscal Year 1986: Hearings before the Subcomm. on Civil and Constitutional Rights of the House Comm. on the Judiciary," 99th Cong. 29 (1985) [hereinafter "FBI Authorization Hearings"].

13. "[T]he scope widened substantively to include surveillance and reporting of political activities and to encompass rank-and-file members as well as leaders...." Senate Intelligence Report, 96. See also ibid., 80.

14. FBI CISPES document, 199-8848-162 (Jan. 11, 1984), reprinted in CISPES Hearings, 271.

15. FBI CISPES document, 199-8848-300X (April 2, 1984), reprinted in CISPES Hearings, 355–61.

16. See Statement of Rep. Don Edwards, Cong. Rec. H707 (March 3, 1988, daily edition), quoted in Gary M. Stern, "The FBI's Misguided Probe of CISPES," CNSS Rep. No. 111 (June 1988), reprinted in CISPES Hearings, 23–24.

17. "Some have questioned whether the FBI may properly investigate an individual or group in the absence of a specific federal criminal violation. It is important to understand that the FBI does have such authority in the international terrorism field." Senate Intelligence Report, 91.

18. FBI CISPES document, 199-8848-128 (Nov. 8, 1983), reprinted in CISPES Hearings, 226–29.

19. FBI CISPES document, 199-8848-146 (Jan. 5, 1984), reprinted in CISPES Hearings, 258–59.

20. FBI CISPES document 199-8848-[not recorded] (Jan. 16, 1984), reprinted in CISPES Hearings, 247.

21. FBI CISPES document, 199-8848-166 (Feb. 2, 1984), reprinted in CISPES Hearings, 313, 317.

22. FBI CISPES document, 199-8848-378 (May 11, 1984), reprinted in CISPES Hearings, 374.

23. FBI CISPES document, 199-8848-436 (Jul. 26, 1984), reprinted in CISPES Hearings, 396–404.

24. FBI CISPES document, 199-8848-483 (Aug. 8, 1984), reprinted in CISPES Hearings, 406.
25. Stern, "The FBI's Misguided Probe of CISPES," 32 (quoting FBI CISPES document 199-8848-482 [Aug. 10, 1983]).
26. FBI CISPES document, 199-8848-492 (Aug. 29, 1984), reprinted in CISPES Hearings, 411–13.
27. FBI CISPES document, 199-8848-492 (Aug. 29, 1984), reprinted in CISPES Hearings, 410–13.
28. FBI CISPES document, 199-8848 [not recorded] (June 4, 1985), reprinted in CISPES Hearings, 430.
29. See "Legislative Initiatives to Curb Domestic and International Terrorism: Hearings before the Subcomm. on Security and Terrorism of the Senate Comm. on the Judiciary," 98th Cong. (1984).
30. See Senate Intelligence Report, 42, 71.
31. Immediately after learning of the scope of the CISPES investigation in early 1988, Rep. Edwards asked the General Accounting Office (GAO) to audit the FBI's international terrorism program. This was the first independent examination ever of the Bureau's international terrorism investigations. Edwards wanted to know whether the CISPES case was an aberration, as the FBI claimed, or whether it reflected broader issues in the FBI's approach to international terrorism. See General Accounting Office, "International Terrorism: FBI Investigates Domestic Activities to Identify Terrorists" (1989) [hereinafter "GAO Report"], reprinted in "FBI Investigation of First Amendment Activities: Hearings before the Subcomm. on Civil and Constitutional Rights of the House Comm. on the Judiciary," 101st Cong. (1989), 112–57.

The GAO found that, between January 1982 and June 1988, the FBI opened and closed about 19,500 international terrorism cases. In 99 percent of the closed cases, the investigative record filled only one or two file folders, indicating that the investigation was not extensive. But the existence of 19,500 cases over a six-and-a-half-year period, even if most were limited to one or two folders of information, means that the FBI collected as many as 30,000 folders of data on groups and individuals in the name of investigating international counterterrorism.

During the same time period of 1982 through 1988, there were twenty-five international terrorist incidents in the U.S., all of them in 1982 and 1983. From 1984 through 1988, there were no international terrorist incidents in the United States.

Nearly 68 percent of the FBI's international terrorism cases studied by the GAO were closed because no evidence was uncovered linking the subject to international terrorism or terrorist acts. Ibid., 115. This further reinforces the finding that most of the FBI's cases do not involve the investigation of actual terrorists, but rather the pursuit of allegations or suspicions later found to be unsubstantiated. In another 22 percent, the cases "were closed because the subject moved or could not be located." Ibid., 117.

32. Ibid., 131.

33. See, e.g., ibid., 133–35 (discussing five cases where basis for investigation was attendance at meeting, participation in religious service, or being listed in foreign newspaper article).

34. Ibid., 132–33.

35. Michael Doyle, "Fresno Group Probed by FBI," *Fresno Bee*, Jan. 29, 1990, A1.

36. Senate Intelligence Report, 80–86.

37. CISPES Hearings, 188.

### 3. The Investigation and Attempted Deportation of the Los Angeles 8

1. FBI, "Popular Front for the Liberation of Palestine (PFLP)" (1986), (report in four volumes), reprinted in part in *American-Arab Anti-Discrimination Committee v. Reno*, No. 96-55929 (9th Cir. 1996), Supplemental Excerpts of Record (vol. 2), at 354.

2. William Overend and Ronald L. Soble, "7 Tied to PLO Terrorist Wing Seized by INS," *Los Angeles Times*, Jan. 27, 1987, 1.

3. *Reno v. American-Arab Anti-Discrimination Comm.*, 525 U.S. 471 (1999), *vacating and remanding* 119 F.3d 1367 (9th Cir. 1997); *American-Arab Anti-Discrimination Comm. v. Reno*, 70 F.3d 1045 (9th Cir. 1995); *American-Arab Anti-Discrimination Comm. v. Meese*, 714 F. Supp. 1060 (C.D. CA. 1989), *aff'd in part, rev'd in part, American-Arab Anti-Discrimination Comm. v. Thornburgh*, 970 F.2d 501 (9th Cir. 1991).

4. "Hearings before the Senate Select Comm. on Intelligence on Nomination of William H. Webster to Be Director of Central Intelligence," 100th Cong. 94-95 (1987).

5. See *American-Arab Anti-Discrimination Comm. v. Reno*, 70 F.3d 1045, 1053 (9th Cir. 1995).

6. FBI, "Popular Front for the Liberation of Palestine (PFLP)," 1.

7. See *American-Arab Anti-Discrimination Committee v. Reno*, No. 96-55929 (9th Cir. 1996) Supplemental Excerpts of Record (vol. 2), at 336.

8. Ibid., 306–7.

9. Memorandum from Investigations Division, INS, "Alien Border Control Committee (ABC) Group IV—Contingency Plans" (Nov. 18, 1986), with attachments, on file with James X. Dempsey.

10. Memorandum from Deputy Attorney General D. Lowell Jensen to INS

Commissioner Alan C. Nelson, "Formation of the Alien Border Control Committee" (June 27, 1986), on file with James X. Dempsey.

11. FBI, "Popular Front for the Liberation of Palestine (PFLP)," 354.

12. Thousands of Americans regularly attended such "haflis" across the United States, and contributed money to support humanitarian aid for those "back home." The events, like everything else in Palestinian culture at that time, were generally associated with one or more of the PLO factions, because most Palestinians identified the PLO as their legitimate political representative. The dinners were attended by large numbers of children, the elderly, and many non-Palestinians. Donations were solicited for humanitarian purposes only, and were directed to U.S. OMEN, an IRS-certified charitable organization that provided humanitarian aid to Palestinians in Lebanon, the West Bank, and Gaza. U.S. OMEN sent the money to various charitable institutions in the Middle East, such as the Ghassan Kanafani Foundation, which operated kindergartens and day-care centers in Lebanon.

13. *American-Arab Anti-Discrimination Comm. v. Reno*, No. 87-02107 (Memorandum opinion, C.D. Cal. 1986), reprinted in *Reno v. American-Arab Anti-Discrimination Comm.*, No. 97-1252 (S. Ct.), Joint Appendix.

14. See *American-Arab Anti-Discrimination Comm. v. Meese*, 714 F. Supp. 1060 (C.D. Cal. 1989), *aff'd in part, rev'd in part, American-Arab Anti-Discrimination Comm. v. Thornburgh*, 970 F.2d 501 (9th Cir. 1991).

15. *American-Arab Anti-Discrimination Comm. v. Reno*, 70 F.3d 1045, 1064 (9th Cir. 1995).

16. *American-Arab Anti-Discrimination Comm. v. Reno*, 119 F.3d 1367 (9th Cir. 1997), *vacated and remanded*, 525 U.S. 471 (1999).

17. *Reno v. American-Arab Anti-Discrimination Comm.*, 525 U.S. 471 (1999).

18. The Court's analysis leaves open the question whether the INS may deport an alien *solely* for engaging in First Amendment–protected political activity. Its decision addressed only whether an alien who faces deportation for some other ground has an affirmative defense where he has been selectively targeted for constitutionally impermissible reasons. The Court held that he does not, thereby unleashing the INS to use its immigration powers selectively to punish politically unpopular ideas.

19. Lisa Belkin, "For Many Arab-Americans, FBI Scrutiny Renews Fears," *New York Times*, Jan. 12, 1991, 1A; Sharon LaFraniere, "FBI Starts Interviewing Arab-American Leaders," *Washington Post*, Jan. 9, 1991, A14.

20. Emily Sachar, "FBI Grills NY Arab-Americans," *Newsday*, Jan. 29, 1991, 6.

21. Belkin, "For Many Arab-Americans, FBI Scrutiny Renews Fears."

22. Sachar, "FBI Grills NY Arab-Americans."

23. "FBI Questions Arab-Americans in New Castle, Ohio," UPI, Jan. 10, 1991.
24. "State Police, FBI Questioning Arabs," *Arkansas Democrat-Gazette*, Jan. 16, 1991.
25. Jim Doyle, "Federal Agents Balancing Rights, Terror Concerns," *San Francisco Chronicle*, Feb. 19, 1991, A7.
26. Jane Friedman, "In the Aftermath of Gulf War, Arab-Americans Assess Standing," *Christian Science Monitor*, March 13, 1991, 9.
27. These documents are now at the not-for-profit National Security Archives in Washington, D.C.

## 4. Intelligence Investigations from Amnesty International to Earth First!

1. "FBI Investigation of First Amendment Activities: Hearings before the Subcomm. on Civil and Constitutional Rights of the House Comm. on the Judiciary," 101st Cong. (1989), 35–36 [hereinafter "First Amendment Hearings"].
2. Ibid., 112.
3. Ibid., 9–15.
4. *Patterson v. FBI*, 705 F. Supp. 1033 (D. N.J. 1989), *aff'd*, 893 F.2d 595 (3d Cir. 1990), *cert. denied*, 498 U.S. 812 (1990).
5. First Amendment Hearings, 31–32.
6. See "FBI Counterintelligence Visits to Libraries: Hearings before the Subcomm. on Civil and Constitutional Rights of the House Comm. on the Judiciary," 100th Cong. (1988) [hereinafter "FBI Library Visits"]. See also Robert D. McFadden, "FBI in New York Asks Librarians' Aid in Reporting on Spies," *New York Times*, Sept. 18, 1987, 1A.
7. FBI Library Visits, 332–33.
8. The federal Court of Appeals for the District of Columbia allowed the FBI to maintain the file and keep it secret, notwithstanding the Privacy Act's prohibition against the maintenance of records on First Amendment activities not pertinent to a legitimate law enforcement activity. *J. Roderick MacArthur Foundation v. FBI*, 102 F.3d 600 (D.C. Cir. 1996), *cert. denied*, 522 U.S. 913 (1997).
9. Susan Page, "AIDS Protest Held Near Bush's Home," *Newsday*, Sept. 2, 1991, 13.
10. In response to the Freedom of Information Act request filed by the Center for Constitutional Rights, the FBI released just twenty-two pages of a file containing 451 documents from sixteen FBI field offices, dating from February 1988 to October 1993. Greg B. Smith, *New York Daily News*, June 21, 1995, 21.

11. David W. Dunlap, "FBI Kept Watch on AIDS Group During Protest Years," *New York Times*, May 16, 1995, B3.

12. Local police sometimes responded to ACT-UP demonstrations with excessive force. On September 12, 1991, a large group of ACT-UP activists greeted George Bush as he entered the Bellevue Hotel in Philadelphia for a fund-raising event. The ACT-UP protesters held up signs criticizing Bush's neglect of the AIDS issue. They blew whistles and yelled "shame." Other demonstrators, including some from NOW and groups representing the homeless and elderly, voiced their own criticisms of the Bush administration in a demonstration of 7,500 in all. The ACT-UP contingent formed the largest and noisiest of the protesters. The Philadelphia police descended upon the ACT-UP members with nightsticks, violently throwing demonstrators into a paddy wagon. See 'Panel: Cops Were Afraid," *Newsday*, March 21, 1992, 9.

13. Greg B. Smith, "FBI to Probe Itself on AIDS Group File," *New York Daily News*, May 18, 1995, 5.

14. "Senate Select Comm. on Intelligence, the FBI, and CISPES," 101st Cong., 1st Sess. 12, 20-22, 88-89 (1989), 5, 102 [hereinafter "Senate Intelligence Report"].

15. Michael Taylor, "2 Earth First! Members Hurt By Bomb in Car; Radicals Reportedly Suspected in Oakland Blast," *San Francisco Chronicle*, May 25, 1990, A1.

16. Rep. Edwards tried to answer Bari's question through the oversight process. In 1991, in response to Edwards's questioning, the FBI responded that it had not had an investigation of Earth First!, Cherney, Bari, or Redwood Summer before the bombing. In 1996, after six years of litigation, Bari's lawyer obtained a complete copy of the form 302 that was written by the FBI agent who responded to the scene of the bombing, in which the agent stated that, at the scene of the bombing, he was advised by the field office that Bari and Cherney "were the subjects of an FBI investigation in the terrorist field." In a teletype to headquarters the day after the bombing, the San Francisco field office noted that "Bari and Cherney were already considered potential suspects in 'Earth Night Action Groups'; DS/T [Domestic Security/Terrorism] OO [Office of Origin]: San Francisco (SF File 100A-SF-80488), which involved the destruction of a Pacific Gas and Electric Power tower in Santa Cruz County." FBI teletype, 174-SF-90788-14 (5/25/90), on file with James X. Dempsey.

17. David Helvarg, *The War Against the Greens* (Sierra Club Books, 1997), 334–35.

18. Ibid., 397.

19. Ibid., 396.

20. Ibid.
21. Ibid., 400.
22. Earth First! was not the only domestic group classified as terrorist. In 1986, the FBI opened under the domestic security/terrorism category a preliminary investigation of eleven acts of vandalism at Chicago military recruiting offices. The perpetrators had left behind leaflets referring to the Veterans Fast for Life, and one of the suspects was identified with Silo Plowshares, another antiwar group. The Chicago field office of the FBI stated in a memo to headquarters that "it does not know the size or scope of this conspiracy although preliminary indications suggest that it is probably nationwide." The case was closed within six months.
23. Information about the civil lawsuit can be found at http://www.judibari .org/legal_index.html.
24. "CISPES and FBI Counterterrorism Investigations: Hearings before the Subcomm. on Civil and Constitutional Rights of the House Comm. on the Judiciary," 100th Cong. (1988) (statement of William Sessions, Director, FBI).
25. See also Associated Press, "Georgia Professor Sues for Access to FBI File," *Washington Post*, Feb. 4, 1999, A9 (FBI agents visited a Georgia State professor in 1994 a few weeks after he invited the secretary of the Office of Cuban Interests in Washington to a symposium).

## 5. Mechanisms for Control of the FBI

1. Criminal offenses are defined mainly in Title 18 of the United States Code. Drug offenses are defined in Title 21. There are other criminal provisions scattered through other titles of the federal code.
2. 18 U.S.C. §§ 2510–2522.
3. 5 U.S.C. § 552.
4. See *Bivens v. Six Unknown Named Agents of Federal Bureau of Narcotics*, 403 U.S. 388 (1971). The ability of citizens to recover damages against the government for law enforcement misconduct is a complex area, well beyond the scope of this work.
5. E.g., 18 U.S.C. § 2384 (seditious conspiracy) and § 2385 (advocating overthrow of government). The Foreign Agents Registration Act, 22 U.S.C. §§ 611-21, widens the scope of the criminal law to reach activities that, in the absence of the Act's registration and disclosure requirements, would be entirely lawful. John T. Elliff, *The Reform of FBI Intelligence Operations* (Princeton University Press, 1979), 33.
6. Between 1987 and 1997, only three law enforcement applications to conduct wiretaps were denied by judges at the federal, state, or local level; 8,594 requests were granted. "Administrative Office of the U.S. Courts,

1997 Wiretap Report" (Washington, DC, 1998), 30, available online at http://www.uscourts.gov/wiretap/table7.pdf. For a brief description of the erosion of the protections in the wiretap laws, see James X. Dempsey, "Communications Privacy in the Digital Age: Revitalizing the Federal Wiretap Laws to Enhance Privacy," 8 *Albany Law Journal Science & Technology* 65, 75–78 (1997).

7. The best source for practical information on the FOIA is Harry Hammitt, ed., *Litigation under the Federal Open Government Laws* (EPIC and the James Madison Project, 2002), in its twenty-first edition at this time and periodically updated. The Department of Justice Office of Information and Privacy publishes a detailed volume entitled "Freedom of Information Act Guide & Privacy Act Overview" and an exhaustive "Freedom of Information Case List," both available from the Government Printing Office. The document "A Citizen's Guide to Using the Freedom of Information Act and the Privacy Act of 1974 to Request Government Records," published by the House Committee on Government Reform and Oversight, 108th Cong., is available online at http://www.fas.org/sgp/foia/citizen.html. For case studies of how the FOIA has worked at the FBI, CIA, and other agencies, see Athan Theoharis, ed., *A Culture of Secrecy: The Government Versus the People's Right to Know* (University Press of Kansas, 1998).

8. See generally Chapter 7; see also Harold Hongju Koh, *The National Security Constitution* (Yale University Press 1990).

9. "FBI Statutory Charter: Hearings before the Senate Comm. on the Judiciary," 95th Cong. 4 (1978) (testimony of Attorney General Griffin B. Bell).

10. See 28 U.S.C. §§ 531–540A (1988). The notes accompanying these code sections contain a number of other uncodified laws governing specific details of a wide range of FBI activities, but none constitutes a significant limitation on those activities.

11. 28 U.S.C. § 533 (1988) (Attorney General may appoint investigative officials).

12. 28 U.S.C. § 534 (Attorney General shall acquire crime identification and other records).

13. 42 U.S.C. § 3744 (1988) (FBI director authorized to establish training programs).

14. 18 U.S.C. §3052.

15. Pub. L. 90-351, Title VI, §1101, 82 Stat. 236, June 19, 1968, as amended by Pub. L. 94-503, Title II, §203, 90 Stat. 2427, Oct. 15, 1976.

16. Elliff, *Reform of FBI Intelligence Operations*, 30–32.

17. 18 U.S.C. § 2385 (advocating overthrow of government—Smith Act);

18 U.S.C. § 2386 (Voorhis Act) (1988); 50 U.S.C. §§ 781–789 (1988) (Internal Security Act of 1950 and Communist Control Act of 1964). While these laws remain on the books, their constitutionality is highly questionable, and they have not been used in many years. See *Scales v. United States*, 367 U.S. 203, 224–30 (1961) (membership clause of Smith Act, which makes it felony to belong to an organization that advocates overthrow of government, held not to violate First or Fifth Amendments when construed to apply only to members with specific intent to further illegal ends); *Yates v. United States*, 354 U.S. 298, 303–11 (1957), *overruled on other grounds, Burks v. United States*, 437 U.S. 1 (1978) (convictions for conspiring to organize group advocating overthrow of government reversed—word "organize" should be strictly construed); *Dennis v. United States*, 341 U.S. 494, 516 (1951) (sections of Smith Act that make it crime to advocate overthrow of government do not violate First or Fifth Amendments as applied to leaders of the Communist Party).

18. 18 U.S.C. § 2384.

19. *United States v. Rodriguez*, 803 F.2d 318 (7th Cir. 1986), *cert. denied*, 480 U.S. 908 (1987).

20. For discussion of the "material support" law, see Chapters 9 and 10.

21. John Mintz and Michael Grunwald, "FBI Terror Probes Focus on U.S. Muslims; Expanded Investigations, New Tactics Stir Allegations of Persecution," *Washington Post*, Oct. 31, 1998, A1.

22. "[I]f credible information comes to the FBI's attention that a group or entity is acting under the direction and control of a hostile foreign power, the FBI may initiate a counterintelligence investigation. Such an investigation could be initiated even though the activities of the group or entity do not, on their face, violate a criminal statute. … A foreign power can be a faction or entity or other similar foreign-directed group, which definition is in [the] unclassified portion of the AG Guidelines and which is the same as that used in the Foreign Intelligence Surveillance Act." Letter from Acting FBI Director John E. Otto to Rep. Don Edwards, June 22, 1987, reprinted in "Break-ins at Sanctuary Churches and Organizations Opposed to administration Policy in Central America: Hearings before the Subcomm. on Civil and Constitutional Rights of the House Judiciary Comm.," 104th Cong., 1st Sess. Serial No. 42 (1987), 545. See also Chapter 2, note 17.

## 6. Reform and Retrenchment

1. This summary is based on the extensive expositions in the report of the Church Committee, "Intelligence Activities and the Rights of Ameri-

cans, Book II, Final Report of the Senate Select Committee to Study Governmental Operations with Respect to Intelligence Activities," 94th Cong. (1976) [hereinafter "Church Comm. Rep. Book II"], and Frank J. Donner, *The Age of Surveillance* (Knopf, 1980).

2. See Church Comm. Rep. Book II, 23–67; "FBI Oversight, Part 2: Hearings before the Subcomm. on Civil and Constitutional Rights of the House Comm. on the Judiciary," 94th Cong., 1st and 2d Sess. (1976), 167–68 (citing General Accounting Office, FBI "Domestic Intelligence Operations—Their Purpose and Scope: Issues That Need to Be Resolved"); see also *Socialist Workers' Party v. Attorney Gen.*, 642 F. Supp. 1357, 1375–77 (S.D.N.Y. 1986) (summary of history relating to FBI's investigation of SWP). See generally Comment, "Ideological Exclusion, Plenary Power, and the PLO," 77 *California Law Review* 831, 837–39 (1989) (discussing Palmer Raids).

3. Church Comm. Rep. Book II, 23.

4. Ibid.

5. Ibid., 23–24. The first of these authorizations was oral and was reflected only in then-secret memoranda written by Hoover. It was based on the ambiguous reference in the FBI's general authorities statute to investigations of "official matters" referred by the secretary of state. In August 1936, at Hoover's urging, Roosevelt asked Secretary of State Cordell Hull to request the FBI to undertake an investigation of "subversive activities in the United States, particularly Fascism and Communism." Hull did so, and in the succeeding years Hoover parlayed this request into approval for a permanent domestic intelligence operation. Donner, *Age of Surveillance*, 52–60.

6. Church Comm. Rep. Book II, 24.

7. Ibid., 32–33.

8. Ibid., 38.

9. Ibid., 45–46.

10. Ibid., 38.

11. "Supplementary Detailed Staff Reports on Intelligence Activities and the Rights of Americans, Book III, Final Report of the Senate Select Committee to Study Governmental Operations with Respect to Intelligence Activities," 94th Cong. (1976), 15.

12. Ibid.

13. See generally Richard Criley, *The FBI v. the First Amendment* (First Amendment Foundation, 1990).

14. For a full description of the FBI's COINTELPRO campaign against the SWP, see *Socialist Workers' Party v. Attorney Gen.*, 642 F. Supp. 1357 (S.D.N.Y. 1986).

15. Church Comm. Rep. Book III, 3.

16. Hampton and Clark were killed in a Chicago apartment on December 4, 1969. Police raided the house, supposedly looking for weapons. The police assertions that they fired into the apartment only after someone fired out seemed to be contradicted by the physical evidence, including the fact that Hampton was killed in his bed. It later emerged that Hampton's bodyguard and chief of security for the Chicago Panthers was an FBI informant, who provided the FBI a map of the apartment. The FBI gave the map first to one local police unit, which declined to raid the apartment, and then to the one that went forward with the raid that resulted in the deaths of Hampton and Clark. "It is fair to say that the FBI was shopping around for a law enforcement unit that was willing to conduct a raid that it, the Bureau, wanted to see carried out, but had no legal pretext for staging on its own. . . . Taken together, the indications were that the Bureau might have tacitly encouraged the unprovoked killing of the two Black Panthers at a time when there was no legal way of pursuing them otherwise." Sanford J. Ungar, *FBI* (Atlantic/Little, Brown, 1975), 466. Ungar's descriptions of the culture and methodology of the Bureau remain highly relevant. The family of Hampton successfully sued the Chicago police and the FBI.

17. See Senate Resolution 400, 94th Congress (the charter of the Senate Select Committee on Intelligence) (1976) and House Rule XLVIII (the charter of the House Permanent Select Committee on Intelligence). These and many other documents on the intelligence oversight process are periodically collected in a booklet by the House Intelligence Committee entitled "Compilation of Intelligence Laws and Related Laws and Executive Orders of Interest to the National Intelligence Community," available from the committee or the Government Printing Office.

18. *New York Times Co. v. United States*, 403 U.S. 713 (1971).

19. *United States v. United States District Court*, 407 U.S. 297 (1972).

20. 50 U.S.C. §1801 *et seq.*

21. See "FBI Domestic Security Guidelines: Oversight Hearings before the Subcomm. on Civil and Constitutional Rights of the House Comm. on the Judiciary," 98th Cong. (1983), 60–66 (Levi guidelines).

22. Curt Gentry, *J. Edgar Hoover: The Man and the Secrets* (Penguin Plume, 1991), 594fn.

23. See generally Athan Theoharis, ed., *A Culture of Secrecy: The Government Versus the People's Right to Know* (University Press of Kansas, 1998).

24. Various experts, including the 9/11 Commission, have concluded that disclosure of the size of the total intelligence budget would cause no harm to the national security. Nevertheless, successive Directors of Central Intelligence have opposed even aggregate disclosure. As a result of litigation by the Federation of American Scientists and the Center for National Se-

curity Studies, the intelligence budget totals for fiscal years 1997 and 1998 were disclosed, but the DCI has refused further disclosures, and the courts have rejected efforts to force disclosure of the figures for subsequent years.

25. The Clinton administration, like the Bush administration, has continued to operate under Executive Order 12333, issued by Ronald Reagan in 1981. E.O. 12333 was published in the Federal Register on December 4, 1981, 46 Fed Reg. 59941. It is also reprinted in "Compilation of Intelligence Laws and Related Laws and Executive Orders of Interest to the National Intelligence Community," published by the House Intelligence Committee (June 2003).

26. Letter from Acting FBI Director John E. Otto to Rep. Don Edwards, June 22, 1987, reprinted in "Break-ins at Sanctuary Churches and Organizations Opposed to administration Policy in Central America: Hearings before the Subcomm. on Civil and Constitutional Rights of the House Judiciary Comm.," 104th Cong., 1st Sess. (1987), 545.

27. See "FBI Domestic Security Guidelines: Oversight Hearings before the Subcomm. on Civil and Constitutional Rights of the House Comm. on the Judiciary," 98th Cong. (1983), 60–66 (Levi guidelines), 67–85 (Smith guidelines).

28. E.O. 12333, *supra* note 25.

29. See generally Theoharis, *Culture of Secrecy.*

30. Each year, the attorney general submits to Congress a brief letter stating the number of applications made to the FISA court in the prior year and the number of orders granted. Steven Aftergood of the Federation of American Scientists has tracked these reports for many years. Aftergood's Project on Government Secrecy is an invaluable resource on issues of intelligence agency secrecy and accountability, available at http://www.fas.org/sgp/.

31. 50 U.S.C. §§ 1821–29, added by the Intelligence Authorization Act for FY 1995, Pub. L. 103-359, 108 Stat. 3443.

32. See "Activities of Federal Law Enforcement Agencies Towards the Branch Davidians: Joint Hearings Before the Subcomm. on Crime of the House Judiciary Committee and the Subcomm. on National Security of the House Comm. on Government Reform and Oversight," 104th Cong. (1995), and "The Federal Raid on Ruby Ridge Idaho: Hearings Before the Subcomm. on Terrorism of the Senate Judiciary Comm.," 104th Cong. (1995).

33. See "FBI Domestic Security Guidelines: Oversight Hearings before the Subcomm. on Civil and Constitutional Rights of the House Comm. on the Judiciary" (1983), 60–66 (Levi guidelines), 67–85 (Smith guidelines).

34. Department of Justice, "Attorney General's Guidelines on General Crimes, Racketeering Enterprise and Terrorism Enterprise Investigations" (May 30, 2002), available at http://www.usdoj.gov/olp/general crimes2.pdf.
35. Attorney General Thornburgh made minor changes in 1989.
36. The Privacy Act would seem to prohibit this. The Act provides that a federal agency shall

> maintain no record describing how any individual exercises rights guaranteed by the First Amendment unless expressly authorized by statute or by the individual about whom the record is maintained or unless pertinent to and within the scope of an authorized law enforcement activity.

5 U.S.C. 552a(e)(7). The courts, however, have declined to rule FBI intelligence gathering as illegal under this provision. In *Jabara v. Webster*, 691 F.2d 272 (6th Cir. 1982), the appellate court held that intelligence investigations are "law enforcement" activities within the meaning of (e)(7) and that it is not necessary to show any relationship to a specific criminal act.
37. Of course, commercially available electronic databases of news stories, such as Nexis, obviate the need for the FBI to clip and index press reports of demonstrations and meetings.
38. Combating Domestic Terrorism: Hearing Before the Subcomm. on Crime of the House Judiciary Comm.," 104th Cong., 1st Sess. 27 (May 3, 1995) (testimony of Louis J. Freeh).
39. Jim McGee, "The Rise of the FBI," *Washington Post Magazine*, July 20, 1997, 10, 25.
40. Department of Justice, "Attorney General's Guidelines on General Crimes, Racketeering Enterprise and Terrorism Enterprise Investigations" (May 30, 2002), available at http://www.usdoj.gov/olp/generalcrimes2 .pdf.
41. Thus both the 9/11 attacks in the United States and the destruction of Pan Am Flight 103 over Lockerbie, Scotland, are international terrorist incidents. The dividing lines between domestic and international terrorism are not always clear. For example, some Jewish extremist groups in the United States have been classified as domestic terrorist groups, despite ties in Israel, while Islamic, Palestinian, and other Arab groups operating in the United States are classified as international terrorists, subject to investigation under the more expansive foreign counterintelligence guidelines. See, e.g., FBI, "Terrorism in the United States 1987."
42. "The Attorney General's Guidelines for FBI National Security Investigations and Foreign Intelligence Collection" (Oct. 31, 2003), redacted ver-

sion available at http://www.fas.org/irp/agency/doj/fbi/nsiguidelines
.pdf. A DOJ "fact sheet" on the guidlines is at http://www.fas.org/irp/
agency/doj/fbi/nsi-fact.html.

43. See *Healy v. James*, 408 U.S. 169, 187 (1972); *Keyishian v. Board of Regents*, 385 U.S. 589, 606-07 (1967). But in *Palestine Information Office v. Schultz*, 853 F.2d 932, 939-42 (D.C. Cir. 1988), the federal court of appeals held that the First Amendment was not implicated by an order shutting down an office funded solely by and representing only one foreign entity. This case, however, did not approve the investigation of groups receiving domestic funding and representing domestic members.

44. The LA 8 case offers the most well-documented recent example of this approach in action. The district court concluded there that the FBI never really devoted much attention to determining whether the individuals it was investigating actually intended to support any illegal activity. Rather, the FBI proceeded on the basis of guilt by association, assuming that it was enough to link the individuals to the PFLP and to show that the PFLP engaged in terrorist violence. The court concluded that the nefarious nature of the PFLP was "irrelevant" under the First Amendment absent specific intent on the part of individuals to further the group's illegal activities. *American-Arab Anti-Discrimination Committee v. Reno* C.A. No. 87-2107 (C.D. Cal. April 29, 1996), *reprinted in Reno v. American-Arab Anti-Discrimination Committee*, No. 97-1252 (S.Ct.), Joint Appendix.

45. "CISPES and FBI Counterterrorism Investigations: Hearings Before the Subcomm. on Civil and Constitutional Rights of the House Judiciary Comm.," 100th Cong., 2nd Sess., Serial No. 122 (1988), 135 (emphasis added).

46. John Kifner, "Roots of Terror: A Special Report—Alms and Arms: Tactics in a Holy War," *New York Times*, March 15, 1996, Al.

47. See, e.g., *Handschu v. Special Services Div.*, 605 F. Supp. 1384 (S.D.N.Y. 1985), 349 F.Supp. 766 (S.D.N.Y. 1972). See generally, Paul G. Chevigny, "Politics and Law in the Control of Local Surveillance," 69 *Cornell Law Review* 735 (1984).

48. Seth Rosenfeld, "FBI Wants S.F. Cops to Join Spy Squad," *San Francisco Examiner*, Jan. 12, 1997, A1.

49. *Alliance to End Repression v. City of Chicago*, 237 F.3d 799 (7th Cir. 2001).

50. See H.R. 50, 102nd Cong., 1st Sess., 137 Cong. Rec. E69 (1991) (Edwards's floor statement). See also H.R. 5369, 100th Cong., 2nd Sess., 134 Cong. Rec. H8140.

51. Pub. L. 103-322, 108 Stat. 2022-23 (1994).

52. Sec. 120005 of Pub. L. 103-322, 108 Stat. 2022, adding 18 U.S.C. § 2339A.

53. White House Fact Sheet, "Strengthening Intelligence to Better Protect America" (Jan. 28, 2003), available at http://www.whitehouse.gov/news/releases/2003/01/20030128-12.html. See also Homeland Security Presidential Directive/Hspd-6, "Integration and Use of Screening Information" (Sept. 16, 2003), available at http://www.whitehouse.gov/news/releases/2003/09/20030916-5.html.

## 7. Constitutional Limits—The Role of the Judiciary

1. 395 U.S. 444, 447 (1969). The case involved the violent rhetoric of the Ku Klux Klan.

    Earlier in the century, the Court had upheld convictions for antidraft speeches and for advocating the overthrow of the government by force. See *Schenck v. United States,* 249 U.S. 47 (1919) (upholding convictions for antiwar, antidraft speeches); *Debs v. United States,* 249 U.S. 211 (1919) (same); and *Dennis v. United States,* 341 U.S. 494 (1951) (upholding conviction under Smith Act of leaders of the Communist Party in the United States). But the deferential approach reflected in these cases gradually gave way with the waning of McCarthyism to a First Amendment theory that acknowledged the value of a much broader range of antigovernment speech. See generally Rodney A. Smolla, *Smolla and Nimmer on Freedom of Speech* (Matthew Bender, 1994).

2. See, e.g., *NAACP v. Claiborne Hardware Co.,* 458 U.S. 886 (1982); *R.A.V. v. City of St. Paul,* 505 U.S. 377 (1992).

3. Beginning with a series of cases in the 1950s and 1960s in which it overturned states' attempts to curb the activities of the National Association for the Advancement of Colored People (NAACP), the Supreme Court recognized that "[e]ffective advocacy of both public and private points of view, particularly controversial ones, is undeniably enhanced by group association." *NAACP v. Alabama ex rel. Patterson,* 357 U.S. 449 (1958).

    The Court over the years rejected direct and indirect attempts at curbing associational activity. In 1958, the Court held that recruiting members for a group is protected under the right of association. *Staub v. City of Baxley,* 355 U.S. 313 (1958) (striking down restriction on solicitation of members for unions and other organizations as violation of First Amendment). See also *City of Watseka v. Illinois Public Action Council,* 796 F.2d 1547, 1558-59 (7th Cir. 1986) (upholding award of damages for First Amendment violation based in part on organization's "inability to recruit new members").

    In 1981, it held that raising and contributing money to a group is a form of "collective expression" also fully protected by the First Amendment. *Citizens Against Rent Control v. Berkeley,* 454 U.S. 290, 295-96

(1981). *Accord, Federal Election Comm. v. National Conservative Political Action Comm.*, 470 U.S. 480, 495 (1985); *Roberts v. United States Jaycees*, 468 U.S. 609, 626-27 (1984) (First Amendment protects Jaycees' "fundraising"); *Village of Schaumburg v. Citizens for a Better Environment*, 444 U.S. 620, 632-33 (1980) (First Amendment protects charitable solicitation of funds).

Furthermore, the Court has held that politically active groups have a right to protect their membership from scrutiny: in one of the earliest NAACP cases, the Court held that groups cannot be compelled to disclose information about their membership. *NAACP v. Alabama ex rel. Patterson*, 357 U.S. 449 (1958). More recently, the Court has held that there is a right to engage in political speech anonymously. *McIntyre v. Ohio*, 514 U.S. 334 (1995).

4. *Healy v. James*, 408 U.S. 169, 186 (1972). In 1961, the Supreme Court warned against the danger "that one in sympathy with the legitimate aims of . . . an organization, but not specifically intending to accomplish them by resort to violence, might be punished for his adherence to lawful and constitutionally protected purposes, because of other and unprotected purposes which he does not necessarily share." *Noto v. United States,* 364 U.S. 290, 299-300 (1961). Holding that this danger of curtailing association was more serious than the threat of illegal activity, the Court ruled that in order for the government to punish an individual's association with the group, it must prove that the individual specifically intended to further the unlawful ends of the group.

Under these principles, the Court has struck down statutes barring Communist Party members from public and private employment, *Keyishian v. Board of Regents*, 385 U.S. 589, 606-07 (1967); *Elfbrandt v. Russell,* 384 U.S. 11, 17 (1966); *United States v. Robel*, 389 U.S. 258 (1967); ballot access, *Communist Party of Indiana v. Whitcomb*, 414 U.S. 441, 448-49 (1974); the right to travel abroad, *Aptheker v. Secretary of State,* 378 U.S. 500 (1964); and the practice of law, *Baird v. State Bar of Arizona*, 401 U.S. 1 (1971); *Schware v. Board of Bar Examiners*, 353 U.S. 232 (1957).

5. Another major development in First Amendment protections was the Pentagon Papers case, in which the Supreme Court refused to enjoin the *New York Times* from publishing classified national security information. The Court's opinion set a very high presumption against prior restraints and has served to ensure that information on matters of national security, once obtained by the press, can almost always be presented to the public. *New York Times Co. v. United States*, 403 U.S. 713 (1971).

However, government officials who publicly disclose information that they learned through their official duties and were supposed to keep secret may be punished administratively, including being fired. Employees of the CIA and others with access to intelligence information may also be required to sign agreements that they will submit any writings, even after they leave the government, for prepublication review to ensure that no classified information is disclosed. The Supreme Court has upheld the use of such agreements as essentially just another contractual agreement, and has held that the government is entitled to forfeiture of the profits of any writings not submitted for review. *Snepp v. United States,* 444 U.S. 507 (1980).

6. *Laird v. Tatum,* 408 U.S. 1 (1972) .

7. *Donohoe v. Duling,* 465 F.2d 196 (1972). *Donohoe* was decided approximately one month after *Tatum.*

8. *Socialist Workers Party v. Attorney General,* 510 F.2d 253 (2d Cir. 1974).

9. *Philadelphia Yearly Meeting of the Religious Society of Friends v. Tate,* 519 F.2d 1335 (3d Cir. 1975)(approving photographing and compilation of records, but not the sharing of the information with private employers or broadcaster). See also *Fifth Avenue Peace Parade Comm. v. Gray,* 480 F.2d 326 (2d Cir. 1973). In *Rizzo v. Goode,* 423 U.S. 362 (1976), the Supreme Court made it more difficult for courts to control police practices in general.

10. *Philadelphia Yearly Meeting of the Religious Society of Friends v. Tate,* 519 F.2d at 1338-39. In a more recent case, a group of Arizona churches brought suit against the United States for conducting an undercover investigation of the sanctuary movement. *Presbyterian Church v. United States,* 807 F.2d 518 (9th Cir. 1989). The agents involved infiltrated four churches wearing recording devices, and recorded prayers, hymns, and Bible readings while attending worship services and Bible study classes. The churches contended that the infiltration and recording of religious services violated their First Amendment rights to the free exercise of religion and association. The churches claimed concrete injury was suffered as a result, since "INS surveillance . . . chilled individual congregants from attending worship services," and that this in turn adversely affected the ability of the church to carry out its religious mission. The trial court agreed and let the case go forward.

11. *Halkin v. Helms,* 690 F.2d 977 (D.C. Cir. 1982).

12. *Socialist Workers Party v. Attorney General,* 642 F. Supp. 1357 (S.D.N.Y. 1986). The court awarded a total of $264,000 in damages and placed restrictions on the use of records illegally compiled by the FBI in the course of the investigation. With one exception, the court denied the SWP's requests for declaratory and injunctive relief because there was no prosecution or threatened activity against the SWP.

13. Similarly, in 1984, the federal court of appeals for the District of Columbia also held that the FBI's COINTELPRO campaign violated the First Amendment. The court stated:

> Government action taken with the intent to disrupt or destroy lawful organizations, or to deter membership in those groups, is absolutely unconstitutional. The Government could not constitutionally make such participation unlawful; consequently, it may not surreptitiously undertake to do what it cannot do publicly.

*Hobson v. Wilson*, 737 F.2d 1 (D.C. Cir. 1984), *cert. denied sub nom. Brennan v. Hobson*, 470 U.S. 1084 (1985).

14. The Alliance to End Repression is a Chicago coalition of civil liberties, civil rights, and community action groups. The Chicago Committee to Defend the Bill of Rights is the Chicago affiliate of NCARL and a member of the Alliance.

15. *Alliance to End Repression v. City of Chicago*, 91 F.R.D. 182 (N.D. Ill. 1981).

16. *Alliance to End Repression v. City of Chicago*, 742 F.2d 1007 (7th Cir. 1984).

17. *Alliance to End Repression v. City of Chicago*, 119 F.3d 472 (7th Cir. 1997).

18. The settlement was invoked again in 1991 when the FBI undertook its interviews of Arab-Americans in Chicago near the time of the Persian Gulf war. *Alliance to End Repression v. City of Chicago*, 1994 U.S. Dist. LEXIS 17052 (N.D. Ill. 1994).

19. *Alliance to End Repression v. City of Chicago*, 66 F. Supp.2d 899 (N.D. Ill. 1999).

20. *Alliance to End Repression v. City of Chicago*, 237 F.3d 799 (7th Cir. 2001).

21. *Socialist Workers Party v. Attorney General*, 642 F. Supp. at 1416.

22. *United States v. United States District Court*, 407 U.S. 297, 320 (1972).

23. *United States v. Ehrlichman*, 376 F. Supp. 29 (1974), *aff'd*, 546 F.2d 910 (D.C. Cir. 1976), *cert. denied*, 429 U.S. 1120 (1977).

24. They relied on *United States v. Butenko*, 494 F.2d 593 (3rd Cir. 1974), *cert. denied sub nom. Ivanov v. United States*, 419 U.S. 881 (1974), and *Zweibon v. Mitchell*, 363 F. Supp. 936 (D.D.C. 1973) (both cases involving wiretapping).

25. 376 F. Supp. at 33-34.

26. *Halperin v. Kissinger*, 807 F.2d 180, 194 (D.C. Cir. 1986).

27. In balancing the government's interest in "self-defense" against the defendants' interest in privacy pursuant to the Fourth Amendment's guarantee of freedom from warrantless searches, the court found not only that no

Fourth Amendment rights were encroached, but also that the transcripts of the alleged conversations need not be revealed to the defendants to allow them to prepare their defense. *United States v. Butenko*, 494 F.2d 593, 608 (3d Cir. 1974)(en banc), *cert. denied sub nom. Ivanov v. United States*, 419 U.S. 881 (1974). A warrantless national security wiretap was also upheld in *United States v. Brown*, 484 F.2d 418 (5th Cir. 1973), *cert. denied*, 415 U.S. 960 (1974).

However, in *Zweibon v. Mitchell*, 516 F. 2d 594 (D.C. Cir. 1975), *cert. denied*, 425 U.S. 944 (1976), the court of appeals, in a case involving a domestic organization, questioned whether any national security exception to the warrant requirement would be permissible, concluding that "an analysis of the policies implicated by foreign security surveillance indicates that, absent exigent circumstances, all warrantless electronic surveillance is unreasonable and therefore unconstitutional."

With the adoption of the Foreign Intelligence Surveillance Act, and its amendment in 1994 to cover physical searches, Congress mooted many aspects of the debate over a national security exception to the Fourth Amendment's warrant clause; the Act requires judicial authorization but grants to a secret court the authority to issue orders for electronic surveillance and physical searches in national security cases.

28. *Hoffa v. United States*, 385 U.S. 293 (1966).
29. *United States v. Aguilar*, 883 F.2d 662 (9th Cir. 1989).
30. 18 U.S.C. App. 3.
31. *Kwong Hai Chew v. Colding*, 344 U.S. 590 (1953) (holding that INS could not subject returning permanent resident alien to "summary exclusion" procedure in which INS would rely on secret evidence).
32. The DOJ has long claimed the authority to use secret evidence to deny discretionary relief from deportation. *Jay v. Boyd*, 351 U.S. 345 (1956). According to an INS statement in February 1998, it had used classified evidence in approximately fifty cases since 1992. Letter dated February 3, 1998, from INS Acting General Counsel Lori Scialabba to Gregory T. Nojeim, on file with James X. Dempsey.
33. *Rafeedie v. INS*, 880 F.2d 506, 516 (D.C. Cir. 1989); *Rafeedie v. INS*, 795 F. Supp. 13 (D.D.C. 1992) (holding unconstitutional the INS's attempt to expel a permanent resident alien on the basis of undisclosed classified information).
34. *American-Arab Anti-Discrimination Comm. v. Reno*, 70 F.3d 1045, 1069 (9th Cir. 1995).
35. *United States ex rel. Knauff v. Shaughnessy*, 338 U.S. 537, 551 (1950).
36. *NAACP v. Alabama ex rel. Patterson*, 357 U.S. 449 (1958).
37. *NAACP v. Button*, 371 U.S. 415 (1963).

## 8. Prologue to the 1996 Antiterrorism Act

1. Omnibus Counterterrorism Act of 1995, H.R. 896, 104th Cong. (1995); Omnibus Counterterrorism Act of 1995, S. 390, 104th Cong. (1995).
2. These last-mentioned provisions were dropped from the Antiterrorism Act, although the posse comitatus changes were enacted later in 1996 on another bill and the roving wiretap changes were adopted in 1998, as discussed in Chapter 10.
3. 18 U.S.C. § 2339A, as added by Pub. L. 103-322, § 120005, 108 Stat. 2022.
4. "International Terrorism: Threats and Responses: Hearings Before the House Comm. on the Judiciary," 104th Cong., 1st Sess. (1995) [hereinafter "Full Committee Hearings"].
5. "Combating Domestic Terrorism, Hearings Before the Subcomm. on Crime of the House Comm. on the Judiciary," 104th Cong., 1st Sess., Serial no. 52 (1995) [hereinafter "Combating Terrorism Hearings"].
6. Ibid., 88.
7. Ibid., 46.
8. Full Committee Hearings, 57–59.
9. Ibid., 65, 72–74, 475.
10. Combating Terrorism Hearings, 33.
11. On May 15, 1995, Rep. Richard A. Gephardt introduced H.R. 1635, embodying the Clinton administration's reaction to the Oklahoma City bombing. On May 25, Judiciary Committee Chairman Henry J. Hyde introduced his own bill, H.R. 1710, which narrowed the scope of Clinton's proposal in some areas while widening it in others.

## 9. The 1996 Antiterrorism Act's Central Provisions

1. Pub. L. No. 104-132, 110 Stat. 1214.
2. 18 U.S.C. § 2339B (Supp. II 1996), as added by Section 303 of the Antiterrorism Act, 110 Stat. 1250.
3. Section 411(1) of the Act, amending 8 U.S.C. § 1182(a)(3)(B) (Supp. II 1996) to add a new subclause, "is a member of a foreign terrorist organization, as designated by the Secretary."
4. Grounds for exclusion or inadmissibility are codified at 8 U.S.C. § 1182 (1994 & Supp. II 1996). Grounds for deportation or removal are codified at 8 U.S.C. § 1227 (Supp. II 1996). The two are interrelated, for a person is deportable (subject to removal) if she was inadmissible at the time of her entry to the United States. 8 U.S.C. § 1227 (a)(1)(A) (Supp. II 1996). Subsequent to the enactment of the 1996 Antiterrorism Act, Congress

passed the Illegal Immigration Reform and Immigrant Responsibility Act ("IIRIRA"), Pub. L. No. 104-208, 110 Stat. 3009, which substantially rewrote the immigration laws. IIRIRA replaced the concept of "exclusion" with "inadmissibility," and the concept of "deportation" with "removal," but we use both the old and the new terms here. For a description of the IIRIRA and for more information about immigration law in general, see Charles Gordon, Stanley Mailman, and Stephen Yale-Loehr, *Immigration Law and Procedure* (Matthew Bender, rev. 1998).

5. Section 401 of the Antiterrorism Act, adding a new Title V to the Immigration and Nationality Act, 8 U.S.C. § 1531 *et seq.* (Supp. II 1996).

6. See footnote 27, *infra.*

7. The effects and constitutionality of these habeas provisions are beyond the scope of this treatment. See, e.g., *Stewart v. Martinez-Villareal,* 523 U.S. 637 (1998) (Antiterrorism Act habeas provisions did not bar review of prisoner's claim that he could not be executed because he was insane); *Williams v. Taylor,* 529 U.S. 362 (2000).

8. The Act's other immigration law changes are not even nominally related to terrorism. Most notable is a provision that severely curtails the ability to claim political asylum, by requiring an undocumented alien entering the U.S. to be immediately sent back to the country he is fleeing unless he can prove, at the border inspection point, a credible fear of political persecution. 8 U.S.C. § 1225 (Supp. II 1996), as amended by Sec. 421 of the Antiterrorism Act.

   The Act also changed immigration law by making aliens who enter the U.S. without inspection (e.g., aliens who did not enter at border crossings) subject to removal by exclusion rather than deportation. 8 U.S.C. § 1251 (Supp. II 1996), as amended by Sec. 414 of the Act. In the past, aliens once in the U.S. were entitled to greater procedural protections. Under the changes brought about by the Act, aliens who enter without inspection are treated as if they never entered at all: they are treated like other applicants for admission, even if they have been in the U.S. for many years.

   The Act's effect on habeas challenges to deportation proceedings has been the subject of several appellate opinions. See *Sandoval v. Reno,* 166 F.3d 225 (3rd Cir. 1999), and cases cited therein.

9. Written testimony of Mary A. Ryan, Assistant Sec. for Consular Affairs, Dept. of State, before the Subcomm. on International Law, Immigration and Refugees of the House Judiciary Comm., Feb. 23, 1994, at 7. See also written testimony of Chris Sale, INS, ibid., 9.

10. Designation of Foreign Terrorist Organizations, 62 Fed. Reg. 52650 (Oct. 8, 1997), discussed in Chapter 10. See also Treasury Department regulations, 62 Fed. Reg. 67729 (Dec. 30, 1997), *codified at* 31

C.F.R. ch. V; Executive Order 13099, 63 Fed. Reg. 45167 (Aug. 25, 1998).

11. 18 U.S.C. § 2339B (Supp. II 1996), as added by Section 303 of the Antiterrorism Act, 110 Stat. 1250.

12. 8 U.S.C. § 1182(a)(3)(B)(i)(V), as added by Section 411 of the Antiterrorism Act, 110 Stat. 1268.

13. 8 U.S.C. § 1189(b), as added by Section 302 of the Antiterrorism Act. See *People's Mojahedin Org. of Iran v. Department of State* 182 F.3d 17 (D.C. Cir. 1999) (rejecting challenges by two designated groups), *cert. denied*, 120 S.Ct. 1846 (2000), and *National Council of Resistance of Iran v. Department of State*, 2001 WL 629300 (D.C. Cir., June 8, 2001) (groups with sufficient U.S. presence are entitled to due process).

14. 8 U.S.C. § 1189(a)(8), as added by Section 302 of the Antiterrorism Act.

15. 18 U.S.C. § 2339B, as added by Section 303 of the Antiterrorism Act and subsequently amended, provides:

> Whoever, within the United States or subject to the jurisdiction of the United States, knowingly provides material support or resources to a foreign terrorist organization, or attempts or conspires to do so, shall be fined under this title or imprisoned not more than 15 years, or both, and, if the death of any person results, shall be imprisoned for any term of years or for life.

16. 18 U.S.C. § 2339A (Supp. II 1996).

17. 18 U.S.C. § 2339A(c) (1994) (repealed 1996), as added by Pub. L. 103-322, § 120005, 108 Stat. 2022.

18. *Elfbrandt v. Russell*, 384 U.S. 11 (1966).

19. In 1987, Congress adopted a temporary provision limiting exclusion and deportation based solely on political activities. The new provision stated that no alien could be denied a visa, excluded from the United States, or deported because of past, current, or expected beliefs, statements, or associations that would be protected by the Constitution if engaged in by a U.S. citizen in the U.S. Foreign Relations Authorization Act for Fiscal Years 1988 and 1989, Pub. L. No. 100-204, §901, 101 Stat. 1331; Foreign Operations, Export Financing, and Related Programs Act, 1989, Pub. L. No. 100-461, §555, 102 Stat. 2268.

At the same time, the courts, recognizing the adverse impact of ideological exclusions on the First Amendment rights of U.S. citizens who wanted to hear the views of controversial speakers, had begun to question the constitutionality of ideological exclusions. See *Allende v. Schultz*, 845 F.2d 1111 (1st Cir. 1988); *Abourezk v. Reagan*, 785 F.2d 1043 (D.C. Cir. 1986), *aff'd by an equally divided Court*, 484 U.S. 1 (1987).

Later in 1996, the exclusion provisions were further expanded by Pub.

L. 104-208, § 342(a)(2), 110 Stat. 3009, which added a new subsection (a)(3)(B)(i)(III) to 18 U.S.C. §1182, making inadmissible any alien who has, "under circumstances indicating an intention to cause death or serious bodily harm, incited terrorist activity."

20. 8 U.S.C. § 1182(a)(3)(B)(i)(IV), as amended by Section 411 of the Antiterrorism Act.

21. See Title IV of the Antiterrorism Act, adding a new title V to the Immigration and Nationality Act, codified at 8 U.S.C. § 1531 (Supp. II 1996) *et seq.*

22. The definition is convoluted, at best, and is not directly linked to the secretary of state's designation of "foreign terrorist organizations." The definition of alien terrorist in the removal provision, 8 U.S.C. § 1531(1), refers to 8 U.S.C. § 1227(a)(4)(B), which in turn refers to 8 U.S.C. §1182(a)(3)(B)(iii). That latter section states that "engage in terrorist activity" means "to commit . . . an act of terrorist activity or an act which the actor knows, or reasonably should know, affords material support to any individual, organization, or government in conducting a terrorist activity." The INS, however, has taken the position that this definition encompasses any providing of material support to an organization that has engaged in terrorism, even if the support is intended to be used, and is in fact used, only for lawful humanitarian or political ends.

23. 8 U.S.C. § 1534(e)(3), as added by Sec. 401 of the Antiterrorism Act, 110 Stat. 1262.

24. Compare this standard with the one under Sec. 6(c) of the Classified Information Procedures Act, which permits the substitution of a summary for classified evidence only if the summary "provide[s] the defendant with substantially the same ability to make his defense as would disclosure of the specific classified information." 18 U.S.C. App. 3 (1994).

25. 8 U.S.C. § 1534(e)(1), as added by Sec. 401 of the Antiterrorism Act, 110 Stat. 1262. The Foreign Intelligence Surveillance Act has a set of procedures intended to balance the rights of individuals against the national security. Those procedures include a requirement that the government give a defendant notice when it intends to use information from a FISA wiretap and allow the defendant to move to suppress the evidence if it was obtained illegally. The Antiterrorism Act makes such provisions, which have been followed in the most serious criminal espionage cases, inapplicable in deportation cases against "alien terrorists."

26. 8 U.S.C. § 1536, as added by Sec. 401 of the Antiterrorism Act, 110 Stat. 1265. Once the court has ruled that an alien is deportable, the attorney general, if she finds it appropriate in view of the foreign policy of the United States, may send the alien to any country willing to receive him or her, including a country where the alien may face torture or death. If no

country is willing to receive a noncitizen ordered deported under the new provisions, the Act states that "the Attorney General may, notwithstanding any other provision of law, retain the alien in custody." Any alien in custody pursuant to this provision "shall be released from custody solely at the discretion of the Attorney General."

27. *Kwong Hai Chew v. Colding*, 344 U.S. 590 (1953); *Rafeedie v. INS*, 880 F.2d 506 (D.C.Cir. 1989), *later proceeding*, 795 F. Supp. 13 (D.D.C. 1992); *American-Arab Anti-Discrimination Comm. v. Reno*, 70 F.3d 1045 (9th Cir. 1995); *Al Najjar v. Reno*, 97 F. Supp. 2d 1329 (S.D. Fla. 2000), *vacated as moot*, 273 F.3d 1330 (11th Cir. 2001); *Kiareldeen v. Reno*, 71 F. Supp. 2d 402 (D.N.J. 1999).

## 10. The Impact of the 1996 Act

1. See generally David Cole, "Secrecy, Guilt by Association, and the Terrorist Profile," 15 *Journal of Law and Religion* 267 (2001); John Mintz and Michael Grunwald, "FBI Terror Probes Focus on U.S. Muslims," *Washington Post*, Oct. 31, 1998, A1; Ronald Smothers, "Secret Data and Hidden Accusers Used Against Some Immigrants," *New York Times*, Aug. 15, 1998, A1.

2. "2nd Presidential Debate Between Gov. Bush and Vice President Gore" (transcript of Oct. 11, 2000, presidential debate), *New York Times*, Oct. 12, 2000, A23.

3. See William Glaberson, "U.S. Asks to Use Secret Evidence in Many Cases of Deportation," *New York Times*, Dec. 9, 2001, B1.

4. It is not entirely clear why the government has failed to use the removal procedures of the 1996 Act. One reason may be that the 1996 Act's procedures require the government to provide to the alien facing deportation at least a summary of the evidence against him, and the government has sought to avoid even that limited concession to due process.

Second, alien terrorist removal proceedings under the Antiterrorism Act would take place before a federal judge who would have the authority to rule immediately on a constitutional challenge to the use of secret evidence. By invoking other provisions of the Immigration and Nationality Act, the government instead has brought its cases before immigration judges who could not declare the procedures unconstitutional. In this way, the INS was able to avoid for years constitutional review of its secret evidence theories.

A third reason may arise from the fact that the secret evidence procedures under the 1996 Act apply only to someone who is an "alien terrorist," which the law defines as someone who "has engaged, is engaged, or at any time after admission engages in any terrorist activity." The definitions section of the removal provision, 8 U.S.C. § 1531(1) (Supp. II 1996), refers to 8 U.S.C. § 1227(a)(4)(B) (Supp. II 1996), which in turn refers to 8 U.S.C. § 1182(a)(3)(B)(iii) (Supp. II 1996). The definitions of "engage in" and "terrorist activity" do not encompass mere membership, and before the 2001 USA PATRIOT Act, they clearly did not include fund-raising for peaceful political and humanitarian activities. Therefore, ironically, the secret evidence procedures Congress adopted in 1996 did not cover many of the aliens against whom the government sought to use secret evidence, for the cases generally involved mere membership and/or fund-raising for peaceful activities.

5. Immigration law has recognized a distinction between the use of secret evidence as the basis for deportation, and the use of secret evidence to oppose discretionary relief such as suspension of deportation, adjustment of status, or asylum, which are forms of relief from deportation normally available to aliens. Prior to the enactment of the "alien terrorist removal" provisions in the 1996 Antiterrorism Act, there was no statutory authority to use secret evidence in deportation proceedings. However, even prior to the Act, the government claimed the authority to use secret evidence to deny certain relief to aliens it was seeking to deport on the basis of technical violations. In those cases, the secret evidence was used not to support the deportation itself, but to deny relief that would otherwise block the deportation, like asylum. The law has further drawn a distinction between "discretionary" relief, such as asylum, adjustment of status or suspension of deportation, and "mandatory" relief, such as withholding of deportation and amnesty. The Supreme Court has allowed the use of secret evidence to deny discretionary relief, although it has never squarely ruled on its constitutionality. It has never accepted the use of secret evidence to deny mandatory relief, and the only lower court to address that issue has barred the use of secret evidence. *American-Arab Anti-Discrimination Comm. v. Reno,* 70 F.3d 1045 (9th Cir. 1995). See also testimony of Walter D. Cadman, INS, before the Subcomm. on Technology, Terrorism and Government Information of the Senate Judiciary Comm., Feb. 24, 1998, and letter from INS Acting General Counsel Lois Scialabba to Greg Nojeim of the ACLU, Feb. 3, 1998, on file with James X. Dempsey. In another 1996 statute, the Illegal Immigration Reform and Immigrant Responsibility Act, Congress for the first time expressly authorized use of secret evidence to oppose discretionary "relief from removal." See 8 U.S.C. 1229 a (b) (4) (B).

6. Mintz and Grunwald, "FBI Terror Probes Focus on U.S. Muslims."

7. William Branigin, "Secret U.S. Evidence Entangles Immigrants; Rarely Used Law Now Falls Most Heavily on Arabs," *Washington Post,* Oct. 19, 1997, A1.

8. Matter of Al Najjar, No. A-26-599-077 (U.S. Imm. Ct. Oct. 27, 2000) (Decision of Immigration Judge). All of the quotes in the following two paragraphs are from this decision. Judicial opinions in the case include *Najjar v. Ashcroft*, 257 F.3d 1262 (11th Cir. 2001); *Najjar v. Ashcroft*, 273 F.3d 2001 (11th Cir. 2001); and *Al Najjar v. Reno*, 97 F.Supp.2d 1329 (S.D. Fla. 2000).

9. Ronald Smothers, "Secret Data and Hidden Accusers Used Against Some Immigrants," *New York Times*, Aug. 15, 1998, A1.

10. *Kiareldeen v. Reno*, 71 F. Supp. 2d 402 (D.N.J. 1999).

11. Matter of Kiareldeen, A77-025-332, slip op. 15 (U.S. Immgr. Ct. April 2, 1999) (Dec. of Immgr. J.).

12. Matter of Kiareldeen, No. A77-025-332, slip dissent 1 (BIA June 29, 1999) (Moscato, J., dissenting to Dec. Denying Request to Lift Stay of Release Order).

13. Ibid., 1–2. The other two judges on this panel declined to lift the stay of Kiareldeen's release order pending appeal, but did not dispute Judge Moscato's characterization of the evidence.

14. Tim Weiner, "6 Iraqis Who Aided C.I.A. Are Ordered Deported from U.S.," *New York Times*, March 11, 1998, A1.

15. R. James Woolsey, "Iraqi Dissidents Railroaded by U.S.," *Wall Street Journal*, June 10, 1998, A18.

16. Ibid.

17. James Risen, "Evidence to Deny 6 Iraqis Asylum May Be Weak, Files Show," *New York Times*, Oct. 13, 1998, A9; Patrick J. McDonnell, "New Files Cast Doubt on Case Against 6 Iraqis," *Los Angeles Times*, Aug. 10, 1998, B1; Vernon Loeb, "Iraqis Detained on Flawed Data, Lawyers Say," *Washington Post*, July 19, 1998, A16.

18. Vernon Loeb, "Iraqi Dissidents' American Dream—and Nightmare," *Washington Post*, Dec. 28, 2000, A1; Dan Weikel, "INS Judge Frees Iraqi Dissident Held for 4 Years," *Los Angeles Times*, Aug. 19, 2000.

19. Nina Bernstein, "Girl Called Would-Be Bomber Was Drawn to Islam," *New York Times*, April 8, 2005; Editorial, "Guilty Until Proven Innocent," *New York Times*, April 12, 2005.

20. The first list of thirty "foreign terrorist organizations" was issued by the secretary of state in October 1997. 62 Fed. Reg. 52650. It included old and new groups, some nearly defunct, others that enjoy major support. Eight of the groups were based in the Middle East and supported Palestinian and/or Islamic causes. Four in Algeria, Egypt, and Iran supported Islamic causes. Two in Israel were radical Zionist groups. The remaining sixteen were spread throughout the world. Dozens, if not hundreds, of groups that have engaged in violent activity in recent years as part of a political movement were not on the list.

21. The delay in issuing the list angered advocates of the Antiterrorism Act, who harshly criticized the government for dragging its feet in the fight against terrorism. "We are bitterly disappointed that . . . the administration has failed to designate a single foreign terrorist organization—even the most obvious and deadly ones," said an official of the Anti-Defamation League of B'nai B'rith. Benjamin Wittes, "Anti-Terrorism Act: Rhetoric vs. Reality," *Legal Times*, June 2, 1997, 1.

Under a separate, earlier law, the State Department is required to report annually on terrorism groups. In 1998, when it issued its report on terrorism, following the designation of the first thirty groups, the State Department included additional groups, but these additional groups were not designated for purposes of the Antiterrorism Act. The State Department report is available at http://www.state.gov/www/global/ terrorism/1997Report/1997index.html.

Under separate authority, the president has designated by executive order certain foreign terrorist organizations with whom it is illegal to have financial transactions. The designation came in the form of a declaration of a state of emergency initially issued in January 1995, and renewed each year since, in the name of dealing with the threat that terrorism poses to the Middle East peace process. 63 Fed. Reg. 3445 (Jan. 22, 1998), continuing Executive Order 12947 (Jan. 23, 1995). In August 1998, the president issued Executive Order 13099, amending E.O. 12947 to add Osama bin Laden and his Islamic Army. 63 Fed. Reg. 45167 (Aug. 25, 1998). The list issued by the secretary of state and that issued by the president are combined in the regulations of the Treasury Department's Office of Foreign Assets Control, Appendix A to 31 C.F.R. Chapter V. The executive order freezes the assets of designated foreign terrorists and organizations, if such assets are in the United States or under the control of U.S. persons in the United States or abroad. It additionally bans dealings or transactions in the property of such terrorists by U.S. persons.

After September 11, President Bush added many more groups to the list, and authorized the secretary of the Treasury to add still more. This authority was used to freeze the assets of several Muslim charities in the wake of September 11, as described in Chapter 13.

22. The plaintiffs also challenged the Act on other grounds, arguing that it invited viewpoint discrimination by the secretary of state because it provided her with unrestricted discretion to designate an organization as terrorist. This open-ended standard allows the secretary to target supporters of politically disfavored groups. In addition, the plaintiffs contended the Act was impermissibly vague by failing to define "material support or resources" and "national security," such that citizens will not understand what conduct is prohibited, and government officials are free to enforce

the Act in an arbitrary and discriminatory manner. Memorandum of Points and Authorities in Support of Plaintiffs' Motion for Preliminary Injunction (May 11, 1998) in *Humanitarian Law Project v. Reno* (C.A. No. 98-1971) (C.D.Cal.).

23. *Humanitarian Law Project v. Reno*, 205 F.3d 1130 (9th Cir. 2000), *cert. denied*, 532 U.S. 904 (2001).

24. *Humanitarian Law Project v. U.S. Dept. of Justice*, 352 F.3d 382 (9th Cir. 2003).

25. *Humanitarian Law Project v. Ashcroft*, 309 F. Supp.2d 1185 (C.D. Cal. 2004).

26. *Humanitarian Law Project v. Gonzales*, 380 F. Supp.2d 1134 (C.D. Cal. 2005).

27. Trial Transcript, Feb. 18, 1998, in *Nasher Ltd. v. Crestar Bank*, Civil Action No. 98-227-A [hereinafter "Nasher Ltd."], 9.

28. Preliminary Injunction, Feb. 27, 1998, in *Nasher Ltd.*

29. Trial Transcript, *Nasher Ltd.*, 15; Government's Brief in Opposition to Plaintiff's Motion for Preliminary Injunction, Feb. 26, 1998, 4 ("At no time has OFAC instructed Crestar Bank to block the account pursuant to the Act . . . [or] made an affirmative demand for a report").

30. Trial Transcript, *Nasher Ltd.*, 15–16.

31. Mintz and Grunwald, "FBI Terror Probes Focus on U.S. Muslims."

32. 10 U.S.C. § 382, added by Sec. 1416 of Pub. L. 104-201.

33. Sec. 604 of Pub. L. 105-272, 112 Stat. 2396, 2413, amending 18 U.S.C. §2518(11)(b).

34. Sec. 601-602 of Pub. L. 105-272, 112 Stat. 2396, 2404, amending the Foreign Intelligence Surveillance Act to add a new Title IV (pen registers and trap-and-trace devices) and a new Title V (access to certain business records). A pen register is a device that records the dialed numbers identifying outgoing calls on a surveilled line; a trap-and-trace device identifies the number of origin of incoming calls on a surveilled line.

35. "Foreign Terrorists in America: Five Years after the World Trade Center Bombing, Before the Senate Judiciary Subcommittee on Terrorism, Technology and Government Information," 105th Cong., 2d Sess. (1998).

## 11. New Challenges, Old Dilemmas

1. Congress first delayed deployment of TIA technologies until the administration answered certain questions about the program. See Consolidated Appropriations Resolution, Pub. L. No. 108-7, Div. M, § 111, 117 Stat. 11, 534-36 (2003). Thereafter, Congress eliminated funding for TIA. See Department of Defense Appropriations Act, Pub. L. No. 108-

87, § 8131(a)-(b), 117 Stat. 1054, 1102 (2004). Similarly, Congress exercised close oversight of the proposed Computer Assisted Passenger Prescreening System (CAPPS II) and, when that program was revamped as "Secure Flight," Congress placed limits on the program and required close GAO scrutiny. See section 4012 of the Intelligence Reform Act of 2004 and § 522 of the fiscal year 2005 DHS Appropriations Act (Pub. L. No. 108-334).

## 12. Detention and Interrogation

1. The Department of Homeland Security reported that as of September 30, 2003, 2,870 persons had been detained pursuant to Special Registration, a program targeted at male foreign nationals from Arab and Muslim countries. U.S. Department of Homeland Security, "Fact Sheet: Changes to the National Security Entry/Exit Registration System," 5, available at http://www.ice.gov/graphics/news/factsheets/NSEERSfactsheet120103 .pdf. According to the 9/11 Commission, 1,139 absconders had been apprehended as of early 2003 under the "Absconder Apprehension Initiative," targeted at aliens from Arab and Muslim countries with outstanding deportation orders. National Commission on Terrorist Attacks upon the United States, "Staff Statement No. 10: Threats and Reponses in 2001," 13, available at http://www.9-11commission.gov/hearings/hearing10/staff_statement_10.pdf. As of November 5, 2001, the last day the Justice Department announced a cumulative total of all those detained in its terrorism investigation, it had detained 1,182 persons. Dan Eggen and Susan Schmidt, "Count of Released Detainees Is Hard to Pin Down," *Washington Post,* Nov. 6, 2001, A10. Taken together, that makes well over 5,000 foreign nationals detained in antiterrorism preventive detention measures in the first two years after 9/11.

2. Only three of these persons were ever charged with a terrorist crime, all in a "material support to terrorism" trial in Detroit. Two of the three were acquitted on the terrorist charges by the jury. The third was convicted, but his conviction was thrown out in September 2004 after the prosecution admitted that it failed to disclose to the defense evidence that its principal witness had lied on the stand and that its own experts had raised serious doubts about its evidence in the case. See Danny Hakim, "Judge Reverses Convictions in Detroit Terrorism Case," *New York Times,* Sept. 3, 2004, A12.

3. The courts rejected efforts to require the government to disclose the names of the detainees. *Ctr. For Nat'l Sec. Studies v. United States* DOJ, 215 F. Supp. 2d 94 (D.D.C. 2002), *aff'd in part and rev'd in part,* 331 F. 3rd 918 (D.C. Cir. 2003), *cert. denied,* 124 S. Ct. 1041 (2004).

4. For details, see David Cole, *Enemy Aliens: Double Standards and Constitutional Freedoms in the War on Terrorism* (The New Press, 2003), 17–46.
5. *Detroit Free Press v. Ashcroft,* 195 F. Supp. 2d 937 (E.D. Mich. 2002), *aff'd,* 303 F.3d 681 (6th Cir. 2002); *Haddad v. Ashcroft,* 221 F. Supp.2d 799 (E.D. Mich. 2002); *North Jersey Media Group, Inc. v. Ashcroft,* 205 F. Supp.2d 288 (D.N.J. 2002), *rev'd,* 308 F.3d 198 (3d Cir. 2002), *cert. denied,* 538 U.S. 1056 (2003).
6. U.S. Department of Justice, Office of the Inspector General, "The September 11 Detainees: A Review of the Treatment of Aliens Held on Immigration Charges in Connection with the Investigation of the September 11 Attacks" (April 2003) (released June 2, 2003).
7. See, e.g., *Ashley v. Ridge,* 288 F. Supp. 2d 662 (D.N.J. 2003).
8. 18 U.S.C. §3144.
9. Steve Fainaru and Margot Williams, "Material Witness Law Puts Detainees in Legal Limbo," *Washington Post,* Nov. 24, 2002, A1.
10. See Cole, *Enemy Aliens,* 35–39; Adam Liptak, "Threats and Responses: The Detainees; For Post–9/11 Material Witness, It Is a Terror of a Different Kind," *New York Times,* Aug. 19, 2004, A1.
11. Special Administrative Measure for the Prevention of Acts of Violence and Terrorism, 66 Fed. Reg. 55, 062 (October 31, 2001) (amending 2 C.F.R. §501.3(d)).
12. Arlie Hochschild, "Arrested Development," *New York Times,* June 29, 2005; Tim McGirk and Kotka Miralam Daud Shah, "A Letter from Guantánamo," *Time,* Oct. 29, 2002, available at http://www.time.com/time/world/article/0,8599,385661,00.html.
13. John Mintz, "Detainees at Base in Cuba Yield Little Valuable Information," *Washington Post,* Oct. 29, 2002.
14. Douglas Jehl, "Pentagon Seeks to Transfer More Detainees from Base in Cuba," *New York Times,* Mar. 11, 2005 at A1.
15. "Britain Frees 5 Citizens Sent Home From U.S. Jail," *New York Times,* Mar. 11, 2005 at A3.
16. *Rasul v. Bush,* 124 S. Ct. 2686 (2004).
17. Geneva Convention Relative to the Treatment of Prisoners of War, Aug. 12, 1949, art. 5, 6 U.S.T. 3316, 3322, 75 U.N.T.S. 135, 140.
18. *Hamdi v. Rumsfeld,* 296 F.3d 278, 283 (4th Cir. 2002).
19. *Hamdi v. Rumsfeld,* 124 S. Ct. 2633 (2004) [hereinafter *Hamdi II*].
20. Four Justices dissented in *Padilla* on the question of jurisdiction, but also noted that they considered the president to lack authority to detain U.S. citizens arrested domestically. *Rumsfeld v. Padilla,* 124 S.Ct. 2711, 2729 (2004) (Stevens, J., dissenting). Justice Scalia joined the majority in *Padilla* on the question of jurisdiction, but his opinion in *Hamdi II* makes clear that on the merits, he would have ruled for Padilla, as he be-

lieves that the Constitution bars military detention of U.S. citizens unless Congress suspends the writ of habeas corpus. *Hamdi II,* 124 S. Ct. at 2660 (Scalia, J., dissenting).

21. *Padilla v. Rumsfeld,* 124 S. Ct. 2711 (2004).
22. *Padilla v. Hanft,* No. Civ.A. 2:04–2221–26A, 2005 WL 465691 (D.S.C. 2005).
23. *Padilla v. Hanft,* 2005 U.S. App. LEXIS 19465 (4th Cir. Sept. 9, 2005).
24. John Hendren, "Detainees May Be Moved Off Cuba Base," *Los Angeles Times,* June 30, 2004, A1.
25. *Hamdi II,* 124 S. Ct. at 2650.
26. *Hamdan v. Rumsfeld,* 344 F. Supp.2d 152 (D.D.C. 2004).
27. *Hamdan v. Rumsfeld,* 2005 U.S. App. LEXIS 114 315 (D.C. Cir. July 15, 2005).
28. Richard A. Serrano, "Prison Interrogators' Gloves Came Off Before Abu Ghraib," *Los Angeles Times,* June 9, 2004, A1; Bob Woodward, "CIA Told to Do 'Whatever Necessary' to Kill Bin Laden," *Washington Post,* October 21, 2001, A1.
29. See, e.g., Mark Bowden, "The Dark Art of Interrogation," *Atlantic Monthly,* Oct. 2003.
30. Office of Legal Counsel, Memorandum to Alberto Gonzales, Counsel to the President, "Re: Standards of Conduct for Interrogation under 18 U.S.C. §§ 2340–2340A" (August 1, 2002), reprinted in *The Torture Papers: The Road to Abu Ghraib,* ed. Karen J. Greenberg and Joshua L. Dratel (Cambridge University Press, 2005), 172 (hereinafter "August 2002 Torture Memo"); "Working Group Report on Detainee Interrogations in the Global War on Terrorism: Assessment of Legal, Historical, Policy and Operational Considerations" (Mar. 6, 2003) reprinted in *The Torture Papers,* 241.
31. August 2002 Torture Memo, 174 (specific intent); 177 (imminent death); 180–81 (drugs); 177 (mental harm); 176 (physical harm).
32. Ibid., 207.
33. White House transcript, http://www.whitehouse.gov/news/releases/2004/06/print/20040610–36.html. See also Dana Milbank and Dana Priest, "Bush: U.S. Expected to Follow Law on Prisoners," *Washington Post,* June 11, 2004, A06.

## 13. The Patriot Act—Unleashing Government Spying, Reducing Oversight

1. Pub. L. No. 107–56.
2. *NAACP v. Claiborne Hardware Co.,* 458 U.S. 886 (1982).
3. USA PATRIOT Act, § 411. The Act defines as a deportable offense the

solicitation of members or funds for, or the provision of material support to, any group designated as terrorist. There is no defense available for those who can show that their support had no connection to furthering terrorism. The government is free to designate any organization that uses or threatens to use violence as terrorist. In addition, the law makes aliens who support even nondesignated groups deportable if the group has engaged in violence, unless the alien can show that he neither knew nor reasonably should have known that his support would further the group's violent activity.

4. See, e.g., *Scales v. United States*, 367 U.S. 203 (1961); *United States v. Robel*, 389 U.S. 258, 262 (1967); *Keyishian v. Board of Regents of the University of the State of N.Y.*, 385 U.S. 589, 606 (1967).

5. Patriot Act, § 412.

6. *United States v. Salerno*, 481 U.S. 739, 746–47 (1987).

7. The Supreme Court recently held that even aliens who have been finally ordered deported have a constitutionally protected liberty interest in remaining free, and that the government's authority to detain them is therefore limited. *Zadvydas v. Davis*, 121 S. Ct. 2491 (2001).

8. *County of Riverside v. McLaughlin*, 500 U.S. 44 (1991).

9. *United States v. Salerno*, 481 U.S. 739.

10. Patriot Act, § 411.

11. REAL ID Act of 2005, Pub. L. No. 109-13, 119 Stat. 231 (enacted May 11, 2005).

12. Patriot Act, § 218, amending 50 U.S.C. §§ 1804(a)(7)(B) and 1823(a)(7)(B).

13. 50 U.S.C. § 1801 et seq.

14. In re Sealed Case, 310 F.3d 717 (Foreign Intel. Ct. Rev. 2002).

15. A copy of this manual is available at http://www.cdt.org/security/011030doj.

16. Patriot Act, Section 213, amending 18 U.S.C. § 3103(a).

17. The prohibition is now codified in 50 U.S.C. § 403–3(d)(1).

18. Fed. R. Crim. P. 6(e).

19. Patriot Act, § 203.

20. USA PATRIOT Act, § 203(a), incorporates by reference the definition of "foreign intelligence" contained in 50 U.S.C. § 401a.

21. Patriot Act, § 215, amending 50 U.S.C. §§ 1862 and 1863.

22. *Doe v. Ashcroft*, No. 04-CIV-2614 (S.D.N.Y. Sept. 29, 2004), available at http://www.nysd.uscourts.gov/rulings/04CV2614_Opinion_092904.pdf.

## 14. Casting a Broad Net, Catching Few Big Fish

1. Roper Center for Public Opinion Research, "Do You Approve or Disapprove of the Use of 'Racial Profiling' by Police?," Gallup poll, December 9, 1999, available at WESTLAW, USGALLUP 120999 R6 009.

2. "National News Briefs: Attorney General Seeks End to Racial Profiling," *New York Times,* March 2, 2001, A20.

3. Sam Howe Verhovek, "A Nation Challenged; Civil Liberties; Americans Give in to Race Profiling," *New York Times,* Sept. 23, 2001, A1; Gregg Krupa, "Most in State Support Screening of Arabs," *Detroit News,* Feb. 28, 2002, A1.

4. Stuart Taylor, "Never Say Never," *Legal Times,* Sept. 24, 2001, 70.

5. *Craig v. Boren,* 429 U.S. 190 (1976).

6. Malcolm Gladwell, writing in the *New Yorker* shortly after September 11, argued that it is cognitively impossible to remain alert in reviewing metal detectors at airports, because the fact that the vast majority of luggage will pose no threat inevitably causes the security personnel to let their guard down.

7. See U.S. Department of Justice, Civil Rights Division, "Guidance Regarding the Use of Race by Federal Law Enforcement Agencies," (June 2003).

8. See James X. Dempsey and Lara M. Flint, "Commercial Data and National Security," 72 *George Washington Law Review* 1459 (2004); Technology and Privacy Advisory Committee, "Safe-guarding Privacy in the Fight Against Terrorism" (2004), available at http://www.sainc.com/tapac/finalreport.htm; Markle Foundation Task Force on National Security in the Information Age, "Creating a Trusted Information Network for Homeland Security" (2003); Markle Foundation Task Force on National Security in the Information Age, "Protecting America's Freedom in the Information Age" (2002). Both reports are available at http://www.markle.org. See also Mary DeRosa, Center for Strategic & International Studies, "Data Mining and Data Analysis for Counterterrorism" (2004); Gina Marie Stevens, Congressional Research Service, "Privacy: Total Information Awareness Programs and Related Information Access, Collection, and Protection Laws" (2003).

9. See, e.g., Robert O'Harrow Jr., "U.S. Hopes to Check Computers Globally; System Would Be Used to Hunt Terrorists," *Washington Post,* Nov. 12, 2002, A4; William Safire, "You Are a Suspect," *New York Times,* Nov. 14, 2002, A35.

10. The Defense Department appropriations act for FY 2004 eliminated funding for TIA. See Department of Defense Appropriations Act, Pub. L. No. 108–87, § 8131(a)–(b), 117 Stat. 1054, 1102 (2004). See also H.R.

Rep. No. 108–283, at 327 (2003), reprinted in 2003 U.S.C.C.A.N. 1168, 1189.

11. General Accounting Office, "Data Mining: Federal Efforts Cover a Wide Range of Uses," GAO-04-548 (2004), available at http://www.gao.gov/new.items/d04548.pdf.

12. See Notice of Status of System of Records; Interim Final Notice: Request for Further Comments, 68 Fed. Reg. 45,265, 45,266 (Aug. 1, 2003).

13. Testimony of James X. Dempsey before a subcommittee of the House Committee on Homeland Security, June 29, 2005, available at http://www.cdt.org/privacy/20050629screeningtestimony.pdf.

14. Stevens, "Privacy," CRS-3.

15. Department of Justice, "Attorney General's Guidelines on General Crimes, Racketeering Enterprise and Terrorism Enterprise Investigations" (May 30, 2002), 21–22, available at http://www.usdoj.gov/olp/generalcrimes2.pdf (accessed June 26, 2004).

16. See Memorandum from the National Security Law Unit, Office of the General Counsel, FBI, to National Security Division, FBI, on "Guidance Regarding the Use of Choicepoint for Foreign Intelligence Collection or Foreign Counterterrorism Investigations" (Sept. 17, 2001), 1 (responding to request from the National Security Division "for advice concerning legal restrictions on the use of ChoicePoint, a data warehousing company, for foreign intelligence collection or foreign counterintelligence investigations"), available at http://www.epic.org/privacy/publicrecords/cpfcimemo.pdf; see also Glenn R. Simpson, "Big Brother-in-Law: If the FBI Hopes to Get the Goods on You, It May Ask ChoicePoint: U.S. Agencies' Growing Use of Outside Data Suppliers Raises Privacy Concerns," *Wall Street Journal,* Apr. 13, 2001, A1.

17. See Homeland Security Act of 2002, Pub. L. No. 107–296, § 201(d)(14), 116 Stat. 2135, 2145–47 (2002).

18. The Patriot Act specified that FinCEN was to provide government-wide access to information collected under the anti–money laundering laws, records maintained by other government offices, as well as privately and publicly held information. Pub. L. No. 107–56, § 361, 115 Stat. 272, 329–32 (2001).

19. See James X. Dempsey and Lara Flint, *Commercial Data and National Security,* 72 G.W. L. Rev. 1459 (2004).

20. See, e.g., 12 U.S.C. § 3407 (2000) (permitting access to financial records with a judicial subpoena under certain circumstances); 20 U.S.C. § 1232g(b)(1)(J)(i) (2000) (providing for access to educational records with a grand jury subpoena); 45 C.F.R. 164.512(f)(1)(ii)(B) (2002) (allowing for disclosure of health records, pursuant to the Health Insurance

Portability and Accountability Act of 1996, Pub. L. No. 104–191, § 264, 110 Stat. 1936, 2033–34 (1996)).

21. See generally Ann Davis, "Why a 'No Fly List' Aimed at Terrorists Delays Others," *Wall Street Journal,* Apr. 22, 2003, A1; Sara Kehaulani Goo, "Sen. Kennedy Flagged by No-Fly List," *Washington Post,* Aug. 20, 2004, A1.

22. In the frenzied aftermath of 9/11, when the government was looking for associates of the hijackers, it arrested a man who had obtained a driver's license at the same motor vehicle office and within minutes of the time one of the hijackers obtained a license. The man was correctly identified, but the inference drawn from his Arab name and proximity in time to one of the hijackers was wrong, albeit in good faith. Tamara Lytle and Jim Leusner, "The Price of Protection: Push for Safety Clouds Individual Rights," *Orlando Sentinel,* Aug. 29, 2002, A1.

23. In December 2002, a former DEA agent was convicted of selling to a private investigation firm criminal history and law enforcement data he obtained from law enforcement computer systems while an agent. *Privacy Times* 23, no. 1 ( Jan. 2, 2003), 10. In another documented case, between 1994 and 2000, an officer with the Los Angeles Police Department searched the police department's computers for information on celebrities and his ex-girlfriend. He used the information on his ex-girlfriend to stalk her and he allegedly sold the information on celebrities to tabloids. *Privacy Times* 23, no. 8 (Apr. 15, 2003), 5. In May 2002, two FBI agents were indicted on fraud charges for allegedly accessing FBI databases to provide information on companies to manipulate stocks. One of the agents used information from the NCIC database to discredit a company executive and lower stock prices. The agents also used confidential records from FBI databases to monitor government investigations of other stock manipulators. *EPIC,* http://www.epic.org/privacy/public records/. An FBI agent in Las Vegas working with a member of the state attorney general's office was accused of selling information from the FBI's NCIC database to organized crime leaders. Ibid.

24. In December 2002, the personal health care information and Social Security numbers of more than 500,000 military personnel, retirees, and family members were stolen from the Phoenix office of TriWest Healthcare Alliance, a contractor administering the Department of Defense's health plan. *Privacy Times* 23, no. 1 ( Jan. 2, 2003), 2.

25. The Supreme Court has noted that there is a "distinction, in terms of personal privacy, between scattered disclosure of the bits of information . . . and revelation of the [information] as a whole." *Department of Justice v. Reporters Committee,* 489 U.S 780, 764 (1989). The Court went on: "Plainly there is a vast difference between the public records that might be

found after a diligent search of courthouse files, county archives, and local police stations throughout the country and a computerized summary located in a single clearinghouse of information."

26. Transportation, Treasury, Independent Agencies, and General Government Appropriations Act of 2005, Pub. L. No. 108–447, Div. H, Title V, § 522, 3268 (2004).

27. Jerry Markon, "Hamdi Returned to Saudi Arabia," *Washington Post,* Oct. 12, 2004 at A2.

28. See Danny Hakim, "Judge Reverses Convictions in Detroit Terrorism Case," *New York Times,* Sept. 3, 2004, A12.

29. Brian Ross, "Secret FBI Report Questions Al Qaeda Capabilities," ABC News, Mar. 9, 2005, available at http://abcnews.go.com/WNT/Investi gation/story?id=566425&page=1.

30. *Whitney v. California,* 274 U.S. 357, 375 (1927).

## 15. Conclusion

1. "Intelligence Activities and the Rights of Americans, Book II, Final Report of the Senate Select Committee to Study Governmental Operations with Respect to Intelligence Activities" (1976), 289.

2. A useful discussion of this and many other issues involving terrorism and civil liberties can be found in Philip B. Heymann, *Terrorism and America* (MIT Press, 1998). This sensitive book serves as a commendable response to the calls of many for substantial curtailment of civil liberties in the name of fighting terrorism. Heymann argues that the current counterintelligence approach of the FBI, properly managed, would produce no intolerable limitations on the First Amendment.

3. Matthew L. Wald, "Tests Show Holes in Airline Security," *New York Times,* Jan. 11, 1999, A1.

4. James Risen and Benjamin Weiser, "Before Bombings, Omens and Fears," *New York Times,* Jan. 9, 1999, A1.

5. See, e.g., Kate Martin, "Domestic Intelligence and Civil Liberties," 24 *SAIS Reveiw* 7 (2004). We do not mean to suggest that terrorism may *only* be dealt with through the criminal justice system. Terrorist attacks like those of 9/11 may also justify a military response. But we address here only the appropriate character of a nonmilitary response.

# Index